The 7 Hidden Reasons Employees Leave

Second Edition

The 7 Hidden Reasons Employees Leave

Second Edition

How to Recognize the Subtle Signs and Act Before It's Too Late

Leigh Branham

American Management Association

New York • Atlanta • Brussels • Chicago • Mexico City • San Francisco
Shanghai • Tokyo • Toronto • Washington, D. C.

Bulk discounts available. For details visit:
www.amacombooks.org/go/specialsales
Or contact special sales:
Phone: 800-250-5308
Email: specialsls@amanet.org
View all the AMACOM titles at: www.amacombooks.org

This publication is designed to provide accurate and authoritative information in regard to the subject matter covered. It is sold with the understanding that the publisher is not engaged in rendering legal, accounting, or other professional service. If legal advice or other expert assistance is required, the services of a competent professional person should be sought.

Library of Congress Cataloging-in-Publication Data
Branham, Leigh.
  The 7 hidden reasons employees leave : how to recognize the subtle signs and act before it's too late / Leigh Branham. — 2nd ed.
      p. cm.
  Includes bibliographical references and index.
  ISBN-13: 978-0-8144-1758-4
  ISBN-10: 0-8144-1758-2
  1. Labor turnover. 2. Employee retention. 3. Job satisfaction. I. Title. II. Title: Seven hidden reasons employees leave.
  HF5549.5.T8B7 2012
  658.3'14—dc23

                                                                        2012005592

About AMA

American Management Association (www.amanet.org) is a world leader in talent development, ad-vancing the skills of individuals to drive business success. Our mission is to support the goals of individuals and organizations through a complete range of products and services, including classroom and virtual seminars, webcasts, webinars, podcasts, conferences, corporate and government solutions, business books, and research. AMA's approach to improving performance combines experiential learning—learning through doing—with opportunities for ongoing professional growth at every step of one's career journey.

Printing number
10 9 8 7 6 5 4 3 2 1

This book is dedicated to the memory of W. Michael Kelly (1938–2010). Michael was Director of Research at Saratoga Institute when I first inquired about analyzing Saratoga's database of post-exit research. He welcomed my analysis and became my partner. With a sharp mind and a generous heart, Michael invested countless hours by phone in helpful and challenging conversations, offering new insights by e-mail, and critiquing my drafts chapter by chapter. I am deeply and eternally grateful for his contributions, which live on in this book and my work. I am glad I was able to finally meet Michael and his lovely wife, Carol, just months before he died unexpectedly.

CONTENTS

Chapter 4

Chapter 5

Chapter 6

Chapter 7

Chapter 8

Chapter 9

Chapter 10

Chapter 11

Appendix A

Appendix B

Yes, the seven reasons employees leave remain fundamentally the same, even after the seismic changes that have shaken the economy and the job market these past few years since the first edition of this book. There have been some noteworthy changes that I have continued to track through our online Decision-to-Leave post-exit survey (www.keepingthepeople.com). I am pleased to be able to report what has changed and what hasn't in this revised edition.

The seven reasons, as you probably know, are hiding in plain sight, invisible only to those who continue to believe that employee turnover is mostly about pay.

In Chapters 2 and 3 of this new edition, you will find the results of more than 1,000 completed post-exit surveys that, when considered along with the original 19,700 Saratoga Institute surveys I analyzed in the original book, add new depth and relevance to the research. The new findings reveal answers to new questions, such as "Was there a triggering event?," "How long did it take until you actually left?," "What could your employer have done to make you want to change your mind and stay?," and "Did you look for another job while still employed?" The response percentages and frank comments may surprise you.

I am grateful to the visitors to my website who have taken the time to complete the Decision-to-Leave survey and have responded with passion and candor. Thanks in advance to all readers who are inclined to take the survey and encourage others to do so in the future.

My thanks also goes to my clients, who have continued to provide me with opportunities to deepen my own learning and enhance their understanding about why people choose to engage and disengage at work; my editor at AMACOM Books, Christina Parisi, who invited me to undertake this revision; my copyeditor, Jerilyn Famighetti, for her many improvements; and to the Saratoga Institute, which made the first edition possible by granting permission for me to analyze the thousands of post-exit surveys it had collected for its clients over the years.

Leigh Branham
January 2012

The 7 Hidden Reasons Employees Leave

Second Edition

CHAPTER ONE

Why Care About Why They Leave?

The greatest obstacle to discovery is not ignorance—
it is the illusion of knowledge

—Daniel Boorstin

It was almost six weeks since Anna had resigned her position with her former employer, but it was obvious that strong feelings were still stirring inside her.

"I was thrown into the job with no training. I asked for some one-on-one time with my manager to go over the project inside out, but he never had the time. I sensed he didn't really know enough to be able to thoroughly brief me, anyway.

"When I got feedback that certain work wasn't acceptable, he wouldn't be specific about how to correct it in the future. . . . He actually enjoyed intimidating people, and he had a terrible temper—he would ask me a question and, if I didn't know the answer, he would make fun of me in front of my coworkers. As it turns out, he wasn't following the right work procedures himself.

"Later, when I was working way below my skill set, I was told they weren't ready to give me a promotion, even though I had mastered everything.

"Finally, when I resigned, they didn't seem interested in why I was leaving. There was no exit interview. They never listened to me when I was there, and they certainly didn't care to listen when I left."

Anna went on to say that she loved her management position with her new employer: "I'm still doing what I love to do, but in a much more professional environment. There's open communication and no game playing. I know where I stand with them at all times."

One more thing—Anna went on to mention that she had hired away a talented colleague from her former company.

In the post-exit interviews I do for client companies with employees they regretted losing, these are the kinds of stories I hear. I know there are two sides to every story and that Anna's former manager might tell it differently. But I also know that there is truth in Anna's story, and in all the stories I hear—more truth than many were willing to tell their former employers when they checked out on their last day of employment.

The good news is that some companies do wake up and realize it's not too late to start listening to both former and current employees. Some grow alarmed at the sudden departure of highly valued workers who leave over the course of a few weeks. Others become concerned about protecting their reputation as a desirable place to work, and most simply want to make sure they have the talent they need to achieve their business objectives.

Why Many Managers Don't Care

The fact is that many managers and even senior executives simply don't care about why their employees are leaving. Their attitude seems to be "If you don't like it, don't let the door hit you in the backside on your way out!" If this sounds familiar, it should, because it describes the prevailing mindset of most managers in American companies today. Most are overworked, and many are frustrated by their inability to meet the demands of the current workforce, much less do exit interviews. And, increasingly, human resource departments are so understaffed that they have little time to do more than ask departing employees to complete perfunctory exit surveys on their last day. You care about preventing turnover, or you wouldn't be reading this book. So why *do* you care? Why even take the time and effort to uncover the real reasons employees leave? It would be much easier just to accept what most employees say in exit interviews. You know the usual answers—"more money," "better opportunity."

There are many ways to rationalize the loss of talent:

- Who has time to stop and wonder why they left, anyway? They're gone.
- They didn't want to be here, so why worry about what they think?
- They were probably just disgruntled or had the wrong attitude or just didn't fit.

- We can't expect to retain everybody we hire.
- There's nobody that isn't replaceable.
- Let's just get on with finding a replacement.

Of course, we cannot hope to keep all our valued talent. But good managers care enough to try to understand why good people leave, especially when the departure could have been prevented. There will always be managers who are too preoccupied, self-focused, or insensitive to notice the signs that employees are becoming disengaged and too uncaring, complacent, blaming, in denial, insecure, or ego-defensive to find out the real reasons they left. They too readily accept turnover as "a cost of doing business." They are too willing to believe the superficial reasons for leaving that employees give in exit interviews. Why? Psychologists call it "motivated blindness"; they cannot handle the truth—that the real reason the employee left may be linked to their own behavior. These managers are actually choosing not to see, hear, or speak the "evil" that plagues them.

As Brad, another employee, told me during an exit interview, "It seems like most managers just don't care enough to go to any effort to retain good people." But many managers do care enough to coach, train, develop, and keep their direct reports engaged. Now what we need are more organizations that make heroes of these managers, not just by praising them but also by measuring their contributions and rewarding them with serious money.

Managers Cannot Hear What Workers Will Not Speak

As we know, when exiting employees come to the question "Why are you leaving?," most are not inclined to tell the whole truth. Rather than risk burning a bridge with the former manager, whose reference they might need, they'll just say or write "better opportunity" or "higher pay." Why would they want to go into the unpleasant truth about how they never got any feedback or recognition from the boss or were passed over for promotion?

So, it is no wonder that in one survey, 89 percent of managers said they believe that employees leave and stay mostly for the money.[1] Yet, my own research,[2] the Saratoga Institute's surveys of almost twenty thousand workers from eighteen industries,[3] and the research reported in dozens of other studies reveal that about 80 to 90 percent of employees leave for reasons related *not* to the level of pay but to the job, the manager, the culture, or the work environment. These internal reasons—also known as "push" factors, as opposed to "pull" factors such as a better-paying outside opportunity—are within the power of the organization and the manager to change and control. But you can't change what you don't know. It is a simple case of "when you don't know what's causing the problem, you can't expect to fix it."

Figure 1.1.

What managers believe about reasons employees leave and why employees say they leave.

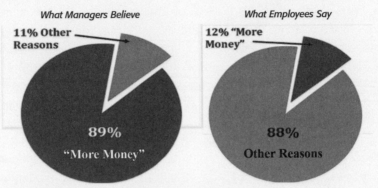

What Managers Believe

11% Other Reasons

89% "More Money"

What Employees Say

12% "More Money"

88% Other Reasons

Source: Harvard Management Update Survey; Saratoga post-exit surveys.

The Real Costs of Avoidable Turnover

This disconcerting disconnect between what managers believe and the reality—the true root causes of employee disengagement and turnover—is costing businesses in the billions of dollars per year. (See Figure 1.1.)

The Saratoga Institute estimated the cost of losing the average employee to be one times annual salary.[4] This means that a company with three hundred employees, an average employee salary of $35,000, and a voluntary turnover rate of 15 percent a year is losing $1,575,000 per year in turnover costs alone. If, for the sake of illustration, 70 percent of this company's forty-five yearly voluntary turnovers—thirty-one employees—are avoidable, then the company, by correcting the root causes, could be saving $1,102,500 per year. This should be enough to make most CEOs raise their eyebrows and take action. Just looking at turnover costs doesn't tell the whole story, however. Long before many employees leave, they become disengaged. Disengaged employees are uncommitted, marginally productive, frequently absent, or, in the case of the actively disengaged, actually working against the interests of the company. The Gallup Organization reports that 70 percent of the American workforce is either disengaged or actively disengaged.[5] (See Figure 1.2.)

Figure 1.2.

Employee engagement survey results.

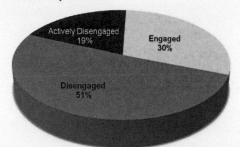

Source: "Engaged Workers Report Twice as Much Job Creation," *Gallup Management Journal*, August 9, 2011.

Actively disengaged workers can be particularly destructive to morale and revenues, for these are the workers who seek to disrupt, complain, have accidents, steal from the company, and occupy the time and attention of managers that would be far better spent dealing with other workers.

The cost to the U.S. economy of disengaged employees is estimated to be somewhere between $254 and $363 billion annually.[6] The cost of absenteeism alone, a signal symptom of disengagement, is estimated to be $40 billion per year.[7]

Most of the mind-boggling costs accumulate from the loss of sales revenue caused by customers' disappointing interactions with disengaged employees, many of whom are turnovers waiting to happen. Simply put, employee disengagement creates customer disengagement, and employee defections create customer defections.

Breaking it down further, Gallup found that "top-quartile workgroups (on employee engagement surveys) have:

- 12 Percent Higher Customer Metrics
- 18 Percent Higher Productivity
- 16 Percent Higher Profitability
- 37 Percent Lower Absenteeism
- 25 Percent Lower Turnover (in Low-Turnover Organizations)
- 49 Percent Lower Turnover (in High-Turnover Organizations)
- 27 Percent Less Theft
- 49 Percent Fewer Safety Incidents
- 41 Percent Fewer Patient Safety Incidents
- 60 Percent Fewer Quality Incidents (Defects).[8]

So, the best reason to be concerned about understanding the root causes of voluntary employee turnover and disengagement is an economic one. It's not about being nice to employees just to be nice, although civility is a standard of behavior to be prized in itself. It's about taking care of employees so that they will then feel good about taking care of customers.[9] The good news is that engaged employees actually create happy customers. So, if we can commit to correctly identifying the root causes of employee disengagement and if we can address these root causes with on-target solutions that increase the engagement of our workers, we will see tangible results in the form of reduced turnover costs and increased revenues.

Turnover: Just an Unavoidable "Cost of Doing Business"?

To review, almost 90 percent of managers believe that their employees are pulled out of the organization by better opportunities or more money, while an almost equal percentage of employees say the opposite—that they were pushed down the slippery slope toward leaving by nonmonetary factors. Where lies the truth? As with many things in organizational life, it's all about differing perceptions. The question is "*Whose* truth?"

From the viewpoint of today's managers, turnover is an acceptable cost of doing business. You've heard them say: "People come and people go"; "You can't expect to hold on to everyone forever"; "Good people get better offers and move on." There is a healthy realism in all these statements.

Recent History: When the Tide Turns, Mindsets Must Change

Let's also not forget that many of today's managers joined the managerial ranks in the 1980s and early 1990s when there were always more baby boomers to take the place of employees who quit. Ever since the first boomers entered the workforce, in 1968, the labor supply has always exceeded the demand. Then, in 1995, there came a tipping point. For the first time in recent memory, the number of jobs started to exceed the supply of workers. The "war for talent" had begun.

For the next six years, the war raged as companies made liberal use of signing bonuses and stock options to attract new employees. Some organizations vied to become "employers of choice" by offering everything from concierge services to massages to take-home meals, even letting their employees bring their pets to work. Employees had moved into the driver's seat.

Yet, a 1998 survey reported that, although 75 percent of executives said that employee retention was one of their top three business priorities, only 15 percent had any plan in place to reduce turnover.[10] It was apparent, by their failure to act, that the majority of managers and executives were stubbornly hanging onto the mindset that had served them so well in their formative years—"turnover is acceptable as a cost of doing business." Those who held on to this mindset soon found themselves competing for talent and losing to a minority of companies whose mindset—"every turnover is a disappointing loss to be analyzed"—was very different, reflecting the same attitude about losing a valued employee that they would have about losing a valued customer. Many of these companies were located in the Silicon Valley, where the war for talent was fiercest.

These companies formed the vanguard of employers who believed that their people came first, built cultures of mutual commitment, lowered their tolerance for bad managers, and came up with clever and innovative best practices for keeping and engaging talent. They were companies like Southwest Airlines, SAS Institute, MBNA, Edward Jones, Sun Microsystems, Synovus Financial, and Harley-Davidson, among many others. They were in the minority, as the best always are.

Then came the economic slowdown of 2001, when employees began "tree-hugging" their jobs and when replacements for those who quit most jobs were plentiful again. CEOs began "high-fiving" one another in celebration of the fact that the war for talent was over. Employers had moved back into the driver's seat. One *Fortune* column featured the headline "The War for Talent Is Over . . . Talent Lost."[11] Once again it seemed entirely appropriate that managers and executives would re-adopt that comfortable old belief that "turnover is acceptable as a cost of doing business."

We had a few good years before the crash and the return of the War for Talent. But, with the financial collapse of 2008, the unemployment rate topped 10 percent, and, once again, the job market turned in the favor of employers. Both managers and employees began adopting the "you're-lucky-to-have-a-job" mindset. Many employees have stayed longer with employers than they would have preferred, swallowed their frustration, and put up with mistreatment, but their restlessness and fatigue have increased along with their workloads. Many high performers—up to 25 percent in one study—are ready to bolt.[12]

It is understandable that managers' mindsets about "human capital" change as the job market changes. It is also easy to see why managers are less worried about employee turnover when there are plenty of unemployed or underemployed job seekers from whom to choose. And, when managers are not as worried about employees leaving, they are also not as likely to be concerned about *why* they are leaving.

But, as forward-thinking companies look ahead at the next several years, their leaders know they must do everything they can to coach and train their managers in how to engage, re-engage, and keep re-engaging talented people. Unfortunately, such leaders are in the minority. A study commissioned in 2011 found that, even though 90 percent of senior leaders said employee engagement impacts business success, 75 percent had no engagement plan or strategy.[13]

In our 2010 book, *Re-Engage*, Mark Hirshfeld and I reported that the employee engagement survey scores of two-thirds of companies participating in *Best Places to Work* competitions nationwide declined during the weeks and months following the crash of 2008. The interesting thing to us was that one-third of participating employers saw their engagement scores go up after the meltdown. As we describe in *Re-Engage*, these employers know that memories last longer than recessions, and they have redoubled their efforts to take special care of their workforces in tough times.

But what's going to happen when the economy improves again to the point where the rate of job creation revs up, just as 75 million boomers start retiring in greater numbers, and the 45 million job-seeking Generation Xers are too few to fill the available jobs?[14] (See Figure 1.3.) As this scenario plays out, the War for Talent will rage again. Employers of choice will once again fight tooth and nail for available talent, and those that lose will not survive as business entities.

This means that no manager can afford to maintain an outdated attitude about turnover. Competitive managers will need to shed the "replacement mindset" and adopt a "retention mindset," which holds that every voluntary avoidable employee defection is a disappointment to be analyzed, learned from, and corrected where possible. Maintaining that mindset means that managers cannot assume they know why employees quit. They cannot assume it was for "better pay" or "better opportunity," although in many cases it may be. Managers and senior executives need to know the truth about why they have lost valued talent, and they need to accept the truth that maybe it was something they did or didn't do that pushed the employee out the door.

Figure 1.3.

Generational labor force composition through 2030.

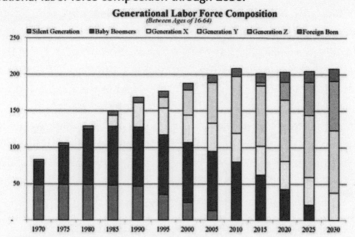

Data drawn from http://ericgarland.posterous.com/generational-labor-force-composition-in-america.

What About HR's Role in Exit Interviewing?

Some managers may say, "What about the human resources department—isn't it their responsibility to do the exit interviews, analyze the data, and report on the reasons employees leave?" Traditionally, these *have* been the responsibilities of human resource departments.

However, available evidence suggests that, in most organizations, HR departments and senior leaders are not providing the kind of meaningful data managers need about the root causes of employee turnover. A comprehensive study by the Saratoga Institute found that, although 95 percent of organizations say they conduct exit interviews, only 32 percent report the data to managers, and only 30 percent follow up with some kind of action. Forty-two percent of HR departments surveyed admitted that their exit interview programs were not effective.[15]

Many companies have concluded in recent years that the best way to understand the true causes of employee turnover is to have a third party contact the departed employee *after* the employee has left the company. Most thoughtful HR professionals understand that even the most skilled company interviewers will not elicit the whole truth from employees who do not wish to burn bridges by speaking negatively of the company or their manager.

HR professionals can play an important role by making sure that post-exit interviews or surveys are done, by linking exit data with engagement survey data, by reporting findings to management, and by partnering with all managers to provide needed resources to ensure that corrective actions are taken.

What must *not* happen is for managers to foist off on HR their own responsibility for keeping and engaging valued talent. HR is their partner in this process, but it should not be the sole accountable party. The key is that the entire organization, beginning with the senior management team, has to adopt a new mindset about talent.

We have seen that the old "replacement mindset" results in superficial understanding of employee turnover, leading to spiraling wage wars and the borrowing of other companies' practices—usually tangible, but off-target quick fixes—that may not be the right medicine for the kind of headache the next War for Talent will bring.

Notes

1. Marie Gendron, "Keys to Retaining Your Best Managers in a Tight Job Market," *Harvard Management Update* (June 1998): 1–4.
2. Decision to Leave post-exit survey, based on 991 responses, 2004–2011, www.keepingthepeople.com.
3. Leigh Branham, *The 7 Hidden Reasons Employees Leave* (New York: AMACOM Books, 2005).
4. Barbara Davidson and Jac Fitz-enz, "Retention Management," a study released by the Saratoga Institute, Santa Clara, California, and published by the American Management Association, 1997.
5. Jim Clifton, *The Coming Jobs War* (New York: Gallup Press, 2011).
6. Ibid.
7. Ibid.
8. Ibid.
9. Hal F. Rosenbluth and Diane McFerrin Peters, *The Customer Comes Second: And Other Secrets of Exceptional Service* (Quill, 1992).
10. Charles Fishman, "The War for Talent," *Fast Company*, August 1998.
11. Geoffrey Colvin, "The War for Talent Is Over . . . Talent Lost," *Fortune*, October 2002.
12. Right Management survey, January 2011.
13. Survey commissioned by ACCOR Services, 2011.
14. Data drawn from http://ericgarland.posterous.com/generational-labor-force-composition-in-america.
15. Davidson and Fitz-enz, "Retention Management."

How They Disengage and Quit

> Some quit and leave ...
> others quit and stay.
>
> —Anonymous

Before I introduce the main reasons employees disengage, it is essential that we understand the dynamics of how they go through the disengagement process. Understanding the unfolding nature of employee disengagement helps us see how we can interrupt the process and salvage key talent at any of several steps down the decision staircase.

The first thing to realize is that employee turnover is not a single event; it is really a process of disengagement that can take days, weeks, months, or even years until the actual decision to leave arrives (if it ever does). Here's what David, an accountant, told me three weeks after resigning:

"On my very first day I started thinking of leaving. I was given an assignment, and I realized very quickly that I was not going to receive any mentoring or support."

For Dave, it was all downhill from there—even though several months elapsed before he resigned, the first day was the turning point.

As the stair-step graphic shows (Figure 2.1), there are actually several sequential and predictable steps that can unfold in the employee's journey from disengagement to leaving.

Of course, many managers are so busy or preoccupied that their employees could walk around with signs pinned to their chests saying "Thinking of Leaving" or "Staying, but Disengaging" or whatever step in the disengagement

Figure 2.1.

Steps in the disengagement-to-departure process.

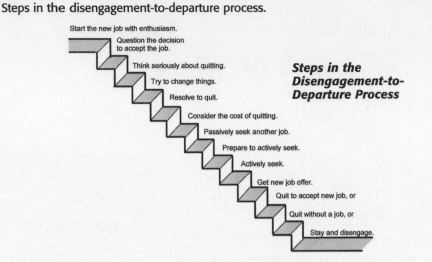

Source: T. R. Lee, T. R Mitchell, L. Wise, and S. Fireman, "An Unfolding Model of Employee Turnover," *Academy of Management Journal* 39 (1966): 5–36.

process they happen to be on, and their managers still wouldn't notice. Not that it's only the manager's responsibility to take the initiative in this process—employees need to understand they have a responsibility to find ways of addressing their concerns and re-engaging themselves in the workplace. But the truth is that many managers are too slow to observe the telltale signs of employee disengagement until it's too late to do anything about it.

The obvious early-warning signs of disengagement are absenteeism, tardiness, and behavior that indicates withdrawal or increased negativity. It is also useful to know that these early signs of disengagement typically start showing up after a *shocking or jarring event* takes place that causes the employee to question his or her commitment.

Events That Trigger Employee Disengagement

Here are some stimulus events that can trigger disengagement:

- Being Passed Over for Promotion
- Realizing That the Job Is not as Promised
- Learning That One May Be Transferred
- Having the Hiring Boss Replaced by New Boss the Employee Doesn't Like

- Being Assigned to a New Territory
- Being Asked to Do Something Unethical
- Learning That the Company Is Doing Something Unethical
- Earning Enough Money to Retire or Pursue New Life Choice (e.g., Windfall or Grubstake)
- Being Subjected to Sexual Harassment
- Being Subjected to Racial Discrimination
- Learning That the Company Has Been Purchased
- Realizing That One Is Underpaid Compared to Others Who Are Doing the Same Job
- Realizing That One Is Not in Line for an Expected Promotion
- Realizing That One's Own Performance or Behavior Has Become Unacceptable
- Receiving a Sudden Outside Job Offer
- Being Pressured to Make an Unreasonable Family or Personal Sacrifice
- Being Asked to Perform a Menial Duty (e.g., Clean the Bathroom)
- Being Subjected to a Petty and Unreasonable Enforcement of Authority
- Being Denied a Request for Family Leave
- Being Denied a Request for Transfer
- Having a Close Colleague Quit or Be Terminated
- Disagreeing with the Boss
- Having a Conflict with a Coworker
- Receiving an Unexpectedly Low Performance Rating
- Receiving a Small or No Pay Increase

The "Last Straw" That Breaks the Employee-Employer Bond

Sometimes, departed employees use the term "last straw" as they describe these events.

As a nurse named Karen told me:

"I was happy there two years ago, but my manager left, and my new manager was not a good mentor or coach. She was just coasting to retirement, but she was moody and unprofessional. . . . And then one day she yelled at me. I went to her manager about it, but she just excused her behavior, saying, 'That's just the way she is.' That was the last straw for me."

Here are excerpts from other post-exit interviews that illustrate the turning-point phenomenon:

"The head of our department changed, and I felt the new one didn't seek my input or recognize my contributions. Then, the work started becoming more administrative than technical. . . . I felt like I was just shuffling papers and not designing anything. That's when I started looking elsewhere, and a coworker referred me to the company I now work for." (Dan, an engineer)

"My managers made it very clear they didn't want my input. They could have made such good use of my language ability, but I got the cold shoulder. They had an old boy network mindset. . . . I went to a national company meeting because my manager couldn't attend—it was 95 percent male, and no one even came up and introduced themselves. That did it for me. After that, I started looking and I had a new job in six weeks." (Janine, business analyst)

"I wasn't being challenged. . . . And then I came across payroll information while doing some project costing and discovered that I was paid 15 percent less than everyone else in my group. That was the turning point." (John, financial analyst)

"I had a degree from a prestigious university, and my manager would take pot shots at me in front of others. . . . Then he started giving me menial work to do, like taking things to mail and Fed-Ex. He would say, 'It's more cost-effective for you to do this than for me to do it.' I started looking for a job after only three months on the job." (Pamela, technical writer)

Here's a sampling of the comments from our Decision to Leave website (www.keepingthepeople.com) survey in which employees described "the last straw," starting with comments about respondents' immediate managers:

- "Being told that my best skills (organization and time management) were the ones I needed to work on."
- "When my boss unfairly required me to arrange doctor's appointments on evenings and weekends."

- "Promotion denied; found out that the boss did not even show up to the meeting to discuss it."
- "My employer didn't want to 'offend' two inefficient coworkers, tried to be a buddy to everyone."
- "I couldn't go get my son from daycare when he was sick without getting reprimanded."
- "Got negative reaction when I took time off to care for a terminally sick family member."
- "Was denied a benefit that was given to another employee in the same position."
- "The coworker the boss was sleeping with got promoted over me."
- "Public recognition for someone who was not a team player/did not carry her weight."

Many comments refer to actions taken by more senior leaders:

- "Seeing an unethical manager promoted."
- "Company owner swearing at a customer in an open Internet forum."
- "The arbitrary termination of half of the employees within one week."
- "Announcement that WorldCom was buying MCI—Bernie Ebbers was just too sleazy for me."
- "Significant staff turnover without a change in governance from the Board."
- "Management treating professional staff like imbeciles, top-down communication only."
- "They began to push the founder out, then fired her friends, it was not a good place to be."
- "Was berated by an SVP who made me feel incompetent for making a small mistake."
- "I saw the owner taking money from the till, and I quit the next morning."
- "When my employer groped me to see if I was wearing underwear."
- "Workload was excessive and the senior HR management were not listening to the concerns."

- "Fell back on promise to pay me back for my real estate course that they asked me to take."
- "They moved me for my 'protection' instead of removing the bullying manager and her minions."

More of the triggering-event comments pointed to higher-up executives than singled out the direct manager, providing a bit more evidence to support our finding in my recent book, *Re-Engage* (coauthored with Mark Hirschfeld and based on our analysis of 2.1 million employee engagement surveys), that the actions of senior leaders figure slightly more significantly than those of direct managers in the employee engagement equation.

Other turning points mentioned in the survey were less specific about the root cause of a decision to leave, but no less emotional:

- "I couldn't sleep at night thinking of having to go back in."
- "I realized my job was literally making me sick!"
- "Realization that coworkers were not the people I wanted to be with professionally."
- "Had a heart attack at work."

Pull-factor triggers or turning points mentioned were diverse:

- "My Dream Job opened up at my professional society."
- "New opportunity to work in a creative environment."
- "Was accepted to grad school."
- "We had our first child and decided we wanted to be closer to our parents and siblings."
- "Received a $7,000 annual increase in pay with guaranteed work-from-home opportunity."
- "Mental health issues."
- "The end of a 3-year $400 million project."
- "Paying my tuition."

Sometimes the push-and-pull turning points occurred at the same time:

- "Opportunity to spend more time with family as the company was quickly failing."

- "Resolve that nothing would change and I needed to leave. Exciting new opportunity presented itself."

The Bottom Line for Leaders and Managers

Keeping employees engaged is just as much about avoiding the triggers for disengagement as it is about doing the proactive things that spark engagement. We cannot prevent all turnover, nor do we want to, but, if we are alert to the kinds of events that precipitate thoughts of leaving and other behavioral warning signs, we may be able to re-engage the employee before it's too late.

Figure 2.2 shows the percentages of yes/no responses to our Web survey question about whether there was a turning-point event in the employee's decision to leave.

Figure 2.2.

Decision to Leave survey of 1,000+ respondents, 2004–2012.

Q: "Was there a triggering event?"

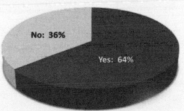

Source: www.KeepingthePeople.com.

Dr. Thomas Lee, a business professor at the University of Washington, who has extensively researched what he calls "the unfolding model of turnover,"[1] reports several interesting findings about how and why people disengage and leave:

- The majority of voluntary turnovers—63 percent—are precipitated by some kind of shocking event.
- Very few employees start thinking of leaving because of shocking events related to pay.
- About 20 percent of departing employees leave without having another job in hand.

- Some leave when the job offer is "likely," not waiting until it is in hand.

- Temporary, part-time, and marginal workers are more likely to quit suddenly or impulsively after a shock rather than enter into a drawn-out period evaluating the situation.

- Many talented employees keep an eye out for other jobs while working and interview for outside opportunities for practice, to create a "plan B," or to test their marketability.

- Many employees leave because of "personal shocks" unrelated to their workplace, such as marriage, pregnancy, inheritance, having the last child leave home, deciding to relocate, becoming a caregiver for a family member in health crisis, or paying off one's mortgage.

- Exit surveying or interviewing that doesn't uncover the shock (turning point) and get the employee to discuss the deliberation process, if there was one, will not reveal the root cause. Dr. Lee also points out that there are two distinct periods in an employee's process of thinking about leaving. The first period is the time between an employee's first thoughts of quitting and the subsequent decision to leave. As an example, one ex-employee said, "After the merger, I gave it a year to see what the company would be like, and I tried to keep my attitude positive, but things were no different, so I started looking." Another man I interviewed recounted how, the day his promotion took effect, no letter of notification went out, which he took as a personal slight. He first started thinking about leaving later when he felt he had proved himself in his current position and asked for more responsibility but was turned down. Because he had lived abroad for a year, apart from his wife and son, he felt the company owed him a new opportunity. Instead of getting the job he wanted, he was transferred.

The Active-Seeking Phase of the Departure Process

The second period in the process of departure is the time between the employee's decision to leave and the actual leaving. (See Figure 2.3.) As you might expect, the chances of a manager re-recruiting and successfully gaining renewed commitment from an employee are greater during the first period, when the employee is just thinking about leaving, than during the second period of active seeking. This is why it is important for managers to be alert to the signs that an employee is just starting to disengage when there is still time to do something about it. Since most disengagements begin with some

Figure 2.3.

Decision to Leave survey of 1,000+ respondents, 2004–2012.

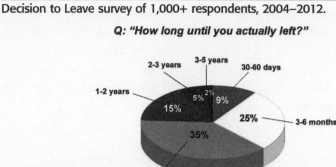

Source: www.KeepingthePeople.com.

kind of shocking event like those listed, managers need to keep their antennae up for signals that a valued employee may have experienced such a shock.

Or, better yet, because it is often hard to read the feelings of employees from the looks on their faces, managers should simply sit down with their direct reports on a regular basis and ask, *"How are things with you?"* The talent losses described earlier might have been avoided if the managers had cared enough to sit down with the employees at some point in their disengagement/deliberation process and ask a simple question: "How are you feeling about things in general?" (See Figure 2.4.) That might have opened a discussion that could have led to a resolution of the employee's issue.

Figure 2.4.

Decision to Leave survey of 1,000+ respondents, 2004–2012.

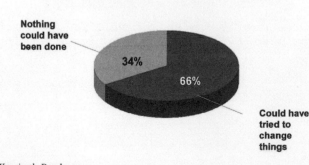

Source: www.KeepingthePeople.com.

Perhaps the employees could have done more on their own initiative to resolve the situations, or maybe they did all they could, or perhaps the managers simply couldn't accommodate the employees' wishes. (See Figure 2.5.) We will never know. The point is that, if the manager does not regularly initiate such discussions and the discussions never happen, it is the manager and the organization that risk suffering the loss of talent and the many costs of employee turnover, including the lost productivity incurred during the active seeking phase.

Figure 2.5.

Decision to Leave survey of 1,000+ respondents, 2004–2012.

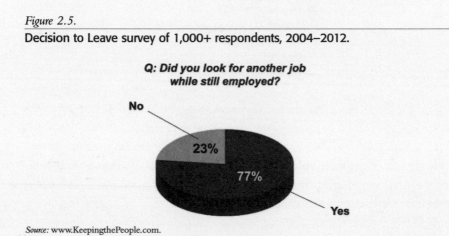

Source: www.KeepingthePeople.com.

When we consider the gradual, unfolding nature of employee disengagement and the research that reveals that 70+ percent of employees are not engaged, there can be but one conclusion—that the need for managers to initiate action to engage and re-engage employees is critical and that the daily opportunity to do so is ever present.

Note

1. T. W. Lee, T. R. Mitchell, L. Wise, and S. Fireman, "An Unfolding Model of Employee Turnover," *Academy of Management Journal* 39 (1966): 5–36.

CHAPTER THREE

Why They Leave: What the Research Reveals

The Root Causes of Employee Disengagement and Turnover

Sometimes if we cut through the brain
and get to the gut, we learn the truth.

—JAC FITZ-ENZ

If you were to compile an alphabetical list of all the reasons people give for leaving their job voluntarily from the exit surveys of dozens of organizations, it would look something like this:

Better-Paying Job

Bureaucracy

Career Change

Commuting Time or Distance

Concerns About Organization's Future

Conflict with Coworker

Difficulties with Immediate Supervisor

Discrimination Based on Race, Gender, Religion, or Other Factors

Dishonest or Unethical Leaders or Managers

Excessive Workload

Favoritism

Fear of Job Elimination

Geographic Location of the Job

Health Concerns

Ideas Not Welcomed

Inability to Master the Job

Inadequate Benefits

Inflexible Work Hours

Insufficient Challenge

Insufficient or Inappropriate Training

Insufficient Resources to Do the Job

Job Elimination

Job Itself

Job Responsibilities

Job Security

Lack of Advancement Opportunity

Lack of Caring Leadership

Lack of Earnings Potential

Lack of Teamwork

Lack of Trust or Confidence in Senior Leaders

Lack of Work-Life Balance

Little or No Empowerment

Little or No Growth or Developmental Opportunity

Little or No Performance Feedback

Negative Work Environment

No Authority to Do the Job

No Career Path

No Consequences for Nonperformers

No Way to Voice Concerns

Not Allowed to Complete the Job

Not Allowed to Do the Job as the Employee Prefers

Not Paid Competitively

Not Paid in Proportion to Contributions

Not Recognized for Contributions

Organization Culture

Organization Instability or Turmoil

Organization Politics

Outdated or Inadequate Equipment

Physical Facility Noisy, Dirty, Hot, Cramped, or Otherwise Unpleasant

Poor Communication

Poor Treatment

Retirement

Return to School

Self-Employment

Sexual Harassment

Small or No Bonus

Spouse Relocation

Stress

Timeliness of Pay Increases

Too Many Changes

Unfair Pay Increases

Unfair Performance Appraisal Process

Unfair Promotion Practices

Unfair Rules, Policies, or Procedures

Unwanted Change in Job Duties

Unwanted Relocation

Vacation Policy

These sixty-seven reasons were, in fact, culled from exit survey responses completed by thousands of exiting employees. Even this long list may be incomplete. When you take away the *seemingly* unpreventable reasons—lack of advancement opportunity, better-paying job, career change, commuting time or distance, geographic location of job, job elimination, retirement, return to school, self-employment, and spouse relocation—that still leaves fifty-seven preventable reasons for voluntary turnover out of the sixty-seven total reasons on the list. I have read and categorized the comments made by more than four thousand employees who voluntarily left their employers since 1998, as surveyed by the Saratoga Institute[1] and through my own open-to-the-public Decision to Leave post-exit Web survey.[2] As I read them, I could not help being touched by the emotions expressed—disappointment, frustration, anger, disillusionment, dismay, resentment, betrayal, to name the most common. There were many positive comments and emotions, as well, but the negative ones were somehow more poignant, powerful, and instructive. It occurred to me that very few of the "reasons" for turnover were based on reasoned thinking; they were mostly rooted in strong feelings such as those just mentioned.

As I analyzed the reasons for leaving and grouped them into categories or themes, peeling layers off the onion in search of root causes, I found some common denominators. It became clear to me that employees begin to disengage and think about leaving their employers when at least one of four fundamental human needs is not being met.

The four fundamental needs are:

1.   *The Need for Trust:* Expecting the company and management to deliver on their promises, to be honest and open in all communications, to invest in you, to treat you fairly, and to pay you fairly and on time.

2.   *The Need to Have Hope:* Believing that you will be able to grow professionally, use and develop your skills on the job and through training, and, for many employees, have the opportunity for advancement or career progress, leading to higher earnings.

3.   *The Need to Feel Worthy and Respected:* Feeling confident that if you work hard, do your best, demonstrate commitment, and make meaningful contributions, you will be recognized and rewarded accordingly, shown respect, and regarded as a valued asset, not a cost, to the organization.

4.   *The Need to Feel Competent as You Gain Mastery:* Expecting that you will be matched to a job that makes good use of your talents and is challenging and that you will receive opportunities to learn to perform the job capably, prepare for future roles, be allowed to see the end results of your work, and obtain regular feedback on your performance.

Why Employees Say They Leave

When I read through the reasons employees gave for leaving their jobs in confidential third-party surveys,[3] it became obvious which of these needs were not being met. Frequently, what appears to be a simple statement of dissatisfaction actually points directly to one of these four themes.

As we see in the breakdown of reasons for leaving presented in Figure 3.1, the responses to the question "Why did you leave?" on the Saratoga survey can be grouped according to the four primary needs.

As you can see, lack of trust was the most common of the four themes, representing 31 percent of the total. This supports the research finding of the Great Place to Work Institute that trust is the single most important driver of employee engagement and commitment.

There were also unavoidable reasons—those generally considered unpreventable by the organization. These amounted to only 5 percent of the reasons given and include excessive commuting distance, retirement, birth of a child, childcare issues, relocation, other family issues, career change, too much travel, return to school, and death or illness in the family.

Figure 3.1.

Saratoga Institute post-exit survey reasons for leaving, categorized by four unmet needs of workers.

Lack of Hope	**Lack of Trust**	**Lack of Worth**	**Lack of Competence**
Limited career growth or advancement opportunity (16%)	Lack of respect or support by supervisor (13%)	Inadequate compensation (12%)	Boring or unchallenging job duties (11%)
	Supervisor's lack of leadership skills (9%)	Inflexible or undesirable work hours (6%)	
	Favoritism by supervisor (4%)	Lack of recognition (4%)	
	Poor senior leadership (2%)	Poor working conditions (3%)	
	Supervisor's lack of technical skills (1%)	Lack of training (3%)	
	Discrimination (1%)	Inadequate benefits (1%)	
	Harassment (1%)		
	Coworker issues (1%)		

What Caused Workers' Initial Dissatisfaction?

As noted in Chapter 2, employees often experience an initial shock or disappointment that may ultimately result in their leaving the organization. The Saratoga Institute used to include the question "What caused your initial dissatisfaction?" in its post-exit survey, but it dropped the question after reviewing the first 950 responses. It turned out that the reasons for leaving as shown in Figure 3.1 were identical to the reasons for initial dissatisfaction and in the same order from top to bottom! This lends added weight to the conclusion that most people ultimately leave for a reason that had as its genesis an event that may have occurred months earlier. Again, the key reminder and the good news in this for managers is this: *There is a built-in period of possible "rescue time" during which they have the opportunity to identify the employee's dissatisfaction and attempt to correct it*—if they care enough to do so.

Survey Comments Confirm the Survey Data

To get below the surface of the survey responses, the Saratoga Institute conducted focus groups with respondents to probe further into their reasons for leaving. It then analyzed the content of the written survey comments. When employees were asked to give open-ended feedback, either in writing or open discussion, they were no longer just responding to prefabricated questions—they were speaking from their hearts about the needs that were not met.

Here, in order, are the ten most frequently mentioned issues that surfaced in departed employees' written and spoken responses to Saratoga's question: "What did your employer do poorly?"

- *Poor Management:* Comments focused mostly on uncaring, incompetent, and unprofessional managers; there were also complaints about being overworked, not getting respect, not having their ideas listened to, and being put in the wrong jobs, as well as the company's making no effort to retain staff, emphasizing speed over quality, and being abusive. There were also many comments about poor or nonexistent methods of selecting managers. (Unmet needs: trust, worth, hope, and competence)

- *Lack of Career Growth and Advancement Opportunity:* Comments were mainly about having no perceivable career path, but also mentioned companies' failure to post jobs or to fill jobs from within and unfair promotions or favoritism. (Unmet needs: hope, trust, and competence)

- *Poor Communications:* Comments were mostly about poor top-down communication from managers and senior leaders and lack of openness with information, but also mentioned poor communications between departments, from the human resources department, from corporate offices to field offices, and following mergers. (Unmet needs: trust and worth)

- *Pay:* Comments were mostly about not being paid fair market rates and not being paid in proportion to their contributions and hard work. Respondents also complained of pay inequities, slow pay raises, favoritism in giving raises and bonuses, and ineffective performance appraisal processes. (Unmet needs: trust and worth)

- *Lack of Recognition:* This issue is connected to issues of pay and workload, but there were many comments about the organization's culture not being one that encourages recognition of employee contributions. (Unmet need: worth)

- *Poor Senior Leadership:* Comments asserted that companies don't care about, listen to, or invest in employees but also mentioned leaders being isolated, remote, and unresponsive, failing to provide an inspiring vision or direction, sending mixed messages, and making too many changes in direction and poor organizational structure. (Unmet need: trust and worth)

• *Lack of Training:* Comments were mainly about employees not receiving enough training to do their current jobs properly, but also cited the poor quality of training, being rushed through superficial training, not being allowed to attend training, lack of new-hire training, poor management training, and lack of training for future advancement. (Unmet need: worth, hope, and competence)

• *Excessive Workload:* Commenters mainly spoke about being asked to do more with fewer staff, but also mentioned that quality and customer service are sacrificed to "make the numbers." (Unmet needs: worth and competence)

• *Lack of Tools and Resources:* Comments cited a range of issues, including lack of office supplies, malfunctioning computers, outdated technology, and insufficient staffing. (Unmet needs: worth, hope, and competence)

• *Lack of Teamwork:* Commenters spoke about lack of cooperation and commitment to get the job done among coworkers but also mentioned a lack of coordination between departments or different locations (Unmet needs: trust and competence)

As you can see (and probably expected), the root causes for leaving mentioned in the survey and in focus-group comments closely parallel the root causes identified in Saratoga's quantitative data as shown in Figure 3.1.

Have the Reasons for Leaving Changed Since the Great Recession?

With the near-collapse of the global economy in the fall of 2008, which brought on new waves of downsizings, wage freezes, and cuts in health benefits, it's not unreasonable to suspect that the reasons employees leave might have changed. This is why I continue to track reasons for leaving through my Decision to Leave post-exit Web survey, which anyone who has ever left an employer can complete (by visiting www.keepingthepeople.com and clicking on Resources, then Surveys).

Since the Decision to Leave post-exit Web survey went up in 2004, just more than one thousand visitors to the Keeping the People website have taken the time to complete it. Respondents represent all major industries, position levels, functions, and age groupings. Hourly and salaried nonexempt account for 37 percent of the survey-takers, with the rest professional/technical workers, managers, and executives. As expected, a significant portion—22 percent—are HR professionals. Respondents are asked to think of a job they voluntarily left in the past and then respond to survey questions as they recall the reasons for and the circumstances surrounding their decision to leave and their eventual departure.

The survey presents respondents with a list of thirty-nine possible reasons for leaving and asks them to select up to five that most prominently entered into their decision to exit. Here is the exact wording: "From the list below, please check up to, but no more than, five factors that first caused you to start thinking seriously about leaving your organization." The question was worded this way in order to bring to the surface the root cause of the exit, which is not necessarily the same reason the employee might give during an on-site exit interview.

Of the thirty-nine reasons, twenty-eight are "push" factors related to an issue originating within the workplace and eleven are "pull" factors indicating an external attraction. Here, then, in order, are the reasons people give for leaving a job, with the percentages of respondents who selected them in parenthesis:

Reported Reasons for Leaving:	Exit Factor
1. Lack of Trust in Senior Leaders (10.6%)	Push
2. Insufficient Pay (5.7%)	Push
3. Unhealthy or Undesirable Culture (5.5%)	Push
4. Company's Lack of Concern for Development (5.1%)	Push
5. Lack of Honesty, Integrity, Ethics (4.9%)	Push
6. Unfair Treatment (4.8%)	Push
7. Lack of Open Communication (4.6%)	Push
8. Lack of Encouragement of Input or Ideas (4.6%)	Push
9. Lack of Teamwork Among Coworkers (4.5%)	Push
10. Excessive Workload (4.4%)	Push
11. Lack of Opportunity for Training and Development (3.9%)	Push
12. Lack of Recognition (3.9%)	Push

Reported Reasons for Leaving:	Exit Factor
13. Lack of Clear Expectations (3.8%)	Push
14. Uncertainty About Future of Company (3.8%)	Push
15. Uninteresting or Unchallenging Work (3.6%)	Push
16. Lack of Needed Resources (3.2%)	Push
17. Pay Not Based on Performance (2.6%)	Push
18. Lack of Encouragement of Input or Ideas (2.3%)	Push
19. Unfair Pay Practices (2.1%)	Push
20. Uncertainty About Job Security (2.0%)	Push
21. Lack of Work-Life Balance (1.9%)	Push
22. Negative Relationship with Coworker (1.7%)	Push
23. Decision to Change Careers (1.7%)	Pull
24. Unexpected Job or Career Opportunity (1.6%)	Pull
25. Lack of Focus on Quality (1.5%)	Push
26. Lack of Feedback (1.5%)	Push
27. Inflexible Work Arrangements (1.3%)	Push
28. Lack of Focus on Productivity (1.2%)	Push
29. Unsatisfactory Benefits (1.0%)	Push
30. Desire to Spend More Time with Family (.09%)	Pull
31. Excessive Travel Demands (.08%)	Push
32. Desire to Relocate (.07%)	Pull
33. Desire to Start a Business (.05%)	Pull
34. Desire to Return to School (.05%)	Pull
35. Desire to Start a Family (.04%)	Pull
36. Family Emergency/Illness (.04%)	Pull
37. Spouse or Partner Relocation (.03%)	Pull
38. Retirement (.03%)	Pull
39. Inheritance or Monetary Windfall (.005%)	Pull

What the New Data Reveal

An analysis of these data reveals several key points:

- *Most turnover is avoidable.* The vast majority of respondents—94 percent—*report leaving more for push reasons than for pull reasons.* This percentage is almost exactly the same as that reported in Saratoga's post-exit data, as presented in the first edition of this book, in 2005 (Figure 3.2).

Figure 3.2.

Degree of employer/employee control over decision to leave.

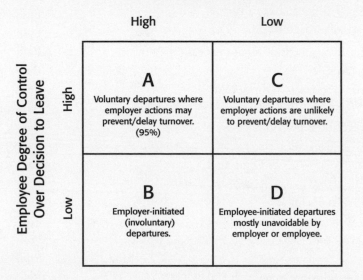

Source: *The 7 Hidden Reasons Employees Leave,* by Leigh Branham (New York: AMACOM Books, 2005), citing Saratoga Institute (Santa Clara, California) research on employee commitment, satisfaction, and turnover, conducted from 1996 to 2003.

As we see in Figure 3.2, depending on the degree of employee control over the decision and the degree of employer influence over that decision, there are four possible categories.[4] If we look back at the list of four needs that are at the root of why employees leave their employers and subtract the unavoidable situations over which the employer had little or no control (e.g., retirement, unacceptable commuting distance, return to school, desire to start own business, family illness/circumstances), we see that about 95 percent of the remaining reasons fit into quadrant A (voluntary and preventable by managers and senior leaders).

The more recent findings support the earlier finding to a remarkably precise degree—within 1 percent—and reaffirm that most turnover is potentially preventable if there is a commitment to re-engage and keep the individual. Of course, we may not care to prevent some employees from leaving even though their departure may be avoidable. We should also acknowledge that a manager or organization cannot always prevent an employee from leaving or even delay the decision to leave.

Toward the end of the Decision-to-Leave Web survey, we ask respondents to choose, from three possible choices, the one that best describes their motivation to leave their former employer. The responses are shown in Figure 3.3.

The finding that people are more than five times more likely to leave a job because of an internal issue than in response to an outside opportunity would come as a surprise to significant numbers of managers.

Figure 3.3.

Decision to Leave web survey, 2004–2012.

Q: *What motivated your decision to leave?*

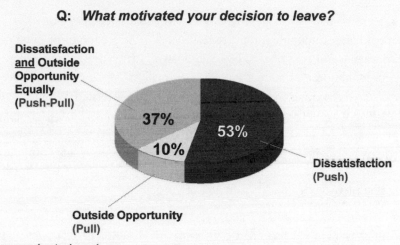

Source: www.keepingthepeople.com.

There were several additional findings in the Web survey data:

- *Lack of trust in senior leaders is a major problem.* This was the #1 reason for employee resignations. This finding may surprise some and certainly runs counter to the conventional wisdom that employees leave because of their managers, usually interpreted to mean one's immediate boss. However, this finding confirms the conclusion Mark Hirschfeld and I presented in our analysis of 2.1 million engagement surveys from ten thousand employers, as described in our book, *Re-Engage*—that caring, competent, and trustworthy senior leadership is the number one driver of employee engagement.

We believe this may be related to the events of the past ten years— the fall from grace of CEOs found guilty of malfeasance, reports of disproportionate CEO compensation, and the greed of Wall Street senior executives before and after the financial collapse of 2008. Sadly, many employees now consider CEOs guilty until proven innocent instead of innocent until proven guilty. The Center for Work-Life Policy (according to *Bloomberg Businessweek*) reported in 2011 that the percentage of Americans who trust their organizational leaders has dropped from 79 percent to 37 percent.[5] This generalized distrust may be having a dual and counterintuitive effect—increasing employee cynicism while at the same time making many employees so much more acutely aware of leader misbehavior that they hope for and even expect better CEO behavior at their own employers.

• *Pay is a significant push factor for some.* Insufficient pay (cited by 5.7 percent as being among their top five reasons) was the second most-cited reason for leaving and continues to be a "dissatisfier" that causes some employees to begin looking for a different employer. Actually, as you may have noticed, three of the thirty-nine website-survey reasons are pay-related. When we add reasons #17 (pay not based on performance—2.6 percent) and #19 (unfair pay practices—2.1 percent), the percentage of respondents who selected pay-related reasons increases to 10.4 percent, still second to problems with senior leadership but nonetheless a significant root cause for many, one that is statistically consistent with Saratoga's finding of 12 percent.

Note that reasons #17 and #19 have more to do with dissatisfaction with the way pay is determined than with the amount of pay per se—an important distinction. Keep in mind also that respondents were asked to cite up to five reasons for leaving, so pay may not be the respondent's number one reason for leaving but one among a handful of others.

• *Leaders and managers can prevent the push factors.* The third most cited reason in the Web survey—unhealthy or undesirable culture—is mostly influenced by the values, mindsets, and standards of senior leaders, but it is also impacted by managers who must be counted on to uphold the cultural values and people practices. Most of the remaining push factors in the list of reasons for leaving can be influenced and prevented by the actions of both senior leaders, managers, and supervisors. "Lack of work/life balance," for example, is influenced by staffing/budget decisions and work/life policies made at the most senior levels, but also by the daily decisions of direct managers about matters such as granting time off to care for sick children and family emergencies.

• *The twenty-nine push factors from the Web survey still fall easily into the seven major themes or categories* as initially described in *The 7 Hidden Reasons Employees Leave* when it was first published in 2005.

In conclusion: Most of the reasons employees disengage and leave are consistent, predictable, and avoidable, if the employers have the desire to retain and are willing to invest the time to take preventive or corrective actions. This is good news, since most such actions don't require significant monetary investment. They generally do cost time, and, yes, time is money; but the cost of disengagement and turnover is greater than the cost of trying to retain valued employees.

A Few More Words About Pay

In spite of the fact that hundreds of employees surveyed had worked for companies that did not pay salaries competitive with those of other companies in their industries, compensation issues still were behind no more than 12 percent of all decisions to leave.

This finding is consistent with the conclusion of Saratoga's comprehensive report, in which the authors, Barbara Davison and Jac Fitz-enz, stated in their chapter on why employees leave:

> Pay . . . is often a smokescreen, not a primary reason that employees leave one organization and move to another. Competitive pay is fundamental to retention; however, the ramifications of continually 'buying' employees are not always in the best interest of the organization. The remaining employees are always affected, pay plans become ineffective, and the financial impact can be far-reaching.... However, maintaining a competitive pay plan on the front end and facing up to job and working conditions has a greater positive effect.[6]

One of the first laws of retaining employees is to pay at or above what the market is paying for similar jobs. Competitive pay is merely the ticket to admission for organizations wishing to qualify as employers of choice, yet survey results make it clear that many companies have not yet purchased that ticket.

Regarding the individual employee's decision to stay or leave because of concerns about pay, Saratoga's former director of research, W. Michael Kelly, observed, "The rule of thumb is that an unhappy employee will bolt the company for a five percent pay increase, but it will take at least an increase of 20 percent to compel a satisfied employee to jump ship."[7] Of course, pay is more important to some people than it is to others. We know that many employees who struggle to pay their bills can understandably be enticed to leave by increases of less than 5 percent. Several studies have also shown that, in general, salespeople are more motivated by money than are most other workers. And, at the other end of the spectrum, we all know individuals whose loyalty to their employer or to their manager is so strong that they have turned down offers of 30 percent or more because they could not imagine being treated better or finding a more satisfying job elsewhere.

In reviewing survey comments about pay from both leavers and stayers, it is striking how few comments have to do with the actual amount of salary, bonus, or other incentive. Rather, the key issue seems to be fairness or the lack thereof. Employees seem to be frustrated about pay because they have observed what they consider to be several kinds of inequities:

- Superior performance reviews have little effect on pay increases.
- Experience is discounted when new hires are paid as much as veterans.
- Higher education levels do not translate into higher pay levels.
- Increasing stress and aggravation aren't worth the money.
- Working more and more hours make the pay worth less and less.

As Dr. Kelly commented, "What is most disturbing about these beliefs is that they fly in the face of an employee's desire to know and understand the formal and informal rules for attaining higher pay levels—performance, experience, education, willingness to sacrifice, and undergo hardships. If these are not linked to increases in pay, they ask, then what is? Pay policies and practices that do not encourage and support employee commitment present obstacles that even the most capable supervisor will find formidable, if not impossible, to deal with."[8]

Respecting the Differences

It's worth noting that the seven major reasons employees leave were distilled from the comments of employees at all position levels in a wide range of industries—financial, industrial, medical, technology, manufacturing, distribution, insurance, health care, telecommunications, transportation, computer services, electronics, consumer products, consumer services, business services, consulting, and other services.

In reading exit survey comments, it quickly becomes apparent that two or three key areas are glaringly in need of attention within a given organization. This is not unexpected, but it reminds us that, while most employees want the things that bring satisfaction, every organization's culture is different, and companies usually suffer from a few issues and turnover root causes that cry out to be addressed.

We also need to keep in mind that, while all employees want the big four—trust, hope, worth, and mastery—they may differ as to which ones they value the most, depending on their age or their tenure with the organization. For example, with younger employees, the hope and expectation of career growth in the company may be paramount, whereas older workers may be more concerned about health-care benefits. Tech workers will want the latest technologies; some employees will want to be recognized in public, while others will not. When it comes to engaging and retaining one employee at a time, effective managers will always respect these individual differences.

Who Has the Power to Meet These Needs?

As the saying goes, "People join companies, but they leave managers." Well, sometimes they leave companies, too, and the senior leaders who run those companies. It is the senior leaders who set the direction, who shape the culture, who approve the pay ranges and the training budget, whose demands bring excessive stress and overwork, and whose strategies bring either growth (and career growth opportunities) or stagnation. For proof of the pervasive power of the senior executive, we need look no further than to companies like Zappos, W. L. Gore, Rackspace Hosting, SAS Institute, and countless others where committed and caring CEOs have built "employer-of-choice" cultures.

In upcoming chapters, I will make clear how managers, senior leaders, human resource executives, and, yes, the employees themselves can partner to create reciprocal commitment.

The Next Seven Chapters: Hidden Reasons and Practical Action

It is not a naive platitude to point out that complaints are just negatively stated solutions. People complain of poor management when what they want is good management. They complain of favoritism when what they prefer is an even playing field. And so, in presenting the seven main reasons that people leave, we are really only a coin flip away from describing what it takes to make people want to stay and be more fully engaged. Delivering those engagement and retention best practices is the real purpose of this book.

Considering all the possible reasons that employees say they leave, as we have in this chapter, you may wonder how I winnowed them down to a select seven. The truth is that it was not that difficult because the Saratoga findings confirm my own research and the findings of dozens of other studies on the causes of employee turnover.

From my desire to present root-cause reasons that are well known yet hiding in plain sight, that are supported by the research findings, that are precisely identifiable and separable from one another, that can be addressed or prevented by managers or senior leaders, and that are few enough in number to be manageable, I isolated these seven as the ones I was compelled to describe and dissect:

1. The job or workplace was not as promised.
2. There was a mismatch between job and person.
3. There was too little coaching and feedback.
4. There were too few growth and advancement opportunities.
5. Workers felt devalued and unrecognized.
6. There was stress from overwork, conflict, and work-life imbalance.
7. Workers had lost trust and confidence in senior leaders.

The order in which these reasons are presented does not reflect their relative importance or frequency; the first two are listed first simply because they tend to occur early in an employee's life cycle. Any of the reasons, however, may cause an employee's early departure. In the next seven chapters, we will:

●   Begin with selected survey comments that illustrate each hidden reason and also convey the depth of emotion surrounding it.
●   Look at the visible signs that one or more of your employees may be disengaging for each of the root-cause reasons.
●   Present the predictable obstacles that stand in the way of preventing or correcting each root cause.

- Most important, review innovative ideas and practical, proven best practices that you and your organization can use to address each root cause.

- Finally, we will focus on what employees can and must do to assume their own share of the responsibility for keeping themselves engaged.

Notes

1. Leigh Branham, *The 7 Hidden Reasons Employees Leave*, 1st ed. (New York: AMACOM Books, 2005), citing Saratoga Institute (Santa Clara, California) research on employee commitment, satisfaction, and turnover, conducted from 1996 to 2003 and involving 19,500 current and former employees in eighteen different organizations.
2. Decision to Leave post-exit survey, based on 1000+ responses, 2004–2012, www.keepingthepeople.com.
3. Branham, *The 7 Reasons Employees Leave.*
4. Paul R. Ahr and Thomas B. Ahr, *Overturn Turnover: Why Some Employees Leave, Why Some Employees Stay, and Ways to Keep the Ones You Want to Stay* (St. Louis, MO: Causeway, 2000), p. 65.
5. Chip Conley, "Mastering the Anxiety Equation: A Remedy for Fearful Times," *Huffington Post,* November 18, 2011, http://www.huffingtonpost.com.
6. Barbara Davidson and Jac Fitz-enz, "Retention Management," a study released by the Saratoga Institute, Santa Clara, California, and published by the American Management Association, 1997.
7. W. Michael Kelly, conversation with the author, March 17, 2004.
8. Ibid.

CHAPTER FOUR

Reason #1:
The Job or Workplace Was
Not as Expected

Between the idea
and the reality
Between the motion
and the act
Falls the Shadow.

—T. S. ELIOT

Years ago, when I was an employee career counselor at Disneyland's on-site career center, one day a young woman walked into my office, sat down almost in tears, and blurted out, "This is *not* the happiest place on Earth."

My amusement was tempered with empathy because her disappointment was deep and sincere, almost as if she had truly expected that her work experience in the Magic Kingdom would be as carefree as that of a five-year-old visiting the park for the first time. But, alas, she had become disillusioned. She was having a conflict with her boss, whom she believed had shown favoritism in promoting a coworker instead of her.

Disappointment about promotions was not uncommon at Disneyland, especially among summer workers, ride operators, and other entry-level and part-time employees. The fact was that the organization had an "Eiffel Tower" organizational structure—wide at the bottom and much narrower at the top than a pyramid—and there were relatively fewer rungs on the promotional ladder to which younger workers could realistically aspire.

What this employee, and many others at Disneyland, needed to understand and accept was that there would come a time when it was best for them to let go of their illusions of long-term employment at "the happiest place on

Earth" and move on. That was a key reason that Disney had created the career center in the first place—to help these employees assess their talents, develop new goals, even prepare new resumés, and make a successful transition to organizations where their careers were more likely to advance. It was a smart strategy because it recognized that these young, disillusioned workers had become disengaged and that disengaged workers cannot deliver the kind of world-class customer experience for which Disney had become famous.

Every day, new hires enter organizations with a wide range of illusions and unrealistic expectations. Some stay and adapt, some disengage and stay, and many disengage and leave. Here are a few word-for-word comments, chosen from among Saratoga's exit surveys and my own, of some who chose to stay but who were less than fully engaged:

- "HR personnel lied to me about wage increase, bonus program just to get me there, then they never followed through with the wage increase! The rotating hours were never discussed."
- "Improper representation of job description and hours of work."
- "They do not deliver promises made as far as advancement, of potential growth within the corporate ladder. This forces one to make some very hard internal choices on the reasons for staying."
- "Thing are not explained well by HR when you are hired."
- "When I hired on, it was with the clear understanding that I would be working three days a week for what I was being paid. Then, after I started the job, my manager said no, that we agreed to five days a week. He acted like we had never had the conversation. That made me really angry. I agreed to stay on full time because I needed the job, but I'm still looking for another part-time job."
- "Our manager makes a lot of promises that are not kept."
- "Supervisors do not keep their promises in terms of promoting employees."
- "I was not at all satisfied with the training I received when I started working for ABC Company. I was sitting at my desk for 3 or 4 hours a day for the first three weeks, as a result I began looking for another job. I felt that management didn't care."
- "XYZ Company does not provide a training program course for any new employee. You are thrown into a new position and are expected to do all things that are required of your position immediately."

- "ABC Company is very good at lying to prospective employees during interviews. He deliberately misrepresents the position in order to get more qualified candidates than necessary for the position."

- "Length of time from interview to hiring was totally unacceptable. When you are told in the interview you will be hired pending check of references and drug test, 6 weeks is too long to wait."

- "They do not give to employees. For example, on my first day of work I was not able to take a lunch. Another example—I am not able to spend any money on my employees to show appreciation for a job well done."

At the root of all these comments is an expectation that was not met.

In some cases, the employee's expectations may have been unrealistic, and, in some cases they, no doubt, were not. In the big picture, it doesn't matter. The point is this: Unrealistic and unmet expectations cost businesses untold millions of dollars. The cost of losing one professional is generally accepted to be one times annual salary. If the average salary is $50,000, then losing twenty employees over the course of a year because of unmet expectations adds up to a tidy total of $1 million.

You may never see an exit survey with a checklist of reasons for leaving that includes the choice "unmet expectations," but it may well be the number one reason most employees leave, and leave quickly. It is the main reason 4 percent of employees walk off the job on the first day.[1] It is most certainly the main reason that more than 50 percent of American workers quit in the first six months.[2] And it is probably a key factor in the failure of 40 percent of new executives to last more than 18 months in their new positions.[3]

A Disastrous First Day

"I'd said at the interview that I planned to take a holiday the following month, and my manager said that would be fine and to give him the dates when I'd booked it. On my first day, when I told him the week I planned to be away, he went bright red, slammed his fist on the desk, and barked that I clearly had no commitment to the company, and what message was it sending out to my team if I went away so soon? I survived another day and another showdown before I took one long permanent holiday."[4]

Hidden Mutual Expectations: The Psychological Contract

In his classic article "The Psychological Contract: Managing the Joining-Up Process," John Paul Kotter defined "the psychological contract" as "an implicit contract between an individual and the organization which specifies what each expects to give and receive from each other in the relationship."[5] (See Figure 4.1.) Matches and mismatches can occur on the basis of the four sets of expectations in this hidden contract.

Figure 4.1.

The Psychological Contract.

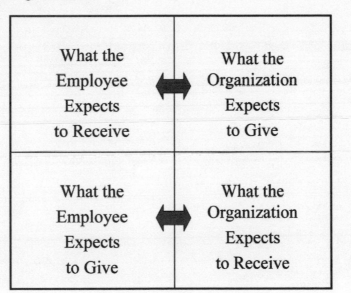

For example, when a new hire expects to receive a promotion after one year on the job and the employer is not prepared to give a promotion that quickly, there is a mismatch. When the employer can and does promote the new employee after a year, there is a match. Kotter's research confirmed what most of us would expect—that the more the mutual expectations match, the greater the likelihood of job satisfaction, productivity, and reduced turnover.

To illustrate further, here are some common mismatches that occur between what Gen Xers may expect to get from an employer and what Boomer managers may expect to give:

Gen Xer may expect to get:	**Boomer manager may expect to give:**
Plenty of Vacation Time	Three Weeks' Vacation only After Five Years
Promotions Based Purely on Merit	Promotions Based Largely on Experience
Hands-Off Supervision	Close Supervision
Self-Paced Computer Training	Classroom Training Only
Frequent Constructive Feedback	Feedback only When the Employee Screws Up

Not all mismatches occur because of generational differences, but most of us have observed such situations and can vouch for the fact that, if not openly discussed, any single mismatch can lead to conflict, lost productivity, and turnover.

Allstate's Written "Psychological Contract":

A Partnership Statement

Some employers, such as Allstate Insurance Company, have actually created formal statements outlining what employee and employer can expect from each other. Because the company believes employee loyalty improves when both company and employees clearly know what is expected, Allstate provides this "partnership statement" to every employee:

You should expect Allstate to:

- Offer work that is meaningful and challenging.
- Promote an environment that encourages open and constructive dialogue.
- Recognize you for your accomplishments.
- Provide competitive pay and rewards based on your performance.
- Advise you on your performance through regular feedback.
- Create learning opportunities through education and job assignments.
- Support you in defining career goals.
- Provide you with information and resources to perform successfully.
- Promote an environment that is inclusive and free from bias.
- Foster dignity and respect in all interactions.
- Establish an environment that promotes a balance of work and professional life.

Allstate expects you to:

- Perform at levels that significantly increase the company's ability to outperform the competition
- Take on assignments critical to meeting business objectives.
- Willingly listen and act upon feedback.
- Demonstrate a high level of commitment to achieving company goals.
- Exhibit no bias in interactions with colleagues and customers.
- Behave consistently with Allstate's ethical standards.
- Take personal responsibility for each transaction with customers and for fostering their trust.
- Continually improve processes to address customers' needs.[6]

Here are some other pertinent findings about psychological contracts:

- As touched on in Chapter 2, when an employee realizes that the employer cannot meet a key expectation, there is often a feeling of having been betrayed, as if a real contract has been broken in bad faith, which can become the "shock" or turning point that begins the downward cycle toward disengagement and departure.
- The more open discussion takes place about mutual expectations, the greater the probability of a satisfactory match. This doesn't happen as frequently as it should, partly because interviewees often feel powerless in the interview process and are reluctant to ask questions, partly because interviewers are too rushed or are simply afraid that if they tell the whole truth about the job or workplace, the interviewee will not accept the offer.
- The more clearly an employee understands his or her own expectations, the higher the probability of a match. Many new employees fresh out of college, however, are only dimly aware of their wants and needs. The problem is compounded when the organization is also not clear about what it expects, which is often the case.
- Companies frequently make the mistake of thinking in terms of offering "the most" or receiving "the best" when they would be better advised to think in terms of "fit." For example, many companies seek to hire only the "top graduates" with the highest grade-point averages, when some of these individuals, because of their cerebral bent or analytical nature, may not fit the company's expectation that they become outgoing, street-smart sales people.

- If an employee and an employer discover after the hire that they have a serious mismatch of expectations, it may be in their best interests to shake hands and part ways. Of course, this is not always easy to do.

- The psychological contract changes over time as the expectations of the employee and the organization change. With each change in expectation, open communication serves to keep both parties in alignment, or may lead to a mutual agreement to renegotiate or break the contract.

How to Recognize the Warning Signs of Unmet Expectations: During and After the Interview

It is obviously far better to read the signs of *potential* unmet expectations prior to hiring than afterward, so be alert to the following signs during the interview process.

During the Interview

- ☑ The interviewee asks few questions or no questions.

- ☑ The interviewee asks lots of questions about one particular issue, and you have doubts about your ability or willingness to meet the implied expectation.

- ☑ The interviewee's previous employer had a culture and working conditions that are very different from your own organization's.

- ☑ When you ask the question "Why did you leave your former employer?," the interviewee mentions a reason that raises doubts about your own employer's ability to meet the implied expectation.

- ☑ You feel rushed to get through the interview.

After the Interview

- ☑ You cannot recall discussing your expectations or those of the interviewee.

Look for these danger signs that the employee may have begun to disengage after realizing that an important expectation will not be met:

- ☑ There is a sudden change in the employee's demeanor, indicating either suppressed anger or withdrawal.

- ☑ The employee stops greeting you or making eye contact.

- ☑ The employee stops participating in discussions at meetings.
- ☑ You observe a drop-off in performance.
- ☑ The employee exhibits increased absenteeism.

Of course, you may not need to watch for any of these warning signs if the employee is assertive enough to come to you and voice his or her dissatisfaction directly. However, as we know, many employees, especially younger and less experienced ones, are often reluctant to do so.

Obstacles to Meeting Mutual Expectations

There are several obstacles to forging an unwritten psychological contract with a new employee, not the least of which is the fact that the "contract" is not typically put into writing, thus greatly increasing the potential for misunderstanding. Here are a few more obstacles to use as a checklist:

- ☑ The job candidate lacks self-knowledge about wants, values, and expectations.
- ☑ The hiring manager is inexperienced at interviewing.
- ☑ The hiring manager is in a hurry to hire and rushes to get through the interview.
- ☑ The hiring manager and search team have created such a long list of ideal candidate characteristics that no single candidate could realistically possess them all.
- ☑ The hiring manager or other managers in the organization are increasingly unwilling to adapt to the changing expectations of younger generations of workers or to accommodate the expectations of diverse populations.
- ☑ The hiring manager believes that new hires should adapt to whatever is asked of them and be happy just to have a job.
- ☑ The organization's human resource policies and management practices are outdated when compared to those of competitors for talent in the industry and the community.
- ☑ The organization's recruitment advertising and related literature make implied promises that the organization cannot deliver.
- ☑ The hiring manager is aware of negative working conditions the new hire will encounter, such as an as-yet unannounced downsizing or merger or conflict within the immediate work team, and is afraid

that mentioning it will cause the new hire to withdraw from the interview process or to decline an offer.

Engagement Practices 1–8: Matching Mutual Expectations

The following best practices for fostering realistic mutual expectations are commonly used by employer-of-choice organizations and have been found to significantly raise the probability of new-hire success, satisfaction, and retention.

 Engagement Practice #1:
Train all hiring managers and recruiters to give RJPs–
"Realistic Job Previews"—with every job candidate.

This practice is the most common way of addressing potential unrealistic expectations. It involves initiating a frank and open discussion of job activities, performance expectations, the immediate work team, working conditions, rules and policies, the work culture, the manager's style, the organization's financial stability, and other topics where surprises need to be minimized. Because of the need to sell applicants on the position and the company, RJPs should obviously accentuate the positives but not gloss over or sugarcoat potential negatives that, when experienced later, after hiring, could cause the new hire to abruptly quit or disengage.

This is a controversial practice among many managers who fear the risk of scaring off and losing talented candidates. The experience of companies that have implemented this practice has shown that some candidates will indeed withdraw when an organization's "warts" are openly discussed. On the other hand, candidates who turn out to be good fits for the organization and culture tend not to be turned off by the truths they hear in RJPs. Rather, in many cases, they are often actually more motivated to meet the challenge head on.

For example, an Ingenix subsidiary, GeoAccess, of Lenexa, Kansas, makes sure that all job applicants are made aware of the way people communicate in the company's fast-paced culture. It's a style of interacting that is direct, frank, spontaneous, and sometimes blunt. In meetings, coworkers give one another feedback that is honest but that may hurt. The company's human resource director, Greg Addison, wanted to make sure that job applicants are made aware of this aspect of the company's culture. "Many companies don't understand their own culture," he says, "so they select misfits."

If you do lose candidates by divulging the truth about the job or work-place, then you probably would have lost them anyway within the first few months on the job. By discussing the truth up front and allowing candidates to opt out, you have actually saved the cost of having to replace and retrain.

Some managers even go so far as to mention former employees who quit or were terminated because they could not adapt to a particular aspect of a challenging job, a working condition, or the company's culture.

Two important cautions about conducting realistic job previews. First, before opening the company's kimono and showing its warts, interviewers should be trained to ask the candidate about his or her expectations. Often, in listening to the applicants' answers, interviewers can see clearly that the applicant will not fit the job or the culture, and they can save themselves the necessity of revealing the bad and the ugly to them. Second, interviewers should be careful how they describe the negative aspects of the company's culture. Some hiring managers have been known to go overboard in describing the negatives or inaccurately describe them because they have not personally experienced them. After all, what appears to be a negative to a hiring manager may actually be seen as a challenge by an applicant.

There is an art to conducting a realistic job preview without having it turn into a horrifying job preview. It is honest, but not necessarily alarming, to say:

"You should be aware that there are negotiations going on that could result in the company being acquired. Should that happen, it could mean significant new career opportunities for many employees. It could also mean that a few people could lose their positions. Your position is one that we do not expect to be adversely affected. For those who might be impacted, we would provide career transition services to help them land on their feet in a new position."

On the other hand, it can be brutally frightening to say: "You should be aware that our company might be acquired, in which case your job could be eliminated. There are no guarantees." Whatever is said in realistic job previews should definitely be approved at higher levels so that managers all deliver basically the same message in the best possible way.

To strengthen the RJP process, it is strongly recommended that organizations faithfully conduct exit interviews or exit surveys that allow departed employees to make comments. By analyzing the exit comments, management can quickly figure out what aspects of jobs have been glossed over, over-promised, undelivered, or misunderstood. These are the issues that need to be more openly discussed during the pre-employment period.

Engagement Practice #2:
Increase hiring from temp-to-hire, adjunct staff, contract consultants, and part-time worker pools.

As the saying goes, before dyeing the whole cloth, it is best to first test-dye a small piece of it. When workers come aboard on a contingency basis, they have a chance to experience the ups and downs of the job firsthand before they and the organization commit to a full-time relationship. Many of those who wouldn't fit the culture or who would find it not to their liking can decide to self-select out. Those who decide to stay and perhaps take on a full-time role will have gone through the most realistic job preview of all.

Engagement Practice #3:
Increase hiring from employee referrals.

The research shows that the first-year turnover rate for employees hired through employee referrals is significantly lower than the rate for those hired through more formal recruiting methods, such as want ads.[7] Why? The main reason is that current employees tend to realistically describe the job and workplace to those they are referring. Because they have a vested interest in maintaining the friendship, they are generally motivated to minimize surprises and "inoculate" the referred individual against possible disappointments.

Many companies have begun the practice of offering attractive monetary incentives or other types of rewards to encourage employees to refer potential new hires.

Engagement Practice #4:
Create a realistic job description with a short list of the most critical competencies.

When search teams create too long a list of job requirements and competencies that the "ideal candidate" must have, they are unwittingly narrowing their pool of candidates, since fewer candidates are able to pass the screening. They are also laying the groundwork for another problem later on—that the performance expectations of the new hire will be impossible to meet.

To prevent either of these problems, take care to create a realistic list of only the five or six most critical competencies needed for success, preferably stated as natural, motivated talents, not as technical or knowledge requirements. The more your organization determines which competencies distinguish top performers from average performers in various job categories, the easier it will be to do this.

Engagement Practice #5:
Allow coworkers to participate in the interviewing process.

When those who would work with the new hire as teammates are allowed to take part in the interviewing process without the manager being present in the room, they are free to answer candidates' questions forthrightly. Likewise, candidates are likely to feel less inhibited about asking questions of their peers that they might be uncomfortable asking in the presence of the boss. This practice has two added advantages—thanks to the "two-heads-are-better-than-one" factor, it typically leads to better candidate selection, and it also creates greater participation and "buy-in" from team members while sending them the message that their opinions count.

Engagement Practice #6:
Increase hiring from within.

This one is easy to understand. When you hire or promote from within, you are taking less of a risk of turnover due to the fact that the inside candidate is already wise to the ways of the organization. It's also a great way to increase morale by encouraging all workers about their career prospects within the company. However, be advised—to be on the safe side, you still need to give them the same realistic job preview you would give to an outside candidate.

Engagement Practice #7:
Conduct the interview or selection process in a way
that provides a sample of on-the-job experience.

A traditional way of doing this is by asking the candidate a hypothetical question, such as "What would you do if an unhappy customer threatened to go to your manager and complain about your service?" An even better method is to ask a behavioral question, in the following way: "This job will frequently challenge you to deal effectively with unhappy customers. Can you tell me about a time when you dealt with a particularly unhappy customer?"

Better yet, many companies have begun using CD-ROMs that simultaneously test the applicant's aptitude for the position and provide a glimpse of on-the-job realities. Wells Fargo Bank, for example, requires bank teller candidates to watch a CD-ROM containing a series of customer-service-dilemma scenarios. One vignette, for example, shows an angry customer approaching to complain about an incorrect account balance; then the video freeze-frames and the teller applicant is asked to select from among three possible responses to indicate how he or she would respond. The bank generally eliminates those with the lowest percentage of right answers but also finds that another 20 percent withdraw their employment applications after viewing the various scenarios that preview the actual on-the-job experience. The company considers this a good outcome, as it has eliminated the expense of hiring and training new hires who would eventually leave.

After Federal Express realized that 10 percent of first-time managers were leaving the company, it began conducting an eight-hour class called "Is Management for Me?" Aspiring managers must attend the class before they can officially become candidates for management positions. During the class, current FedEx managers speak to the aspirants, realistically describing the daily challenges of being a manager—the longer hours, the increased workload, and the headaches related to people management and discipline, plus the fact that they are never "off-the-clock." Like Wells Fargo, FedEx considers this program a success, partly because FedEx, like the bank, experienced a 20 percent candidate drop-out rate. FedEx believes that the program helps weed out management candidates who would not adapt well and who might be motivated to get into management for the wrong reasons, such as a belief that it is the only way to advance.

 Engagement Practice #8:
Have new hires complete post-hire questionnaires.

In recent years, many employers have started the practice of having recent hires complete evaluations of their experiences during the company's recruiting and new-hire orientation processes. From this feedback, received from written questionnaires, personal interviews, or both, the organization learns what the new hires were surprised to learn during their first thirty days on the job, what they expected and have not received, and what was not discussed in interviews that should have been. Companies figure that it doesn't make sense to wait until after new hires have left to find out what they were disillusioned about—better to find it out while there is still an opportunity to do something about it.

How Prospective Employees Can Do Their Part

The main thing that a job candidate can do to gain a more realistic under-standing of the job or workplace is ask questions. Some applicants will ask questions, and others will not. A hiring manager must not wait for job candidates to ask questions but should make it clear that all questions are welcome and that no question will be considered a stupid one. Hiring managers and everyone on the interviewing team should always invite more questions in every job interview with every candidate, even after they have given realistic job previews.

All recruitment materials should also invite candidates to ask questions, particularly the literature that is used in on-campus recruiting efforts and lit-erature that is distributed to entry-level recruits.

The Beginning or the End of Trust

Forging the psychological contract with a new employee in the interviewing and orientation phases is fundamentally a matter of establishing trust. If it is discovered that the employee lied about having a college degree, the trust is broken. If the employee realizes that the manager lied about how much trav-el would be involved in the new job, the opportunity for trust is lost.

Without trust, there can be no viable working relationship. Without tak-ing the time and making the effort to establish trust from the start, managers are risking the waste of their most precious asset.

Engagement Practices Checklist: Meeting Expectations

To score yourself on the engagement best practices described in this chapter, check those that you perform as a hiring manager:

Engagement Practice #1. ____ Conduct realistic job previews with every job candidate.

Engagement Practice #2. ____ Make a significant percentage of hires from pool of temp, adjunct, contract consultants, and part-time workers.

Engagement Practice #3. ____ Make a significant percentage of hires from current employee referrals.

Engagement Practice #4. ____ Typically allow candidate's future coworkers to participate in job interviews.

Engagement Practice #5. ____   Make a significant percentage of hires from pool
                               of current employees.

Engagement Practice #6. ____   Invite all job candidates to ask questions in every
                               interview with all interviewers.

Engagement Practice #7. ____   Build into the interviewing process a way for
                               candidates to gain a "sample" on-the-job
                               experience.

Engagement Practice #8. ____   Survey or interview new hires to find out how
                               to minimize new hire surprises in the future.

   Your next step: *Resolve to take action on the practices you believe are most critical and most appropriate for your situation and objectives.*

Notes

1. "First Day at Work" report, Reed Company, UK, January 2003.
2. B. L. Brown, "Career Mobility: A Choice or Necessity?," *ERIC Digest*
    no. 191, ERIC Clearinghouse on Adult, Career, and Vocational
    Education, Center on Education and Training for Employment, Ohio
    State University, Columbus, 1998.
3. Kelly Beamon, "Just Say No," Employment Briefs, *National Business
    Employment Weekly*, November 24, 1998.
4. Emma Lunn, "Foibles . . . the First Day," *The Guardian*, September 29,
    2003.
5. John Paul Kotter, "The Psychological Contract: Managing the Joining-
    Up Process," *California Management Review* 15 (Spring 1973): 91–99.
6. Allstate Insurance Company website,
    http://allstate.com/careersculture.aspx.
7. Brown, "Career Mobility."

Reason #2: The Mismatch Between Job and Person

> By treating people with diverse skills as an
> undifferentiated resource . . . companies forfeit the
> chance to make substantial gains in productivity,
> profitability, and personnel development.
>
> —Vivek Agrawal

Research conducted over the past twenty-five years has shown that 80 percent of workers feel they are *not* using their strengths on a daily basis.[1] We hear the voices of these workers in the survey comments of both those who left and those who stayed:

- "Job functions are boring and monotonous."
- "My job responsibilities are not challenging."
- "ABC Company does not take full advantage of the employee skills that exist internally."
- "Employees are considered a billing number and their skill sets and hopes are not important."
- "ABC Company hires overqualified employees into positions with low titles or grades."
- "They do not structure the positions to include job variety and challenge, which leads to a boring, routine job very quickly."
- "Employees are often in positions they are not qualified for."
- "XYZ Company doesn't understand the concept of utilizing their employees' skills to the fullest extent."

- "Our company just created a new training program for the operations group. In each department, they now have a skills coach. I am that person in my department. The thing is that I wasn't asked if this was something that I would like to do."

- "Job responsibilities are broken down too much. Too many people are doing jobs that can be combined with another job."

- "The company hires anyone."

- "They have the wrong type of people in certain positions."

- "Moving a person into a job that they don't want, even to prevent them from losing a job, is not a good policy. And if they don't take that job, then they receive no outplacement assistance."

- "In cross-training they give you the opportunity to learn a new task, but move you again before you learn it."

- "Managers are not good about giving employees extra responsibilities. They want to be in control of too much and don't want to let the employees help out once in a while."

- "There is too much control at the top and not enough delegation."

- 'There was not enough authority pushed down. There were very talented people in the local office who truly had no authority."

- "My supervisor said I didn't deserve a raise because I didn't do anything new."

These are the comments of workers whose fundamental need to exercise competence and achieve mastery has not been met. They offer sad testimony to an inestimable and scandalous waste of human talent and loss of productivity. How does this happen?

A closer look at the comments reveals some of the answers:

- Many managers don't care or notice if their people are bored or unchallenged.

- Many managers don't delegate enough to make jobs more interesting or challenging.

- Employees do not know their own strengths and the kind of work that would fit them best.

- Many organizations have no way of effectively assessing the talent of their employees.

- Employees are reluctant to discuss their dissatisfaction with their managers.

- Many jobs are so overly defined and narrowly drawn that almost anyone placed in those jobs would be underemployed.

- Managers are in such a hurry to hire that they end up just hiring warm bodies.

- Some organizations are simply inept or oblivious when it comes to evaluating talent and matching people to the right jobs.

- For many managers, helping their employees grow and use new talents is not a high priority.

What's Missing—A Passion for Matching

With all these examples of talent management malpractice, it's almost surprising that 20 percent of the working population *does* get to use their strengths every day. It is also a reminder of how rare and special it is to have a manager who cares about matching talent to the job and does it well.

The key missing ingredient in so many companies is management's lack of passion for getting the right people in the right jobs. It has been said that the best managers are the best matchmakers. This is truer today than it has ever been because of the preeminence of talent in an economy now dominated by service industries, encompassing everything from health care to retail, from business services to education. Distinguished business executives and management scholars have never been more in agreement about the importance of maintaining a relentless focus on talent:

> "Over time, choosing the right people is what creates the elusive sustainable competitive advantage." (Larry Bossidy, chairman and former CEO of Honeywell Corporation)[2]

> "The best thing we can do for our competitors is hire poorly. If we hire a bunch of bozos, it will hurt us because it takes time to get rid of them . . . then they start hiring people of lower quality. . . . We are always looking to hire people who are better than we are." (Microsoft recruiting director)[3]

> "Leaders of companies that go from good to great . . . start by getting the right people on the bus, the wrong people off the bus, and the right people in the right seats." (Jim Collins, *Good to Great*)[4]

Acknowledging the new realization that talent is king, many large companies have even created senior executive positions with the title "Chief Talent Officer."

So, if matching people to the right jobs is generally recognized to be the key to business success, why do so many businesses lack the passion and commitment to get managers at every level to take it seriously and excel at it?

There are many obstacles to consider, but the greatest of them all is a basic lack of understanding about the nature of human talent. Here are some of the most common misconceptions about talent:

• *Misconception #1: Employees are interchangeable parts to be moved into whatever slots most need to be filled.* It is truly amazing that so many managers seem to hold such a belief in this day and age, but, judging by the way so many managers move employees around like stick figures, they obviously still do. As a corollary to this belief, many managers also believe that anyone can do certain jobs, especially lower-level ones, so they end up just hiring anyone who can "fog a mirror," many of whom are not well matched to the work and end up as turnover statistics.

Truth: People are "hard-wired" to perform certain activities better than others and to prefer using a handful of these talents more than others. These preferred natural gifts and talents are sometimes referred to as "motivated abilities," meaning that people are naturally self-motivated to use them and will make every effort to use them in their jobs, even if their jobs do not appear to require them. If a job does not allow employees to use their motivated abilities, they will find a way to use them in their leisure time because it is intrinsically satisfying to exercise these select few talents.

• *Misconception #2: Skills and knowledge are more important than talent.* It is easy to understand why so many managers believe this. It all begins with the hiring process when someone sits down to make a list of job requirements and writes down the basic requirements for eligible candidates. At the top of that list are the minimum skills, knowledge, certifications, degrees, or training needed to perform the job. Because these requirements are so often the primary focus for screening candidates out and in, many managers frequently lose sight of the natural abilities that will ultimately determine excellence in the job.

Truth: While job-content skills and knowledge are important as basic job requirements, they are much less important than natural talent for long-term success on the job. The distinction that hiring managers fail to make is between *eligibility* to do the job based on trainable skills and *suitability* to do the job based on personality factors and natural talent. The problem is that natural talent is so much more difficult to identify than are trainable skills, causing many managers to make very little effort to do so, and many do not know how. The result is that they hire trained individuals who lack the talent to achieve true competence and screen out or fail to consider many trainable external applicants or internal candidates who do possess the right talents for success.

• *Misconception #3: With the right training and coaching and the proper attitude, people can learn to do well in almost any job.* This myth is related to that great American idea that "you can do anything if you just set your mind to it." Many managers confront their employees with this very challenge, urging competent employees to take on "stretch" assignments outside the range of their natural talents and even promoting them into management positions when what they truly enjoy is doing the work, not delegating it.

Truth: Yes, people are extremely adaptable and can be "bent, folded, and mutilated" to perform many roles adequately. But, unless they are in the roles that match their motivated abilities, they will not excel or enjoy the work. Instead, they will become disengaged, possibly burning themselves out, search for ways to change the role, or leave the job altogether.

What's really going on here, in many cases, is that managers are far more interested in their own needs to fill a slot than they are in the best use of employees' talents. They may say they are trying to develop their people by challenging them, and they may even convince themselves they are doing the right thing and feel very self-satisfied and well intentioned, but the fact is that they are misusing and disrespecting their most precious asset.

Employees also buy into this process by not being sufficiently aware of their own best talents or confident enough in them to turn down an inappropriate assignment or proactively seek a better fit when the job has gone stale.

♦ ♦ ♦ ♦ ♦ ♦ ♦ ♦ ♦

The bottom-line assumption in all three of these misconceptions about talent is that the needs of the organization supersede the needs of the individual and that it is the individual who must adapt. Of course, individuals have always adapted, especially during hard economic times, and they always will adapt when job security and survival are at stake. And organizations are certainly limited in their ability to accommodate every employee's talents.

But, when times get better and companies are competing for talent, good performers will have other choices outside the organization, and they will pursue them. At that point, organizations will start waking up to the fact that perhaps a way can be found to meet the employee's needs *and* the needs of the organization, and both parties will be better served for the company's having made the effort. That can be a turning point in companies becoming true employers of choice.

Recognizing the Signs of Job-Person Mismatch

An employee may be mismatched with the job if he or she:

- Did not seem excited when first assigned to the job.
- Complains that the job content is not what was expected.
- Is not achieving the results or standards you expected.
- Starts making uncharacteristic mistakes.
- Is stressed and overmatched by the demands of the job.
- Starts asking that some job tasks be reassigned to coworkers or outsourced.
- Appears bored or unchallenged.
- Keeps coming around asking for a new project.
- Keeps mentioning a talent that the employee would like to use in the job.
- Starts spending discretionary time on an activity that is more satisfying to perform. but may not be important to the job.
- Requests a reassignment or starts lobbying for a promotion.
- Starts applying for other jobs in the organization.
- Generally appears less engaged or energized on a daily basis.

Most Common Obstacles to Preventing and Correcting Job-Person Mismatch

Many of the obstacles to effective job-person matching are based on deficiencies of organizational leadership and the human resource department, while others are attributable to the manager and others to the individual employee. These are some of the most common:

- The organization does not have basic job descriptions.

- The organization is using outdated job descriptions as the basis for screening, interviewing, and hiring.

- The organization has so narrowly defined the activities of a job that employees who occupy that job feel they have no room to perform in a way that makes best use of their strengths.

- The organization has not forecast critical talent needs growing out of clear strategic business objectives.

- The organization has not analyzed jobs according to key targeted results to determine the critical few talents that distinguish top performers from average performers in each role.

- The fast pace of the organization and/or the manager creates a tendency to rush through the interview process and leads to hires made without careful evaluations.

- Senior leaders have failed to establish a rigorous talent evaluation process, both for new hires and for current employees, as part of the career/succession planning process.

- Senior leaders and managers overpromote the idea of "selecting the best" instead of "selecting the *best fit*," which often results in the hiring of college graduates with the best grades or from the best schools who do not always fit the culture or excel in the roles for which they were chosen.

- There is an excessive focus on eliminating employee weaknesses through coaching and training when it would be wiser in many cases to put those employees into new roles where they can better capitalize on their greatest strengths.

- Organizational values, structures, and policies reinforce the idea that the only way to grow professionally is to be promoted.

- Hires are made from a limited talent pool, which can greatly limit the chances of finding an acceptable match.

- Managers fail to delegate.

Engagement Practices for Matching Job and Person

Companies with strong reputations for selecting the right talent and keeping employees well matched with their jobs do seem to have certain best practices in common. These practices fall into three main areas—selection, engagement through job task assignment and ongoing re-engagement/reassignment as needed, and job enrichment.

Best Practices for Talent Selection

 Engagement Practice #9:
Make a strong commitment to the
continuous upgrading of talent.

The best employers do not have a cavalier, seat-of-the-pants approach to recruiting and interviewing. Instead, they have a serious and resolute mindset about talent that begins with a fundamental belief that the organization's future depends on getting and keeping the right people in the right jobs. This means they leave little to chance.

It usually begins with a CEO who is driven to create an intense focus on strengthening talent levels across the *organization*. The CEO makes it clear that this is the top priority of every manager and typically insists that every manager not delegate hiring. This means that the hiring process is owned by the hiring managers, not by human resources, which operates as a key resource and full partner to support the hiring managers.

Upgrading Quality of Hire at CDW

The technology products and services provider CDW had to support its rapid growth by accelerating its hiring of account managers, IT specialists, and engineers. The company, named among *Fortune*'s 100 Great Places to Work, was receiving more than twenty-six thousand applications a year. Still, with its ambitious growth plans, it undertook a comprehensive review of its recruiting and selection practices. "We took a deep dive into our process for selecting talent," Dennis Berger, CDW's senior vice president of coworker services, recalled. "We found that it was very recruiter heavy—a lot of muscle, but not very smart."[5]

After a six-month review, Berger and his team realized that the company was restricting its talent pipeline by focusing almost exclusively on college recruiting. After reviewing requirements for the account manager position, the company decided that a high school diploma and two years of training were sufficient for success and revamped its sourcing strategy. It added radio spots in key locations, expanded its sourcing efforts through social media, continued its online job boards, and hired more recruiters.

Because turnover was high for account managers in their first few months on the job, Berger's team realized that there was a problem with job expectations and fit. "We found that we were bringing in people who really didn't know what the job was about." The company created a three-minute realistic job preview video that features current coworkers describing their roles and responsibilities and the working environment. This video is embedded in CDW's careers home page for potential candidates to view prior to applying online.

After six weeks of training, the new account managers spend their first six months on the job in the CDW "sales academy," where they receive one-on-one skill development training from sales learning specialists while performing account manager duties. With new hires trained and coached through the early months on the job, attention then turns to meeting the two-year mark.

The company knows that the time and energy spent sourcing and selecting will be wasted unless there is at least an equal emphasis on training and retention.

Engagement Practice #10:
Follow a consistent and thorough talent forecasting and success-factor analysis process.

Before beginning the recruiting process, the best companies engage in a talent forecasting process based on key business objectives. The business objectives drive talent needs, with special attention focused on pivotal jobs that will create the most value for the organization. For auto dealerships, these are general managers, sales people, and finance managers. For grocery stores, these are store managers, department managers, and checkers. For mutual fund companies, these are fund managers. Often, they are lower to midlevel workers who have the most direct customer contact. In some service-driven organizations, 80 percent of the value (revenues/profits) derives from the results generated by 20 percent of the jobs (talent) in the organization.

The next phase of the preselection process involves understanding what makes top performers successful in all positions, especially those that create the most value. Many companies validate a selection instrument by having their top performers—the ones they would clone if they could—take a battery of personality and ability assessments, which they then scrutinize to identify common traits and capabilities. The more top performers take the assessments, the more valid the conclusions that can be made from them. Many organizations find this process helpful, but it is fallible in one sense—not all successful people use the same talents to succeed in the same job. Still, top performers tend to share a select few critical characteristics that are worth the effort to uncover.

How One Company Matches the Personality to the Role

The security-guard leasing firm Weiser Security has significantly decreased turnover by implementing a one-hundred-question assessment that helps to screen candidates and slot them into one of four possible roles and work settings. The company has defined these as:

Greeter: Best suited for lobby and information desk settings.

Gratifier: More service focused, often used as airport preboard screeners.

Graveyarders: Comfortable with solitary assignments, such as night watchmen.

Grinders: Closed-circuit TV monitoring.

The assessment also screens applicants for inability to follow instructions, tendency toward high absenteeism/turnover, and dishonesty. Weiser has found that security officers who are comfortable with their posts report more job satisfaction, which contributes to better performance, lower turnover, and fewer problems all around. On its website, Weiser reports that the Gallup Organization scored the company 89 percent better than other organizations at selecting the right person for the job.[6]

The essential idea here is to supplement an in-depth interviewing process by using a standard battery of assessment instruments to screen job candidates in search of those whose profiles look most like the profiles of top performers.

Some companies add depth to the validation process by conducting focus-group interviews with top performers. One large hotel chain gathered eight of its best housekeepers from around the world into a room to find out what they had in common. They described how they try to see the rooms through the eyes of the hotel guests (empathy) and put on a show for the guests by doing things like arranging children's toys and stuffed animals on the bed to make it look like they were interacting (desire to please and delight).[7]

Other companies may go one step further and conduct one-on-one "behavioral event" interviews with "water-walkers" in key jobs in which they are asked to tell detailed stories about exactly how they achieved a previous successful outcome for a customer or client. Interviewers listen carefully, probe with clarifying questions, and take notes about the talents the worker was using in each achievement. Still others use consultants to observe successful workers while they go about their daily tasks, taking notes and questioning as appropriate to gain a deeper understanding of how and why they do what they do.

Whatever combination of methods is used, the desired outcome is a short list of critical success factors for each job, no matter how low it is in the organization's hierarchy. The mistake most companies make here is that they invite too many people to help construct a list of skills, talents, and traits they would like the ideal candidate to possess. By the time the employment requisition and job ad are written, there are so many job requirements that not even Superman could meet them all. As a result, many perfectly qualified candidates are screened out, and the job goes unfilled for weeks or months.

Finally, it is a cardinal rule that no outdated job descriptions should be used as the basis for constructing employment ads and interview questions. In an ideal world, every job description would be updated every time a new person is hired, reflecting the particular needs of the organizational unit at that moment in time.

What Qualities to Look for and Why

Hire and promote first on the basis of integrity; second, motivation; third, capacity; fourth, understanding; fifth, knowledge; and last and least, experience. Without integrity, motivation is dangerous; without motivation, capacity is impotent; without capacity, understanding is limited; without understanding, knowledge is blind. Experience is easy to provide and quickly put to use by people with all the other qualities.[8]

—Dee Hock

 Engagement Practice #11:
Cast a wide recruiting net to expand your
universe of best-fit candidates.

The logic is simple—the larger the selection, the greater your chances of finding the right fit. There are three ways to expand your labor pool—first, by not imposing too many restrictions in your job requirements; second, by changing the job itself; and, third, by creatively considering new sources of talent that you have never before tapped. Here are guidelines for each of these:

- *Loosening Job Restrictions:* As mentioned previously, many organizations create job descriptions with too many requirements, many of which are optional but not really essential. This means you may need to challenge many of the technical requirements that often appear on the long laundry lists that circulate before you begin the recruiting process. This is especially important when the labor market is tight or when the supply of talent for the position to be filled is limited.

● *Changing the Job Itself:* Every time you fill a job, you have the opportunity to take a second look at and question the way the job is being done. "Because we've always done it that way" is not the answer you are looking for. The next time a position opens up, don't just rush to fill it. Instead, start with a clean slate by asking yourself, "What is the work that needs to get done?" and take a fresh look at the needs behind the job, not just the job description.

It may be that doing the job in a new way will actually result in increasing the availability of applicants. United Parcel Service, for example, was experiencing excessively high turnover among its drivers. When it asked drivers why they were leaving, the overwhelming response was that they hated having to load and unload the delivery trucks. UPS decided to eliminate loading and unloading as a job requirement for drivers and to create a whole new job category—loader. Their reasoning made perfect sense—the supply of drivers is smaller than the supply of potential loaders, so why unnecessarily restrict that supply? As it turned out, the rate of turnover among loaders was also high, but they were easier to replace than drivers, so the solution was a good one. *Creatively consider new sources of talent.*

In my previous book, *Keeping the People Who Keep You in Business,* there is a list of fifty-four creative sources for expanding the talent pool. One of the most overlooked is the pool of internal candidates. Many hiring managers can actually become victims of their own limited perceptions. Failure to consider administrative assistants for management positions because they are stereotyped as second-class workers is a common one.

Another self-imposed way of restricting our own talent supply is to persist in keeping a job requirement that has become outdated, such as continuing to demand specific programming knowledge when today's software packages have made it easier for more internal workers to learn the software and be redeployed into those jobs. The same holds true for job restrictions related to heavy lifting and words-per-minute requirements for word processors that may no longer be needed. Another example is the imposition of dress codes in call centers that may have previously screened out workers who prefer a more informal way of dressing; are they really necessary?

According to Dr. John Sullivan, former chief talent officer at Agilent Technologies and recruiting guru to many forward-thinking employers, "only 10 percent of the recruiters in business today are using innovative methods to help their companies attract and retain talent. The other 90 percent of companies are still using old tools." Here are some of the newer practices that Dr. Sullivan recommends that more companies consider:

- Host open houses by invitation by asking current employees to bring in friends they believe would be good employees.

- Build a website that puts prospects into e-mail contact with current satisfied employees (like Cisco's "Make a Friend at Cisco" capability). Put streaming video on the website that shows the work environment.

- Make your website more interactive, offering applicants the opportunity to list their ideal job criteria, then showing jobs that most closely match those criteria and linking them to current openings.

- Train all hiring managers to be more proactive as talent scouts by coaching them on where to look for new recruits and how to sell them on the company and the job.

- Build a contact database of the best talent in your industry and reach out to build relationships with them through e-newsletters or by phone so that they will think of coming to work with your company when they are ready to make a job change.

- Make every employee a recruiter by creating or revitalizing employee referral programs, as this method remains, when used appropriately, the most effective method of attracting talent that stays.[9]

 Engagement Practice #12:
Follow a purposeful and rigorous interview process.

Most companies with excellent track records for keeping a high percentage of the people they hire use a highly focused and systematic interviewing process and have trained all hiring managers to follow the process religiously. Here are some of the most effective components that these companies use:

- *Train all hiring managers in "behavioral interviewing."* This means that the company must first make the commitment to thoroughly analyze each job in terms of critical success factors and have hiring managers develop questions that require applicants to respond with stories of how they demonstrated those success factors in their past experiences. Most behavioral questions are asked in the form of "Tell me about a time when you . . ." (e.g., "Tell me about a time when you had to deal with a difficult customer and how you did it."). If an applicant does not have a story to tell, it is quite difficult to make one up on the spot. Well-qualified applicants can usually come up with illustrative stories to tell right away, while unsuitable candidates cannot.

The principle that makes this method effective is that actual past behavior accurately predicts future behavior. Companies considering use of behavioral interviewing should realize that it requires discipline for a manager who is in a hurry to fill a position to slow down enough to create behavioral questions and remember to conduct a behavioral interview with every potential hire. Human resource staff can be valuable partners by assisting with the pre-employment job analysis and the preparation of behavioral questions.

* *Use multiple interviewers.* The chances of hiring the right person go up when several interested parties are invited to participate in interviewing candidates. The interviewing team typically consists of peers and others with whom the new hire will have frequent interaction. It is a good way to involve team members in an important decision process while also getting valuable input and differing perspectives from those with a vested interest in seeing the right person hired.

Whether the company uses serial one-on-one interviews or has the interviewee face a panel, we highly recommend that the interviewing team meet beforehand to plan what questions will be asked, how, and by whom. Afterward, the team will need to meet and discuss each candidate, as well.

At Whole Foods, the Whole Team Hires

At Whole Foods Markets, teams—and only teams— have the power to approve new hires for full-time jobs. Store leaders screen candidates, then recommend them for jobs on a specific team. After the team interviews the candidate, a two-thirds vote is required for a hire; then the candidate doesn't become a permanent employee until after a thirty-day trial period. Teams routinely reject new hires before the thirty days are up if they turn out not to have the right stuff. Not everyone fits the Whole Foods profile, which is people who are "serious about food, have a knack for pleasing customers, and can tolerate the candid give-and-take that's necessary for a workplace democracy."

Another reason Whole Foods team members are so tough on new hires is that the company's gainsharing program ties directly to team performance. If team members vote for someone who doesn't perform, their bonuses will be less.[10]

- *Check several references without fail.* Many managers do not check references because of the time it takes and because many references are reluctant to speak for fear of a lawsuit. Still, smart hiring managers know how to overcome these obstacles, and they know that the information to be gotten is worth taking the extra time. There are several books that provide tips for better reference checking, among them Dr. Pierre Mornell's *Hiring Smart!* and my earlier book, *Keeping the People Who Keep You in Business*.

Engagement Practice #13:
Track measures of hiring success.

Many companies track cost per hire, but fewer than 10 percent of companies track the most meaningful hiring measure of them all—quality of hire.[11] Here are recommended ways of tracking the measure that comes closest to quantifying the match between person and job:

- Have each hiring manager set quarterly and first-year objectives for the new hire, expressed in terms of expected quantifiable results, and, in partnership with human resources, track the quality of hire, based on the achievement of those results. Some organizations use the first-year performance appraisal to track quality-of-hire.

- Base results on customer satisfaction surveys, achievement of timely results, cost reduction, or achievement of targeted quantitative objectives.

- Track first-year retention rates of all new hires.

- Track employee engagement survey scores of first-year employees as a group.

- Each year, have hiring managers complete quality-of-hire ratings on all new hires.

- Gather 360-degree feedback ratings on all new hires at the end of the first year.

It is recommended that all hiring managers meet with human resources staff once a year to review the quality of hires and to discuss any mistakes made, lessons learned, new strategies, and plans for improvement.

Best Practices for Engaging and Re-Engaging Through Job Task Assignment

There is potentially no more powerful motivator than the intrinsic satisfaction to be gained from using one's motivated talents. Managers can easily lose sight of this untapped source of motivational power by getting caught up in extrinsic factors like pay, bonuses, and benefits. Because so many workers have never had jobs that are inherently satisfying to perform, they, too, have come to accept external rewards as their due "compensation" for the trade-off they have made in job satisfaction.

Your job as a manager of people is to get the work done by allowing the maximum possible use of your employees' motivated abilities to achieved targeted results. This is not an easy task because it means taking the time to get to know each employee's unique combination of talents. It also means trying to dole out the available work so that it matches those talents. This is not always possible to do in a way that is perfectly acceptable to all, which can be frustrating.

The job of assigning the right tasks to the right talent becomes even more difficult when the manager's own style gets in the way, as when the manager:

- Believes there is only "one best way" to do the job and insists that the job be done that way.
- Doesn't trust people to make the right choices to reach the end result.
- Attempts to "idiot-proof" jobs by overprescribing exactly how they will be done through detailed rules, regulations, and procedure manuals.
- Micromanages employees because of constant fear that they might be doing the wrong thing or taking advantage.
- Exerts pressure on the employee to comply with demands instead of trying to gain voluntary commitment to performance goals (see Figure 5.1).
- Tries to correct employees' weaknesses at the expense of developing their strengths.
- Doesn't spend time trying to understand employees' best talents.

Figure 5.1.

How commitment differs from compliance.

Compliance	Commitment
Management defines the tasks.	Individual defines task.
Management defines the behavior required to perform tasks.	Individual defines the behavior required to perform tasks.
Management defines performance goals.	Management and individual jointly define performance goals that are challenging for the individual.
Manager defines the importance of the goal.	Individual defines the importance of the goal.

Source: Adapted from Chris Argyris, "Empowerment: The Emperor's New Clothes," *Harvard Business Review on Managing People,* Harvard Business School Press, 1999.

Admittedly, there are some jobs where safety, security, and financial accuracy dictate that they be done in a certain way, but in most jobs there is wide berth for the use of an individual's talent. With that exception, managers who engage in the behaviors I have described are limiting their own ability to engage and retain their workers.

Organizations can step in to correct these kinds of management practices by implementing better processes for selecting managers in the first place, providing multi-rater feedback to all managers, training and coaching managers in better talent identification and people management skills, rewarding and recognizing top talent managers, and holding all managers accountable for talent-related objectives.

We next discuss some practical tools and ideas that managers can use now to assign tasks so that workers can be more engaged through the use of their motivated abilities.

 Engagement Practice #14:
Conduct new-hire "entrance interviews."

Meet with the new hires during their first week on the job with the specific purpose of uncovering their greatest strengths and talents. Now that the employee already has the job, you can expect responses to be less calculated to impress you than when you asked similar questions in the job interview. Let employees know it is in your best mutual interests to get at the truth about their talents in order to put them to greatest use. Ask the following questions, even if you already asked similar questions in job interviews:

- What do you consider your greatest strengths?
- What do you consider your greatest weaknesses?

- Which of your talents was most underutilized in your last job?
- Which of your talents would you most like to use in this job?
- Which would you rather work with most—data, people, or things?
- How would you like to be challenged in the coming year?
- What other goals do you have for yourself in the coming year and beyond?
- How often would you like to meet to discuss your progress?
- As you read the job description, which activities appeal to you most and least?
- Which of your talents would you most like to develop further?

Be clear that it may not be possible to make use of employees' talents in exactly the way they prefer, but at least they will know that is your intent. Let them know that you value their talents and look forward to helping them succeed. Invite them to come and let you know if they begin to feel that their best talents are being underused.

Best Practices for Job Enrichment

Years ago, job enrichment researchers Richard Hackman and Greg Oldham identified five factors that contribute to job enrichment:

- *Skill Variety:* A desired mix of skills and activities is needed to carry out the work.
- *Task Completion:* The job is undertaken as a whole, allowing the employee to complete an identifiable piece of work from beginning to end with a visible outcome.
- *Task Significance:* The job has a recognizable impact on the overall mission or on other people inside or outside the organization.
- *Autonomy:* The job offers substantial freedom, independence, and discretion in scheduling the work and in choosing the procedures to be used in carrying it out.
- *Feedback:* The job provides feedback—by the observable progress and results of the job itself or from customers, coworkers, and manager.[12]

Hackman and Oldham's research yielded strong evidence that employees display high levels of self-motivation, work satisfaction, performance, customer service, commitment, and retention when their jobs have all five of these elements.

Engagement Practice #15:
Work to enrich the jobs of all employees.

Some jobs are more easily enriched than others, but it can be surprisingly easy to implement a change that has significant impact. A housecleaning company, for example, started allowing workers to switch jobs as they moved from house to house (skill variety). This meant that, instead of having one individual vacuum all day long and other workers perform other tasks, they would swap jobs at the next house. After instituting this change, the company noticed increased productivity and retention among the workers.

Task completion, task significance, and autonomy can all be increased by one management decision, as when a manager decides to give sales or customer service people the authority and resources to resolve customer problems on the spot instead of passing them on to one person, then another. Customers seem to appreciate this, as well.

Feedback can be increased simply by starting to have more frequent meetings with employees to give feedback on their performance or by sharing customer satisfaction surveys, profitability figures, production results, or other data now made available via company intranets or through increasingly sophisticated information systems. One high-tech manufacturing company even had each of its production teams stamp its own phone number on every product shipped from the plant. The phone calls received from customers who had problems with a product served as a highly direct feedback mechanism that also served to motivate workers to achieve higher levels of quality.

Here are a few other ways to enrich jobs:

- Combine several small tasks performed by separate people into one more fulfilling job.
- Place workers into teams or natural work units organized by the types of clients, industries, or geographies they serve.
- Gradually give more autonomy to workers by delegating first one task, then another, from a higher-level job or from a manager's job to workers at lower levels.
- Establish more direct contact between workers and customers.
- Create teams and task forces with the power to solve problems or create new products, services, or mini-enterprises.
- Allow people doing stand-alone tasks in various locations to connect with employees doing other phases of the work.

Very few jobs are as fixed as they used to be. These days, jobs constantly change, and the opportunity to enrich them will be there if you choose to take it. This also means that, once a job has been enriched, it will not stay enriched unless manager and employee work together to make it happen. Finally, it is considered a realistic rule of thumb that if 80 percent of a job is enriched, it is probably a good job.[13]

 Engagement Practice #16:
Delegate, delegate, delegate!

Today's younger generations of workers don't have the patience to pay their dues as their parents did. You may disparage their impatience, but they will move on to another company that will give them the keys to the car as soon as they come in the door. No matter how many dues you paid as you climbed the ladder, no matter how you slowly prepared yourself for a more meaningful role and deliberately acquired valuable knowledge, that model of gradually taking on incremental challenges is no longer acceptable to most younger workers, who have a more short-term focus. They want meaningful work roles now.

This means you will need to employ the job enrichment guidelines I have suggested and, in many cases, start delegating tasks that you may have been uncomfortable delegating in the past.

Here are some reasons you may be reluctant to delegate:

- You're afraid the employee will screw things up.
- There's no time to train employees to the point where you can trust them not to screw up.
- You believe employees need to pay their dues first, as you did.
- You like doing the work yourself too much to let it go.
- You're afraid that empowering your workers means giving up your power.

If you can identify with any of these concerns, you will need to work to overcome them. For practical guidelines on how to do that, refer to the twenty-three steps toward better delegation and empowerment that I suggest in *Keeping the People Who Keep You in Business* (Retention Practice #18—Give Autonomy and Reward Initiative).[14]

The Employee's Role in the Matching Process

As with all the seven reasons employees leave, it's not just the manager who has all the responsibility. Employees need to be reminded that there is much they can do to achieve the best match of their own talents to the job. For example, they can:

- Ask questions during the interview to make sure the job is one that will make good use of their talents.

- Know their values well enough to resist being recruited into a work culture that would not be a good fit.

- Seek assistance with identifying their talents through a private career coach, psychologist, community college, or university career center if talent assessment workshops or inventories are not offered at the organization.

- Take the initiative to meet with the manager to discuss how they would like the job to be changed if they feel the manager is not making good use of their talents.

- Put themselves in the manager's shoes and be prepared to explain how enriching their own job will also benefit the work unit or organization as a whole.

- Seek whatever training they need to earn the trust of the manager and to give the manager the confidence to delegate more to them.

- Keep themselves engaged by seeking new challenges instead of getting too comfortable when they have mastered a job.

- Ask for feedback when they feel they are not getting enough of it.

Engagement Practices Checklist: Job-Person Matching

To score yourself on the best practices described in this chapter, check those you and your organization perform.

To select the right talent for the job:

Engagement Practice #9. __   Have a strong commitment to the continuous upgrading of talent.

Engagement Practice #10. __   Makes sure that all hiring managers follow a consistent and thorough talent forecasting and success-factor analysis process.

Engagement Practice #11. __   Cast a wide recruiting net to expand the universe of best-fit candidates.

Engagement Practice #12. __   Follow a purposeful and rigorous interview process.

Engagement Practice #13. __   Track measures of hiring success.

To make the right job task assignments:

Engagement Practice #14. __   Conduct "entrance interviews" with all new hires.

Engagement Practice #15. __   Work to enrich the jobs of all employees.

Engagement Practice #16. __   Delegate tasks to challenge and enrich the jobs

Your next step: *Resolve to take action on the ones you believe are most critical and appropriate for your situation and objectives.*

Notes

1. Marcus Buckingham and Donald O. Clifton, *Now, Discover Your Strengths* (New York: Free Press, 2001).

2. Larry Bossidy and Ram Charan, *Execution: The Discipline of Getting Things Done* (New York: Random House, 2002).

3. Edward L. Gubman, *The Talent Solution: Aligning Strategy and People to Achieve Extraordinary Results* (New York: McGraw-Hill, 1998).

4. Jim Collins, author of *Good to Great: Why Some Companies Make the Leap and Others Don't* (New York: HarperBusiness, 2001), based on a study of how 11 companies out of 1,435 went from good to great financial performance, in a Web-exclusive interview for *Fast Company,* October 2001, http://www.fastcompany.com/magazine/51/goodtogreat.html.

5. Fay Hansen, "Overhauling the Recruiting Process at CDW Corp.," Workforce Management Online, April 2007, http://www.workforce .com/article/20070411/NEWS02/3041199966.

6. InnerView™ Guard Performance and Assignment Profile, 2011, www.weisersecurity.com.

7. Marcus Buckingham and Curt Coffman, *First, Break All the Rules: What the World's Great Managers Do Differently* (New York: Simon and Schuster, 1999).

8. M. Mitchell Waldrop, "Dee Hock on Management," *Fast Company,* October/November 1996.

9. Jodi Spiegel Arthur, "Talent Scout," *Human Resource Executive,* June 2, 2000.

10. Charles Fishman, "Whole Foods Is All Teams," *Fast Company,* April 1996.

11. "Quality Now," *Staffing.org Metrics Update e-newsletter,* January 8, 2003.

12. J. Richard Hackman and Greg R. Oldham, *Work Redesign* (London: Addison-Wesley, 1980).

13. Edward E. Lawler III, *Treat People Right! How Organizations and Individuals Can Propel Each Other into a Virtual Spiral of Success* (San Francisco: Jossey-Bass, 2003).

14. Leigh Branham, *Keeping the People Who Keep You in Business: 24 Ways to Hang On to Your Most Valuable Talent* (New York: AMACOM, 2001).

CHAPTER SIX

Reason #3: Too Little Coaching and Feedback

> When you don't manage for progress,
> no amount of emotional intelligence
> or incentive planning will save the day.
>
> —TERESA AMABILE AND STEVEN KRAMER,
> *THE PROGRESS PRINCIPLE*

Just in case you need more evidence that a lack of performance coaching and feedback is a major cause of employee disengagement and turnover, here are some survey results to consider:

- The number one cause of performance problems in 60 percent of companies is poor or insufficient feedback from supervisors.[1]

- A survey of 1,149 people at seventy-nine different companies found that manager feedback and coaching skills were consistently rated as mediocre.[2]

- Forty-one percent of employees believe their managers have no effect whatsoever on their performance, and 14 percent said their manager actually made the job harder.[3]

- Only 39 percent of managers said that their company is very effective at providing candid feedback.[4]

- Only 35 percent of workers identified by their companies as highly talented feel the company tells them openly and candidly where they stand.[5]

- It has been estimated that approximately 50 percent of the nonperformance problems in business occur because of the lack of feedback, and about 50 percent of what appear to be motivational problems in business are actually feedback problems.[6]

Post-exit survey comments of voluntarily departed employees in my own survey and in Saratoga's testify to the role that lack of feedback and coaching played in their decisions to leave:

- "Not enough feedback from supervisors."
- "There is not much feedback on job performance."
- "Managers need to coach employees."
- "There is no feedback from any of the supervisors on how jobs are being done."
- "In my three years of working at XYZ Company, I never had a job description or an evaluation."
- "ABC Company needs to pay a lot more attention to letting employees know how they perform."
- "As an employer, XYZ Company doesn't keep its employees updated enough on their errors, so that we know where we stand in our positions. We don't know what we've done wrong until an error is made because we aren't notified of process changes ahead of time."
- "Management needs to take a little more time to explain what they expect so I would be more inclined to work and perform."
- "The formal performance evaluations are geared more toward the number of mistakes rather than the number of positive contributions."
- "Managers are never around, never seem to keep up on reviews, and pay increases always seem to be delayed."
- "Managers don't handle issues with troubled employees well. They seem to not like confrontation with employees who don't produce or don't give good customer service."
- "This company tends to have managers who are more involved in the small-time politics of the workplace rather than rewarding and disciplining based on performance. There have been times when supervisors have acted in a vindictive, self-serving manner."
- "Managers should start following up with disciplinary measures for those who blatantly disregard the rules."
- "The company will bend over backwards to keep employees that are performing below average."
- "ABC Company does not expeditiously hire, discipline, or terminate employees."
- "XYZ Company must pay more attention to letting employees know how they perform."

- "They tell you everything you do wrong and nothing you do right."
- "I'm not sure that this statement applies to all of ABC Company, but as far as the office I work in, they dwell too much on what an employee does wrong, far more than what an employee does right."
- "XYZ Company needs to address negative issues of employees because these negative issues affect the department as a whole."
- "ABC Company does not communicate expectations, provide timely feedback, or conduct timely performance evaluations. There is also a lack of trust between employees and management."
- "Performance reviews are given out on a whim, it seems."
- "I feel like nobody cares about the work I am doing."

These comments provide ample evidence that opportunities to build competence, trust, hope, and worth through coaching and feedback have been lost. They also reveal several underlying problems:

- Many managers are not paying attention to the people they supervise.
- Performance feedback is occurring irregularly or not happening at all.
- Basic expectations and changes in work procedures are not being communicated.
- Nonperformance is not being addressed.
- Too much emphasis is being placed on criticism and not enough on praise.
- Managers are allowing themselves to be influenced by politics, favoritism, and other factors besides objective performance.
- Employees themselves may be reluctant to seek feedback.

Why Coaching and Feedback Are Important to Engagement and Retention

Performance coaching and feedback are essential for employees because they help them to answer four basic questions:

1. Where are we going as a company?
2. How are we getting there?
3. How do you expect me to contribute?
4. How am I doing?

The answers to these questions constitute much of what gives meaning to an employee's efforts. We all have a basic need to exercise competence and to know that our talents have been used to make a valuable contribution. At times, our own ability to see the impact of our contributions is clouded by the fact that we may be removed from the end result or limited by our own narrow perspectives.

Companies need to give feedback and coaching to make sure that employees' efforts stay aligned with organizational and unit goals and the expectations of direct supervisors. This alignment is a necessary precondition for employee engagement.

One survey found that 80 percent of employees who had been coached by their managers felt a strong sense of commitment to their organization, while only 46 percent of employees who received no coaching reported feeling the same.[7]

The goal of retaining employees through coaching and feedback is really a secondary one. The engagement of employees to enhance performance is the main goal. Much of the coaching and feedback managers offer will always be directed at unsuccessful attempts to get nonperformers to meet expectations. Knowing when to continue coaching and when to discontinue and make the tough decision to terminate is a decision all managers will inevitably have to make. Just as you don't have a goal of making everyone you meet a lifelong friend, you will likewise not try to retain every employee you manage and attempt to coach.

Why Don't Managers Provide Coaching and Feedback?

There are many possible answers to this question. Generally, managers don't provide coaching and feedback because:

- They fear or dread confronting an employee with criticism without hurting, offending, creating defensiveness, alienating the employee, getting into an argument, or losing control of their own emotions.
- Too many of them are simply pressed into service on so many projects that they feel they have little time to actually observe an employee's progress over the long haul.
- They fear they will fail. True coaching and genuine, responsible feedback are higher-order people skills, but they are not taught to managers as anything more complicated than "useful techniques."
- True progress is gradual, and managing step-by-step employee

development requires greater proximity—both physically and emotionally—to workers than most management jobs permit.

- A world filled with virtual assignments, domestic and global travel,
  interminable meetings, and endless client contacts simply does not
  allow for the required immediacy of the effort—if you wait a day to
  give feedback on something, the effect is lost.

- They have never received skilled feedback or positive coaching
  themselves or have worked too long in a culture that doesn't
  encourage it.

Reviewing this list makes one wonder how any feedback and coaching
ever get done, and it should raise our levels of appreciation and admiration for
the managers who somehow do make time for it in their weekly schedules.
Many managers actually believe they are providing sufficient feedback and
coaching, but, if you talk to their direct reports, you hear a different story.

Larry Bossidy, former CEO of Allied-Signal, believes that most CEOs are
unaware of the lack of feedback their direct reports are receiving. "If you ask
any CEO if their direct reports know what the CEO thinks of them," said
Bossidy, "the CEO will slam the table and say, 'Absolutely! I'm with them all
the time. I travel with them. We are always discussing their results.'" But, he
added, "If you then ask the direct reports the same question, nine out of ten
will say, `I don't have a clue, I haven't had a performance review or any feed-
back in the last five years.'"[8]

In the sports world, it would be unimaginable to think of a coach not giving feedback to a player for extended periods of time. Consider this ridiculous
scenario: A basketball coach begins the season by telling his players, "OK, here's
the deal. You're going to go out there and play thirty games, and at the end of
the season I'll sit down with each of you and we'll go over how you did and
how you can get better in the future." And yet, this is exactly what is happening in untold numbers of companies, where managers give feedback to
employees once and only once each year—at the annual formal performance
appraisal meeting.

Recognizing the Signs

Any of the following behaviors may indicate that your direct reports are not
receiving the feedback and coaching they need to improve or maintain desired
performance levels:

- You realize that the last time you gave feedback to one of your direct reports was months ago, during that person's most recent performance appraisal.

- You have not spent at least one hour in the past three months giving performance feedback to each of your direct reports.

- You give feedback only when an employee requests it.

- You find yourself procrastinating about giving feedback to an employee until days or weeks after you first intended to give it.

- Your direct reports have tried to schedule meetings with you for feedback and coaching, and you have had to cancel or postpone them on several occasions.

- After you give feedback, things fail to improve or seem to get even worse.

- When giving feedback, you hold back for fear of hurting the employee's feelings.

- You feel uncomfortable with the whole idea of coaching and giving feedback because you have never been trained in how to do it well.

More Than an Event: It's About the Relationship

Giving good feedback and coaching is about more than having a series of meetings—it's about manager and employee building an open and trusting relationship. Most managers have built comfortable and satisfactory relationships with some employees but have also experienced the opposite, as well—relationships with other employees that never got off on the right footing or went from bad to worse. Perhaps it is that we simply like some employees better than others or that we favor those who are most similar to us, but it is a common phenomenon to place a halo on the heads of some employees and see horns growing on others.

Unknowingly, a manager may actually be contributing to the failure of an employee. As described in a classic article, "The Set-Up-to-Fail Syndrome," there is usually a triggering event that causes the manager to lose faith in an employee—losing a client, undershooting a target, or missing a deadline.[9] The syndrome is set in motion when the supervisor starts to worry about an employee's performance so much that she starts putting him on a "short leash"—constantly checking up on him, requiring approval for all decisions, and generally micromanaging him. The employee interprets this reining-in behavior as a loss of trust and confidence and, in the worst-case scenario, starts living down to the supervisor's low expectations. He begins to withdraw emotionally, may be paralyzed into inaction, and consumes so much of the supervisor's time that he is eventually fired or quits.

This is exactly the kind of downward-spiral disengagement process referred to in Chapter 2. It can be interrupted and reversed by a manager who is aware that it is happening and who is motivated to change the relationship. The prescription: a mixture of coaching, training, job redesign, and a clearing of the air. All this takes courage, an ability to be self-reflective, and more frequent contact and emotional involvement with the employee. But too many managers are not motivated to perform such transformations.

While listening to employees describe how they came to leave their past employers, I have heard many variations of the set-up-to-fail story. One very creative and talented employee I'll call Pam described a turning point with a manager, who was pushing her to tell a prospective client they could deliver a service that Pam knew they were not prepared to deliver. Pam saw this promise to the client as bordering on unethical, while her boss perceived Pam's reluctance as a lack of confidence. After that, the manager began withholding assignments from Pam and giving them to her peers instead. Eventually, the emotional chasm in their relationship became too great, and Pam was let go. With time to reflect, she realized she was quite relieved to be gone.

Could this employee have been salvaged with a different approach to coaching and feedback? Perhaps the disagreement about ethics would have been too great to overcome. But I sincerely believe that at least a third of all terminations could be prevented with better coaching and feedback or by reassigning employees to managers with more compatible coaching styles.

The vast majority of bosses favor some subordinates, treating them as part of an in-group, while consigning others to an out-group. The manager may either totally ignore those in the out-group or oversupervise them to such an extent that they stop giving their best, stop taking the initiative, and become automatons, sending the clear message back to their managers, "Just tell me what you want and I'll do it." This is the very definition of disengagement.

The effects on those in the in-group may also be highly negative. If the manager loses faith in a performer he perceives as weak, he may start overloading those he considers stronger performers, creating resentment on their part and eventually burning them out.

The dynamics of manager-employee relationships are complex, but, in the best-case scenarios, with a good faith effort and the right approach to coaching, employees can be re-engaged.

Engagement Practices for Coaching and Giving Feedback

Engagement Practice #17:
Provide intensive feedback and coaching to new hires.

As the saying goes, you have only one chance to make a first impression. Starting the relationship with the right mix of coaching and feedback will pay big dividends later. As J. Sterling Livingston put it in his now-famous article, "Pygmalion in Management," "Something important is happening in the first year . . . meeting high company expectations in the critical first year leads to the internalization of positive job attitudes and high standards. . . . If managers are unskilled, they leave scars on the careers of young people, cut deeply into their self-esteem, and distort their image of themselves as human beings."[10]

Good managers know that they need to proactively manage the new hires' joining-up process. Here are some specific steps that can jump-start a positive coaching relationship:

- Plan how you want the new hires to spend the first day on the job, and arrange to spend quality time with them at the beginning and the end of the first week.

- Meet with new hires on their first day to reaffirm how their job fits into the organization's mission and objectives.

- Conduct an "entrance interview," as presented in Chapter 5, focused on discovering in-depth the new hire's best talents and professional goals.

- During the first week, discuss your performance expectations in detail for the first ninety days, and ask the new hire to draft a performance agreement that summarizes the stated objectives as targeted results that are specific, measurable, achievable, and realistic.

- Pair up the new employee with a respected peer or senior coworker to be a mentor or buddy during the first six months or longer.

- Make it clear that giving feedback is your responsibility and getting feedback is the new hire's responsibility. In other words, new hires need to understand that, when they feel they are not getting enough feedback, they need to seek it out—from you, from a coworker, from a customer—instead of passively waiting for someone to give it.

- Look for opportunities to directly observe and debrief new employees as frequently as possible during the first few weeks. As events cause changes in first-quarter objectives, revise the objectives as appropriate to make them more realistic or achievable.

- Meet with new employees at the end of the first three months to discuss progress on written objectives and to create new objectives for the next quarter. During this meeting, be sure to ask about any expectations that have not been met so that they can be brought to the surface and openly discussed instead of being allowed to fester.

- Encourage employees to request a performance feedback session with their managers at any time. This is especially important during the employee's first year, and it is a way of signaling to Millennials, who tend to need and want frequent feedback, that sometimes you have to simply "raise your hand" and ask for it.

These same guidelines apply to employees you may inherit when you take over a new group of employees. It is worth keeping in mind that the scarcest commodity in most companies is the manager's attention. When days and weeks pass without new hires, especially younger ones, seeing or hearing from their managers, they tend to assume the worst. As Livingston so eloquently put it, "Managers often communicate most when they believe they are communicating least. . . . The silent treatment communicates negative feelings even more effectively, at times, than a tongue-lashing does. . . . Indifference says to subordinates, 'I don't think much of you.'"[11]

 Engagement Practice #18:
Create a culture of continuous feedback and coaching.

Some companies have cultures where feedback flows freely, and others have cultures where feedback is kept in reserve, saved for "a more appropriate time" that never comes, or kept until performance review time and dumped on the employee all in one sitting. General Electric under Jack Welch was a constant-feedback culture. As described in *Jack: Straight from the Gut*, "In GE every day, there's an informal, unspoken personnel review—in the lunchroom, the hallway, and in every business meeting."[12]

One study found that 64 percent of people prefer informal, on-the-job conversations with their supervisor over formal interviews.[13] Certainly, a frequent-feedback culture is a reflection of a results-driven CEO who wants to make sure that employees have the feedback they need just in time to use it and make a difference for customers. The best way to make sure that feedback is given and received in a meaningful and productive way, however, is to train all managers in how to give it, and all employees in how to receive it. Here are some ideas on which to build a positive feedback culture through training:

- Begin with the assumption that every employee is responsible for getting feedback and not dependent or passively waiting for the manager to give it.

- It is the responsibility of every manager to give timely and frequent feedback to all employees, but the supervisor is not the sole initiator of feedback.

- Make sure that all managers are trained to understand the essential conditions for effective feedback—that the feedback giver is credible and trustworthy and has good intentions; that the timing and circumstances are appropriate; that the feedback is given in a personal and interactive manner; and that the message is clear and helpful.[14]

- Include a training module for employees on how to receive feedback that also encourages them to overcome any resistance they may have to seeking it.

- Emphasize the importance of managers making sure the feedback they are about to give is accurate before they give it.

- Communicate clearly and unequivocally that feedback is not to be reserved for periodic, formal occasions and that it is to be given and sought on an ongoing, continual basis, driven not by the calendar but by the situation.

- Look for logical times to give feedback to an entire team of people, such as at the end of a major project.

- Stress the importance of overcoming people's natural defensiveness about receiving feedback by giving positive feedback along with the negative. Encourage employees to build on their strengths as the preferred strategy for improving performance.

It is not enough to point out shortcomings. Employees need help figuring out what actions they need to take in order to do better.

Because feedback improperly given can have a negative impact on performance, training should include time for managers to practice giving it and employees to practice receiving it.

Along with the training, offer a variety of feedback tools, such as internal and external customer questionnaires, 360-degree feedback instruments, and less formal feedback questionnaires.

Make all managers and employees aware of available feedback tools and training.

How to Become a "Best Place to Work"? Train Managers in Difficult Conversations

The Boston Business Journal selected Winchester Hospital as one of the Best Places to Work in Boston for six years in a row. Anne Lang, Winchester's vice president of human resources, believes the 230-bed hospital's success dates back to a decision that the CEO made years ago to train all managers in how to give honest and constructive feedback.

All management staff received forty hours of training in effective people management and an additional eight hours per year. How do they know it's working? "We know because we can see they are not avoiding confrontations," says Lang. "They come in to me for coaching, knowing they have to have a difficult conversation and often they are dreading it. They ask if I will walk them through how to deal with a tough issue with an employee or sometimes with a peer, physician, or patient." The hospital also achieves high employee engagement by holding managers accountable through its employee engagement survey and performance reviews, by identifying and developing emerging leaders, by keeping employees informed, and by driving decisions "forward to the front lines."

As a result, Winchester achieved a 90th-percentile patient satisfaction rating in the state, its voluntary turnover rate dropped from 15 percent to 7 percent, and its nurse vacancy rate fell to 2 percent, which is unheard of. In an era of nurse shortages, Winchester has a waiting list of applicants.[15]

Getting the Best Results from 360-Degree Feedback

Many companies have initiated the use of 360-degree or multirater feedback that allows employees to receive formal feedback not just from the boss but from their peers, direct reports, and customers. The idea is to give employees a fuller picture of how they are perceived than they can hope to receive only from their direct supervisor. Most companies with experience using 360-degree feedback are reporting that best results are generally obtained when:

- The feedback is used only for self-development, not for rating performance or for making decisions about pay or promotion.
- Employees are given the option of receiving 360-degree feedback, rather than having it mandated.
- Employees are allowed to select the raters in consultation with the direct supervisor.

- There are enough raters to assure anonymity to all raters.
- Those to be rated are trained in how to receive feedback.

After receiving the feedback report, employees are encouraged to seek additional clarifying feedback through follow-up discussions with raters.

 Engagement Practice #19:
Train managers in performance coaching.

While there is no one right way to do performance coaching, most employees know a good performance coach when they have one. One study of great sports coaches found that what many of them describe as their secrets of success—"recruit the right players and inspire them to win"—is not what they do at all. Instead, they carefully observe their players in practice, stop practice to give detailed feedback and teach the proper way, ask questions to make sure the player understands what they are told, watch the player perform the play or movement as instructed, and finally reward with simple praise.[16]

Joe Torre, former Major League Baseball manager, received wide public acclaim in an article that appeared in *Fortune* magazine after he had guided the New York Yankees to yet another baseball world championship. In the article, psychologist Daniel Goleman, author of the book *Emotional Intelligence*, said of Torre, "This guy is a textbook case of an emotionally intelligent leader.'" The article's author describes Torre's principal management tool as "not meetings or motivational talks, but regular one-on-one encounters with his players, which he used to monitor and regulate their psyches." One of his players described how Torre "watches and listens before he says a thing." Another said, "you never see him berating a player . . . or dropping his head in disgust."[17]

Torre and many other managers have the natural gift for coaching, but performance coaching can be learned. One of the best books on performance coaching is Ferdinand Fournies's *Coaching for Improved Work Performance*, which outlines a systematic process based on principles of behavioral psychology. It is a process that provides a workable alternative to what he refers to as "YST—Yelling, Screaming, and Threatening." To quote Fournies, "Instead of pushing solutions on people with the force of your argument, pull solutions out of them."[18]

Fournies's book confronts managers who believe falsely that employees' bad attitudes are unchangeable and that employees choose, against their best interests, to underperform. Instead, he proposes that managers do everything possible to prevent employee failure by pursuing a system of interventions. He identifies sixteen reasons employees don't do what they are supposed to do:

1. They don't know what they are supposed to do.
2. They don't know how to do it.
3. They don't know why they should do it.
4. They think they are doing it (lack of feedback).
5. There are obstacles beyond their control.
6. They think it will not work.
7. They think their way is better.
8. They think something is more important (priorities).
9. There is no positive consequence to them for doing it.
10. There is a negative consequence to them for doing it.
11. There is a positive consequence to them for not doing it.
12. There is no negative consequence to them for not doing it.
13. They have personal limits (incapacity).
14. They have personal problems.
15. Fear (they anticipate future negative consequences).
16. No one could do it.[19]

When these sales managers fire someone they are saying, says Fournies, "I don't have one or two weeks to help you improve your performance, but I have thirty work days to devote to replacing you."[20]

Fournies provides a coaching analysis chart that prescribes what a manager can do to intervene successfully, starting with identifying the unsatisfactory performance, not the *result* of the unsatisfactory performance. Finally, he presents a five-step coaching technique:

Step 1: Get the employee's agreement that a problem exists.

Step 2: Mutually discuss alternative solutions.

Step 3: Mutually agree on action to be taken to solve the problem.

Step 4: Follow up to measure results.

Step 5: Reinforce any achievement when it occurs.

This process is not about placing blame or even assigning motives to employees for their behavior. Rather, it is focused on producing positive behavior going forward. Companies wishing to upgrade the level of performance coaching to more fully engage employees would be well advised to design training for managers in a systematic process such as this one. As Fournies himself points out, "Training compresses time, making people smarter without getting older, and avoids the unnecessary bumps and bruises."[21]

Four Common Performance-Management Routines of Great Managers

1. The routine is simple. (Simple formats allow managers to focus on what to say and how to say it.)
2. The routine forces frequent interaction. (Meaningful feedback happens when it follows on the heels of an event.)
3. The routine is future focused. (Postmortems can lead to recriminations. Positive energy comes from discussing the future.)
4. The routine lets employees keep track of their own performance and learning. (This creates more employee ownership of the self-discovery process.)[22]

Engagement Practice #20:
Make the performance-management process less controlling and more of a partnership.

Over the past twenty years, most companies have been moving to a formal performance review process that reflects the growing trend to create more of a partnership between manager and employee, as Figure 6.1 shows.

Figure 6.1.

A comparison of traditional and partnering approaches to management.

Traditional Approach	Partnering Approach
Manager-Driven	Employee-Driven
Parent-Child Model	Adult-to-Adult Model
An HR Exercise	A Manager's Tool
Subjective Favoritism	Result-Focused
Vague Objectives	Specific Objectives
Yearly Event	Ongoing Discussions
Rate and Rank for Pay	Pay Based on Results

While more than half of all companies have no performance-management system at all,[23] many of those that do still practice the traditional approach. This may help to explain why almost 90 percent of managers who do use performance appraisals do not believe they help to improve worker performance! If a company is trying to become an employer of choice by creating a culture of reciprocal commitment, it is highly unlikely it will achieve that status using an outdated performance appraisal process that is based on anything other than an adult-to-adult relationship. Real commitment comes from partnering agreements in which employees suggest their own objectives and merge them with those of the manager, not from the imposition of goals and objectives from above.

Most experts on performance-management systems report that companies achieve the greatest overall satisfaction and effectiveness with systems that:

- Use no performance ratings or summary judgments, as these have been consistently found to increase defensiveness and reduce receptivity to constructive performance planning.

- Unlink performance discussions from salary discussions. Many companies have eliminated the yearly performance discussion focused on a "final" evaluation in favor of more frequent informal meetings. This avoids the inevitable "gunny-sacking" of supervisor criticisms over several months time until they are all dumped onto the employee in a yearly meeting.

- Further deformalize the process by no longer requiring the employee's signature or placing the plan in a "personnel file." Some companies create more employee ownership of the process by allowing employees to keep the performance plan in their own files and give them the option of providing a copy to the supervisor.

- Call for meetings between manager and employee at least once per quarter and encourage frequent brief performance feedback-and-coaching discussions.

- Emphasize mutual performance analysis over performance appraisal.

- Give the employee the initiative in creating performance goals. The employee is the active agent, not the passive object of a supervisor's appraisal.

- Allow the employee to begin performance review discussions by evaluating personal progress toward self-created objectives.

- Train managers in a discussion process that is simple and memorable,

such as "Get-Give-Merge-Go" (start by *getting* the employee's perspective on performance, then *give* your perspective, then *merge* mutual
perspectives into an agreement, then *go* forward with new objectives).

- Train managers in helping employees set appropriate objectives that are
  specific, measurable, achievable, realistic, and time bound (S-M-A-R-T).

- Put the manager in the role of counselor and co-problem solver, not
  judge. Managers do not coerce or manipulate employees to accept
  organizational goals. The manager is responsible for ensuring that
  the employee's objectives align with the objectives of the unit and
  organization.

- Hold senior executives accountable for following the same performance review and planning processes that every other employee must
  follow.

- Have built-in measures of the system to ensure that it remains
  effective, with measures based on periodic quality and timing
  audits and on surveys of employee opinions about the process.

- Ditch elaborate and complicated ranking systems for determining
  salary increases. Many companies have managers use simple categories
  such as A-players, B-players, and C-players, or "walking on water,"
  "swimming," and "drowning," as initial groups, then provide raises
  based on subjective judgments of overall value to the organization.

Engagement Practice #21:
Terminate nonperformers when best efforts
to coach or reassign don't pay off.

It may seem contradictory to recommend a practice devoted to the termination of poor performance after having recommended another practice
encouraging the commitment to correcting poor performance. However, I do
believe these two practices must coexist in employers of choice. Despite your
best efforts to coach nonperformers or to change the nature of their job
assignments, there will be times when it is simply best to let the employee go.
The problem is that, all too often, other valued employees know when that
time has come long before the manager does, and the manager's failure to act
can adversely impact their commitment.

As one business columnist described the situation, "We're in the middle of
a vast wave of nonfiring. . . . The damage to millions of lives, and the economy, is beyond calculating. . . . Keeping poor performers means that develop-

ment opportunities for promising employees get blocked, so those subordinates don't get developed, productivity and morale fall, good performers leave the company, the company attracts fewer A players, and the whole miserable cycle keeps turning."[24]

This is a theme that appears in all the employee survey results I have seen—good performers consistently complain that underperforming employees are tolerated, even promoted and rewarded with raises, while they themselves are overworked or ignored. When McKinsey asked thousands of employees how they would feel if their employers got rid of underperformers, 59 percent strongly agreed with the option "delighted"—yet only 7 percent believed their companies were doing it.[25]

Jack Welch expressed his feelings on the matter quite clearly in a letter to GE's shareholders, customers, and employees before leaving his post as CEO, saying, "Not removing the bottom 10 percent . . . is not only a management failure, but false kindness as well."[26] This stance opens a highly controversial door—whether to eliminate the bottom 10 percent each year. Some believe this helps to continually upgrade the organization's talent level, while many others believe the "rank and yank" approach eventually leads to the termination of competent employees who just happen to fall into the bottom 10 percent of highly performing teams and can also result in litigation. Conversely, a mediocre employee in a struggling unit may come out looking great. To mitigate this concern, some companies reduce the percentage of employees to be weeded out in successive years, as in 10 percent the first year and 5 percent in the second and third years.

Many proponents of forced-ranking systems believe they force managers to be honest with their employees about how they are doing. Others argue that forced rankings can become a crutch for poor management, making the case that good managers should have the ability to make difficult decisions without having a system force it on them.

No matter where one stands on this issue, there is considerably less doubt about the need to step up and make tough decisions to cut nonperforming employees when all else has failed. Most managers would probably agree with Welch's point about "false kindness." As Debra Dunn, senior executive at Hewlett-Packard, put it, "There is no greater disrespect you can do to a person than to let them hang out in a job where they are not respected by their peers, not viewed as successful, and probably losing their self-esteem. To do that under the guise of respect for people is, to me, ridiculous."[27]

Engagement Practice #22:
Hold managers accountable for coaching and
giving feedback.

If 60 percent of a manager's time is spent fixing people problems, you might think more companies would make special efforts to hold managers accountable for coaching and giving feedback to employees.

Some companies, such as The Security Benefit Group of Companies in Topeka, Kansas, introduced "upward evaluation" systems that allowed employees to give feedback on their managers' people-management and coaching skills. When surveys are completed, results are reported to the manager for use in development discussions. Managers have reported that their results have become more positive since the practice began.

Many other companies have begun incorporating coaching and feedback competencies into the lists of key competencies they require of all leaders. For example, instead of listing "people management" as a single competency for managers, it is more meaningful to select, train, and evaluate managers against competencies that are more specifically defined. People-management skills might be further broken down into more specific competencies, such as human resource planning, employee selection, performance coaching and feedback, training and development, and employee recognition and motivation—with clear definitions provided for each of these.

Management books such as Daniel Goleman's *Emotional Intelligence at Work* and *Primal Leadership* have also made many organizations more aware of the importance of emotional intelligence factors in selecting and promoting managers. Goleman describes the *Coaching* style of leadership as one of the most highly positive of six predominant leadership styles—the others being *Visionary* (most strongly positive), *Affiliative* (positive), *Democratic* (positive), *Pacesetting* (often negative), and *Commanding* (usually negative because it is so often misused). Yet, he concludes, "Despite the commonly held belief that every leader needs to be a good coach, leaders tend to exhibit this style least often."[28]

Regardless of how carefully we spell out competencies and study leadership styles, the only way to ensure that any new practices are working is to hold managers accountable and to create new rewards and consequences. When corporate officers were asked if line managers should be accountable for the strength of the talent pool they are building, 93 percent said they should be, yet only 3 percent said that they actually held line managers accountable for this outcome.[29]

One company that holds managers accountable for people outcomes is Applebee's International, which has installed balanced scorecard measures for its restaurant managers based on results in three areas—financial, people, and customer. The company started holding its area managers accountable for people results in four key areas with significant impact on the bottom line—hourly staffing levels, percentage of employees retained among the top 80 percent of all staff, hourly new-hire retention rates, and progress on succession management. Performance on these four measures accounts for 30 percent of the formula used to determine pay raises. Applebee's also sponsored an annual contest among area managers called "Turn Yourself Over to the Tropics," which awarded top performers who scored well on management turnover measures with vacations in Cancun and cruises to the Bahamas.

How have these new practices worked? The annual turnover rate among hourly employees dropped from 146 percent in the first year to 92 percent in the next, and turnover of restaurant general managers fell from 20 percent to 8 percent over the same period. The drops in turnover were attributable to more than a recessionary economy, as Applebee's turnover rates dropped further and faster than those of most of their competitors in the casual-dining restaurant category. On the basis of avoided hard replacement costs for restaurant managers alone, the company conservatively estimated that it had achieved one-year savings of $1.6 million.

Some companies make it a practice to hold "what's wrong" meetings with managers with low employee-engagement scores or high numbers of employee grievances. Others have "skip-level" meetings where the manager's manager meets with his or her direct reports to get their input on the manager's people-management effectiveness.

Another effective way to create accountability among managers for people results is to promote and select candidates for managerial and executive positions on the basis of who has met the highest standards of management behavior. One of the best-known examples of this came to the attention of the public in early 2001, when Jack Welch, in his annual letter to stockholders, customers, and employees, announced GE's new policy and practice regarding the way managers treat employees.[30] The memo described four types of managers that existed at GE and at all companies (see Figure 6.2).

Figure 6.2.

Four types of managers.

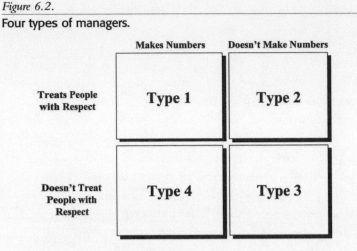

The *Type 1 manager* treats employees with respect and makes the numbers (keep), the *Type 2 manager* treats people with respect and doesn't make the numbers (keep and coach), and the *Type 3 manager* doesn't treat people with respect and doesn't make the numbers (terminate). The problematic type of manager had always been the *Type 4 manager,* the kind of manager who always made the numbers but did not treat people with respect. In the letter, Welch admitted that in the past GE had been guilty of keeping far too many of the Type 4 managers. In the future, he promised, these types of managers would no longer be tolerated at GE; they would be dismissed.

As new jobs are created faster than the supply of workers can keep pace, more and more companies will create "bad manager identification" initiatives. Finding themselves once again in a full-blown "War for Talent" like the one they experienced in the late 1990s, many aspiring employers of choice will realize, as GE has, that they can no longer afford the luxury of keeping any manager who drives talent out the door.

What the Employee Can Do to Get More Feedback and Coaching

The fact that we have covered so much territory encompassing all the things managers and organizations can do to improve performance through coaching and feedback by no means suggests that employees should depend on managers to take the initiative. Here are ways that employees should be expected to seek out and get the coaching and feedback they need when they need it:

- Whenever you believe you are not receiving the feedback and coaching you need, ask for it.
- If you find you are reluctant to seek feedback, start by asking those with whom you feel most comfortable.
- Develop the habit of asking for feedback from peers, customers, direct reports, task force coworkers, administrative assistants, and anyone with whom you might interact, not just the boss.
- If you receive feedback that is too general or too difficult to understand, ask for specific examples.
- If you have never been invited to write your own performance objectives or begin a performance evaluation by giving your own self-assessment, ask to do so.
- If you are not comfortable with your performance objectives or appraisal results, speak up. Try to reach a satisfactory mutual understanding with your supervisor.
- If you feel that changes in circumstances require that changes be made in your performance objectives, request a meeting with your supervisor to rewrite the objectives.
- If your company makes 360-degree feedback assessments available, consider asking whether you can participate in the process.
- Ask whether your company provides off-the-shelf personality and work-style inventories, employee development planning guides, or competency assessments you can take.
- If you feel you are spending more time trying to improve weaknesses than building on your strengths, change your developmental objectives, your supervisor, or your job.
- If your company retains external coaches to assist current employees, ask if they would be willing to provide such coaching at your level.
- If your organization does not retain outside coaches at your position level, consider retaining an outside coach of your own.
- If you work for a supervisor who is not interested in coaching or giving the feedback you need, consider seeking a new position within the company where you can work for a manager who is, or leave the company.

Engagement Practices Checklist: Coaching and Feedback

Review the engagement practices presented in this chapter, and check the ones you believe your organization needs to implement or improve.

To provide coaching and feedback:

Engagement Practice #17. ___ Provide intensive feedback and coaching to new hires.

Engagement Practice #18. ___ Create a culture of continuous feedback and coaching.

Engagement Practice #19. ___ Train managers in performance coaching.

Engagement Practice #20. ___ Make the performance-management process less controlling and more of a partnership.

Engagement Practice #21. ___ Terminate nonperformers when best efforts to coach or reassign don't pay off.

Engagement Practice #22. ___ Hold managers accountable for coaching and giving feedback.

Your next step: *Resolve to take action on the ones you believe are most critical and appropriate for your situation and objectives.*

Notes

1. Ron Zemke, "The Corporate Coach," *Training*, December 1996.
2. Ibid.
3. Ibid.
4. McKinsey Work Force 2000, "Senior Executive and Midlevel Surveys, 2000," http://www.opentec.com/pdf/the_war_for_talent.pdf..
5. Morgan W. McCall Jr., *High Flyers: Developing the Next Generation of Leaders* (Boston: Harvard Business School Press, 1998).
6. Ferdinand Fournies, *Coaching for Improved Work Performance* (New York: McGraw-Hill, 2000).
7. "Career Developments," Newsletter of Career Development Services, September 18, 2003.
8. Ed Michaels, Helen Handfield-Jones, and Beth Axelrod, *The War for Talent* (Boston: Harvard Business School Press, 2001).
9. Juan-Francois Manzoni and Jean-Louis Barsoux, "The Set-Up-to-Fail Syndrome," *Harvard Business Review on Managing People* (Boston: Harvard Business School Press, 1999).
10. J. Sterling Livingston, "Pygmalion in Management," *Harvard Business*

Review on Managing People (Boston: Harvard Business School Press, 1999).

11. Ibid.

12. Jack Welch and John A. Byrne, *Jack: Straight from the Gut* (New York: Warner Books, 2001).

13. Richard Beatty, "Competitive Human Resource Advantage Through the Strategic Management of Performance," *Human Resources Planning* 12 (November 15, 1989).

14. Tom Coens and Mary Jenkins, *Abolishing Performance Appraisals: Why They Backfire and What to Do Instead* (San Francisco: Berrett-Koehler, 2000).

15. Leigh Branham and Mark Hirschfeld, *Re-Engage: How America's Best Places to Work Inspire Extra Effort in Extraordinary Times* (New York: McGraw-Hill, 2010).

16. Zemke, "The Corporate Coach."

17. Jerry Useem, "A Manager for All Seasons," *Fortune*, April 30, 2001.

18. Fournies, *Coaching for Improved Work Performance*.

19. Ibid.

20. Ibid.

21. Ibid.

22. Marcus Buckingham and Curt Coffman, *First Break All the Rules: What the World's Greatest Managers Do Differently* (New York: Simon and Schuster, 1999).

23. Danielle McDonald, "The Impact of Performance Management in Organization Success," Hewitt Associates Study, 1997.

24. Geoffrey Colvin, "Make Sure You Chop the Dead Wood," *Fortune*, April 2000.

25. Ibid.

26. Jack Welch, letter to shareholders, customers, and employees, January 2001.

27. Colvin, "Make Sure You Chop the Dead Wood."

28. Daniel Goleman, *Primal Leadership: Realizing the Power of Emotional Intelligence* (Boston: Harvard Business School Press, 2002).

29. McKinsey Work Force 2000, "Senior Executive and Midlevel Surveys, 2000."

30. Welch, letter to shareholders, customers, and employees.

CHAPTER SEVEN

Reason #4: Too Few Growth and Advancement Opportunities

> In the end, it is important to remember that
> we cannot become what we need to be
> by remaining what we are.
>
> —Max DePree

Comments expressing disappointment with career growth and advancement fall into six categories: limited opportunities for growth or advancement; unfair or inefficient job-posting processes; failure to hire from within; favoritism or unfairness in promotion decisions; insufficient training; and other issues. Here's a sampling of what departed employees had to say in each of these areas:

Limited Growth and Advancement Opportunities

"There is not much opportunity to move up. You get entrenched in a position and you're stuck there."

"Promotions and advancements outside a department within the company are not an easy thing to accomplish. One would think you should be able to advance within a company with ease."

"ABC Company's departments don't work together. In some departments people are promoted each year while other departments never have the money to promote employees."

"The company locks people into their positions for nine months, which stalls advancement. Nine months per position is far too long in most entry-level jobs, especially if the individual has extensive experience."

Unfair or Inefficient Internal Selection Process

"They post positions and then take forever to follow through or proceed, and they don't communicate the status of the posted positions. I applied for a position almost a month ago and have not heard anything back."

"The director was appointed without the posting of the position. Several other candidates had much more integrity, management experience, and education than the director who was selected. It sickened the team."

"XYZ Company did not seem to stick with their own rules. Example: I know that some posted jobs are tailored to fit one employee in particular, and even some jobs are not even posted but renamed and handed off as a promotion."

Not Hiring from Within

"ABC Company hires too much from outside the company instead of promoting from within."

"XYZ Company does poorly regarding promoting from within. We have internal candidates who could step in and do the job quite nicely."

"Promote internally. I have seen four supervisors hired within one year—all of them from other companies."

Unfairness or Favoritism in Promotion Decisions

"In certain cases the manager won't recommend an employee for another position because they do not want to lose that employee. It's not fair for someone to hold you back."

"ABC Company is tainted with politics and favoritism. Employees were given management positions or promotions not for their skill sets but for how well they were liked in the firm."

"I am a working mother of two, and I find it nearly impossible to move up within my department. My hours are structured (nine hours a day), but when I am in the office I work my hardest and strive to achieve my goals. When a project or ongoing activities call for extended hours, I rearrange child care and work as needed. However, on a daily basis I am disheartened that the subject of my hours comes into play. My priority is my family, but my life also includes work that I enjoy. I know there is a delicate balance for working mothers within the workplace, but I'm discouraged there is not more understanding and flexibility. I have heard several times that I need to work longer in order to complete my goals in order to become promoted. If my nine-hour days are not being counted or recognized, I feel worthless, as if my work doesn't matter."

"Discrimination! Too many negative comments regarding women's weight, looks, etc. As a result, many talented people are undervalued."

"Supervisors hire friends as 'team leads' instead of the more competent of the group."

Insufficient Training

"I am disappointed that I am not able to take advantage of certain training/learning opportunities because they do not apply to my current position. I want to be able to grow and learn about all that the company has to offer, but they limit you to only the training that relates to your current job."

"I believe the biggest issue we have is training. I have many employees who would be more satisfied and willing to stay on if adequate training were provided."

"XYZ Company provides poor sales training. If the growth initiatives are to be the number one priority and there is no sales training, how can management expect different results or increased sales?"

"Training!!! If you are not located at the corporate office, training is not available."

Other Issues

"Acknowledge and respect the employee's career goals when assigning work."

"They don't have a clear direction for those who do not know what they want to do. Clearly defined career paths are not available."

"Management and supervisors seem to only care for themselves and don't care about the growth or advancement of their employees."

"ABC Company does not have a career-development workshop."

"Employees need more career counseling."

What They Are Really Saying

Look beneath the surface of these comments, and you will see a number of issues faced by most organizations:

- There are inevitably limited opportunities for career growth in every organization.
- Barriers between departments and position levels constrain internal movement and growth.

- No one at the top of the organization is coordinating internal talent-management activities to create awareness of growth opportunities in all departments and units.

- Fixed time-in-grade policies keep employees from advancing when they are ready.

- Job-posting processes are slow and unresponsive.

- Less-qualified employees are being hired because of manager favoritism.

- Demands for long work hours limit promotional opportunities for single parents despite their sacrifice and hard work.

- Gender-based and other kinds of prejudice create obstacles to career growth.

- Training is restricted to only certain positions, departments, or locations.

- Training is approved only if it is related to employees' current positions and disapproved if it relates to preparation for future opportunities.

- Training is inadequate.

- There is no training at all, even when it is needed to achieve important company goals.

- Managers assign work without considering employees' talents and preferences.

- There is no process to assist employees with unclear career goals.

- Career-path information is unavailable.

- Managers are concerned only about their own careers, not the career growth of their employees.

There are enough issues related to internal career growth and development in most companies to keep several consultants busy for months. Yet, the best employers seem to have fewer such issues. They know that career growth and advancement consistently rank among the top three reasons employees stay at or leave most companies. They understand that top performers seek out and pursue jobs and careers with employers that put extra effort into helping employees learn, grow, and advance internally.

Yet, in a survey by the Conference Board, limited career opportunities were found to be the greatest driver of overall employee dissatisfaction, cited by 59 percent of workers.[1] In another survey, where managers and employees were asked to rate the performance of managers on sixty-seven necessary leadership competencies, "developing direct reports" ranked sixty-seventh—dead last.[2] In a Towers-Watson study, 62 percent of employees cited opportunity to rapidly develop skills as an important expectation, yet only 33 percent said their companies were providing it.[3] The same survey revealed that 43 percent of U.S. workers think that they have to leave their organization to advance in their careers. These kinds of survey results remind us that, with about half of all companies not even trying to develop their people, there is ample opportunity for those who *are* trying to become employers of choice.

Employers of Choice Start by Understanding the New Career Realities

So much has changed in the worldwide business climate and in the way businesses now operate that the impact of these changes on the careers of individuals working in organizations needs to be acknowledged.

Waves of downsizings have changed the loyalty contract and heightened the levels of stress and job security. The continuing focus on short-term, bottom-line results, particularly among public companies, has created tremendous pressure on managers to reduce costs and push workers to produce more with less. Resulting productivity gains have come at the price of reducing job satisfaction, eliminating rungs on career ladders, and forestalling job creation.

The September 11 attacks on the World Trade Center and Pentagon caused many workers to reevaluate the centrality of work in their lives and to seek more time for family, leisure pursuits, or more personally fulfilling career options.

Fewer younger workers now seek traditional full-time jobs or long-term employment with any one company. Many in Generations X and Y prefer the short-term goals of job challenge, vacation time, and new skills acquisition over traditional rewards such as promotion and long-term benefits.

More and more employees are choosing to work from home. After the start of the Great Recession, in 2008, unprecedented numbers became unemployed or underemployed and were seeking part-time or temporary work. Proven and valued older workers who had postponed retirement were poised to at least phase into semiretirement as the economy improves. We are already facing a new era of talent shortages in IT and health care. Millions of companies will experience "leadership gaps" and shortages of workers with basic skills, and the public education system will not be able to prepare workers with the skills needed to do tomorrow's jobs.

The cumulative effect of all these changes has been the creation of a new contract[4] between employer and employee, which many managers (who came of age when the old contract was in place) have been slow to recognize:

Old Career Contract	New Career Contract
Long-term employment is expected.	There are shorter-term expectations, affected by changing business needs (no guarantees).
Reward for performance is recognition and self-satisfaction.	Reward for performance is growth, promotion.
Management controls career progress.	Employees are in charge of their own careers.
Lifetime career is offered.	Employee-employer bond is based on fulfillment of mutual needs.
Clearly defined career paths are changeable.	Career paths are less defined, and more are offered.

Resulting In:	Resulting In:
Fixed job descriptions.	Changing jobs, more use of projects and task forces.
Compensation and benefits that reward tenure	Recognition systems that are based on value and reward creation and results.
Long-term career planning by the employee.	Short-term career planning by organization.
Plateaued workers.	Flexible, task-invested workers.
Dependent workers.	Empowered, responsible workers.

The reality is that the new career contract still has not materialized in many organizations, especially ones that value control over employee autonomy and self-direction. In these old-school organizations, many employees passively wait for managers to take the first step and never learn to manage their own careers. By contrast, most employers of choice clearly communicate that employees must take the initiative with regard to their own career development, but they also provide the tools and training necessary for them to do so, as we shall see in the best practices that follow.

Recognizing the Signs of Blocked Growth and Career Frustration

Your employees may be experiencing restlessness and frustration with career growth and advancement if they:

- Indiscriminately apply for a succession of internal positions, for some of which they are unqualified or unsuited.
- Were recently not selected for another position in the company.
- Have been recently passed over for a promotion.
- Seem to be coasting and appear to be bored or underchallenged.
- Keep asking for new challenges.
- Keep asking for additional training.
- Ask for career-path information.
- Have been in the same position long enough to have long since mastered it.
- Have applied for tuition reimbursement but are unclear about career goals.
- Have recently completed a degree and seem to expect a promotion.

Responsibility for employee career growth and development is shared equally by the employee, the manager, and the organization. Here is the way one organization divided the responsibilities:

Employee's Responsibilities

- Make job performance and creating value your first priority.
- Make your career aspirations known to your manager.
- Assess your own talents, and get frequent feedback on your performance and potential.
- Continually seek new learning and growth opportunities.
- Learn to uncover hidden needs in the organization to create a new job.
- Seek growth through lateral movements and job enrichment, not just promotion.

- Learn how the organization fills jobs internally and how to use the job-posting system.

- Actively seek information about jobs of interest to make sure they are jobs you would truly enjoy and that you would have a realistic chance of obtaining.

- Understand that you, not the organization or your manager, have the primary responsibility for managing your career.

Organization's Responsibilities

- Create systems, policies, and practices that facilitate professional growth for all.

- Provide training and resources to managers to help them develop employees.

- Conduct long-range strategic and human resource planning, and communicate future talent needs to managers and employees.

- Create and maintain a fair and efficient internal job-posting process.

- Provide necessary training to enhance performance and enable career growth.

Manager's Responsibilities

- Identify and continually reevaluate future talent needs in terms of the work to be done.

- Assess the strengths, motivations, and developmental needs of each employee, and match them to the work to be done.

- Maintain person-job fit through frequent coaching, feedback, reassignments, or other corrective action.

- Assist employees in implementing realistic developmental goals and action plans.

If expectations and responsibilities become unbalanced, as when employees expect the organization to create their career plans for them, when a manager fails to discuss career plans with a direct report, or when senior leaders fail to approve necessary training, the system breaks down.

Best Practices for Creating Growth and Advancement Opportunities

Here are the kinds of practices that serve to maintain a balanced approach to providing employees with the growth and development opportunities they need to stay and to stay engaged.

**Engagement Practice #23:
Provide self-assessment tools and career self-management training for all employees.**

Smart companies recognize that employees can have widely ranging degrees of self-awareness and that many highly talented performers may not understand, cannot articulate, and often underuse their greatest strengths. If they misunderstand their own talents, employees may seek jobs for which they are unsuited. They may also borrow the goals and ambitions of successful coworkers and pursue roles incompatible with their temperaments. They may create untold damage by becoming managers of people when the talent to manage people is missing or there is little true interest in that task, except as a means to getting a promotion.

Here are some of the practices in wide use by preferred employers to increase the self-awareness of and to enhance realistic goal setting by employees:

- Provide interactive software for self-directed career self-assessment inventories through the company's intranet.

- Offer voluntary career self-assessment and career self-management workshops, with career self-management guides, to *all* employees. In the first two months after KPMG launched a Web-based training program to better prepare young employees and their managers to talk about building their careers in the company, more than 9,300 employees logged on. Some 2,500 created their own ideal career paths.[5]

- Implement a self-assessment process that places a strong emphasis on identifying an employee's motivated talents and abilities through the analysis of satisfying life and career achievements. Achievement analysis is especially empowering and confidence building.

- Create a "virtual career center" containing self-assessment inventories, along with career planning software programs, career-path-mapping scenarios, position competency definitions, job postings, talent bank profiles, training catalogs, recommended books, and information on professional associations, conferences, courses, articles, and other resources recommended by coworkers.

- Provide tools for independent career management and planning—career guides, individual development plans, and assessment inventories.

- Challenge employees to take the initiative and schedule meetings with their managers to discuss their assessment results and to create a new individual development plan.

"PeopleComeFirst" at Lands' End

Lands' End has developed an online self-service career-development and learning management system called PeopleComeFirst for its eight thousand employees. An employee can create a career-development plan that will be available online for reference and revision. Employees typically meet with managers at least twice a year to work on their development plans, which serve as guides for training and career growth.

The company went to the online process after it found the manual process difficult to track. Now, all information about employees' development and training activity is kept in a central location where both employees and managers can access it. Lands' End has separated the career-development planning process from the annual performance review in order to place maximum focus on the employee's development.[6]

 Engagement Practice #24:
Offer career-coaching tools and training for all managers.

Recognizing that the employee's direct supervisor is the primary agent for achieving employee commitment and satisfaction, more companies are providing tools and training to managers so that they will be better equipped to fulfill their career-coaching responsibilities. Many companies now provide company-sponsored group training for managers on how to conduct career conversations, respond to frequently asked employee career questions, complete individual development plans, and follow through with sponsoring activities or accountability initiatives.

How to Create a Job and Revitalize a Career

Bob Taylor had been with Charles Schwab & Company for twelve years, but he was considering leaving the company. He had begun to lose interest in his work, but, before resigning, he decided to talk things over with his boss. With his boss's go-ahead, Taylor proposed the creation of a job that would combine his technology and business skills—organizational troubleshooter. "The key to my staying was to innovate my own job," said Taylor, whose formal title became vice president of the mobile trading project at Schwab's Electronic Brokerage Group. "To energize someone," advised Taylor, "let them work on what they absolutely love."[7]

Some companies provide individual development-planning forms and feedback tools, such as voluntary manager skill evaluations that employees complete to give managers feedback on their employee coaching and development skills.

To help managers better understand the process that they will be recommending to employees, progressive companies also invite all managers to complete the employee self-assessment and career self-management process for themselves. After all, they are employees, too, and they will be more likely to encourage their employees to complete a process if they have benefited from it themselves.

Engagement Practice #25:
Provide readily accessible information on
career paths and competency requirements.

Some companies understand better than others the need for employees to know how to prepare for future jobs. After using self-assessment tools to look within themselves at their own talents, preferences, values, and motivations, employees need to look outward at career-growth options within the organization. This becomes much easier to do if the organization has invested in the creation of career paths and competency maps for all positions.

Employees need to have access to job descriptions and listings of competencies and educational requirements they will need to qualify for other positions, whether these are shown on a company's intranet via a "virtual career center" or in hard-copy form. Frequently, this information is made available on the company's website for outside applicants to view, as well. Some companies even interview successful employees and publish "career-path profiles," in which they tell the stories of their own advancement, describe key decisions they made and career turning points, and give advice to newer employees about how to progress within the organization. Such stories make clear to anyone who reads them that successful employees in any company often do not progress in a direct, linear path but make lateral moves, leave the organization and come back in higher-level jobs, and accelerate their careers through involvement on task forces, rotational assignments, and short-term projects.

Engagement Practice #26:
Create alternatives to traditional career ladders.

If we truly value all talent for the value it brings to the organization, then we should not penalize top technical performers by forcing them to pursue management positions as their only route to higher pay. Many companies continue to provide only one path to higher pay—the line-management career ladder.

Four Distinct Career Patterns

Michael Driver, a professor in the business school at the University of Southern California, has conducted research that shows that individuals are more or less hard-wired to have different concepts of career success and that there are four distinct patterns:

1. *Linear:* These are people who are naturally motivated to move up the traditional corporate career ladder. They value power and achievement but have been increasingly disillusioned and frustrated in recent years by the disappearance of rungs on career ladders in most organizations.

2. *Expert:* Rather than climb a career ladder, the expert wants to become known as an authority or the best in a selected field or craft. Experts tend to seek training and on-the-job experiences that deepen their expertise.

3. *Spiral:* These are people who aspire to broaden their careers by moving every five to ten years to a position that builds on previous positions but that may involve broader responsibilities. Spirals value growth and creativity and may seek rotational and cross-functional assignments.

4. *Roamer:* They define success by changing jobs often—perhaps every two to three years—and may move on to jobs unrelated to their previous experience. Roamers are generally motivated more by variety and independence than by security, and they can play key roles in start-up situations in companies that are expanding.

Organizations may not be able to accommodate all four of these career patterns at all times. Still, understanding the different career styles that exist among the general population can facilitate the job-person matching process and help managers to assist employees in identifying best-fit advancement opportunities. Managers will need to understand the differing motives of employees through individualized career coaching and work to create career opportunities that meet employee needs and business needs in new ways.[8]

Other companies, especially those whose success depends on product innovations developed by engineers or other technical specialists, have created higher-level technical positions with increasing responsibility and commensurate pay. By doing so, these organizations provide technology-oriented individuals with growth aspirations the opportunity to realize them without leaving the company. They also prevent another damaging outcome: the movement of highly competent technical professionals into positions where their incompetence at managing people can have the unfortunate result of driving good employees out the door.

Companies whose success hinges on the performance of front-line, customer-facing positions, typically labeled "lower-level positions," have recently begun adding career tracks and certification training for them. Costco, which promotes from within 98 percent of the time, is a pioneer in this practice; Xerox Europe's call center staff in Dublin are staying longer because they are systematically assessed and offered training so that they are ready to move up or transfer to a different department requiring a higher skill level. The state of Washington trains low-wage home-care aides through apprenticeships. Basic training requires seventy-five training hours, and advanced training takes an additional seventy hours. Apprentices who complete the program become certified home-care aides. The program is competency based and involves peer mentoring and both online and on-the-job learning. The program director reports that most of the workers experience a paradigm shift as they begin to see themselves as professionals with professional career paths.[9]

Off the Career Ladder and onto the "Swat Team"

Many talented employees have grown tired of patiently serving time on a one-size-fits-all career path. One solution that some larger companies have successfully implemented is to place these restless individuals on unassigned status where they are called on to fill frequently occurring staffing gaps in other departments or divisions.

Those put on "Swat Team" status often find just what they are looking for—a varied mix of responsibilities, new contacts, new opportunities for growth and learning, and greater control over their own schedules.

Swat Team members are often recruited into higher-level positions because of their increased exposure across the organization. By not holding to rigid ideas about traditional career paths, companies can create an exciting, prestigious, flexible alternative that allows the organization to hold on to talent it might otherwise have lost.[10]

Lateral Moves Now Seen as Career Enhancing

After years of economic and career stagnation, 84 percent of employees said they planned to seek other employment in 2011, up from 60 percent the year before.[11] In response to the mounting impatience and restlessness many employees were feeling, some companies began explicitly encouraging lateral moves. Deloitte has been a pioneer in this practice, promoting the idea to its workforce that employees should look at their careers in the company as a "lattice," not a "ladder," thereby endorsing sideways, diagonal, or even downward moves if the end result feels like growth. The insurance giant Chubb has held workshops that addressed how to make the right kinds of lateral moves. The cable provider Cox Communications is also promoting the value of sideways career steps as part of formal development discussions with employees. Erin Hand, Cox Cable's vice president of talent and development, says "Organizations are marketing the lateral move as a development opportunity rather than as a parking spot."[12]

Engagement Practice #27:
Keep employees informed about the company's strategy, direction, and talent-need forecasts.

The best employees seek reassurance that they have hitched their star to a company that will continue to be successful and have a need for their capabilities. This means they need to be kept informed about the company's evolving marketing and growth strategies and the career opportunities that are likely to come with them. Companies such as Sun Microsystems, IBM, Intel, Advanced Micro Devices, 3Com, and Microsoft have carried on the practice of giving open business briefings where senior executives regularly brief employees on decisions and plans that may impact jobs or skills required in the future.

Engagement Practice #28:
Build and maintain a fair and efficient
internal job-posting process.

As we heard in the comments at the beginning of this chapter, employees are frequently suspicious about how jobs get filled inside the organization, particularly when they are filled without being posted, when qualified applicants are not interviewed or never even receive an acknowledgment from human resources that their applications were received, or when they are never told that they were screened out. Because hiring managers often make hires on the basis of factors such as similarity of background, likeability, comfort, and chemistry, there will always be internal applicants who complain that they were more qualified than the outsider who got the job. What is not excusable is the failure of hiring managers or HR managers to post all positions and to give all qualified internal candidates sincere, open-minded consideration.

Much of the employee frustration with job-posting systems arises from the fact that, in many organizations, they appear to be the only valid way to find out about existing or developing positions. As we know, the reality is that, by the time the job opening is formally posted, many internal candidates will have already found out about it through informal means and made themselves known to the hiring manager.

Many employees are passive enough, naive enough, or so overly trusting of the supposed fairness and efficiency of internal systems that they cannot see that using the job-posting system is often the last step in seeking a career opportunity, not the first. Companies that provide formal career self-management workshops and computer modules typically include a section on how jobs are found internally. In these sessions, the importance of informal networking, doing informational interviewing about job and skill requirements, and building relationships with hiring managers can be openly discussed as legitimate career-management activities. Such candid discussion can open the eyes of some employees to the need to be more proactive and can lessen their cynicism about favoritism and office politics.

Engagement Practice #29:
Show a clear preference for hiring from within.

Few things are more frustrating for well-qualified employees than the company's decision to hire an outside candidate or to bring in a consultant without even giving them a shot at interviewing for the job. In fact, such an experience is often a predictable turning point in the disengagement and eventual departure of highly talented employees, who may feel taken for granted.

Employers of choice tend to hire outside candidates only when no internal candidate is available, consistently conducting searches for internal candidates as their first option. Some companies even maintain "talent banks" containing resumes and talent profiles of employees that managers can screen and match against job requirements.

Most companies recognize that it is more cost-efficient to hire a proven internal candidate than to pay recruiter fees, relocation costs, and all the other avoidable costs related to new-hire orientation and training. Current employees already know the culture, have established relationships, and understand the way things are done. But the biggest advantage is the morale-boosting message an internal hire sends to all employees: "Your contributions and talent have not gone unnoticed."

Engagement Practice #30:
Eliminate HR policies and management practices
that block internal movement.

One of the greatest obstacles to the career growth and advancement of high performers is the unwillingness of their own managers to encourage or approve their movement to positions in other departments. Such "blocking" behavior drives top talent out of companies and has caused some CEOs to issue directives to all managers that "there will be no hoarding of talent." Another way of expressing this is "the manager doesn't own the talent . . . the organization owns the talent."

Nevertheless, because some managers will always put their own self-interest before the interests of the organization, this will continue to be an issue. One way to address it is to specifically include wording in competency descriptions, performance appraisals, and 360-degree feedback ratings along these lines: "encourages and approves the movement of employees when they seek professional growth opportunities that also serve the needs of the organization." Another effective way to discourage such blocking behavior is to confront these managers with performance coaching and feedback and, if that does not work, to remove them from positions with responsibility for managing people.

Getting Around the Manager's Career Roadblock

Cerner Corporation of Kansas City created a "career navigation center" where employees could confidentially seek a better position if they felt they were being stifled by their current manager. The company also held seminars for managers to teach them about their retention responsibilities and monitored unit turnover numbers. When the numbers got too high, managers were called in for "what's wrong?" meetings.[13]

From Plateaued to Internal Temps

There will always be employees who reach a plateau and start looking for new challenges. AT&T re-engages and retains "plateaued" employees with a program called Resource Link, which functions as an in-house temporary service. Through this program, employees with diverse management, technical, or professional skills sell their skills to different departments for short-term assignments.[14]

Another kind of blocking that pushes valued employees out the door has to do with outdated and rigid "time-in-grade" policies that require employees to remain in a job for a set period of time before they are allowed to seek other positions. Such policies were often designed to discourage internal job hopping, but they fail to take into account that top performers are often ready to move on sooner than average performers.

 ### Engagement Practice #31:
Create a strong mentoring culture.

Formal mentoring programs have become a popular way for companies to meet three objectives at the same time: increase opportunities for women and minorities, develop future leaders, and enhance the retention of employees at all levels. Mentoring programs have been found to be effective in increasing employee retention in 77 percent of the companies that implemented them.[15]

Mentoring programs are often driven from the top down, with strong endorsement and involvement by the CEO to encourage involvement by managers at all levels. Some companies go with formal programs that require regular meetings and frequent monitoring, while others prefer informal approaches where employees and mentors are free to decide how often to meet. In recent years, "open mentoring," which empowers and enables employees at all levels and locations to participate as either learners or advisors, has become more prevalent. One study found that 88 percent of open-mentoring users agreed that their productivity increased thanks to the program.[16]

From the organizational perspective, there are three types of mentoring: enterprise mentoring that is open to everyone in the organization; people-first learning, where individuals can take the initiative to connect with others when they have learning needs, and networked mentoring, by which employees can connect as either adviser or learner with colleagues across boundaries such as geography, function, job level, and demographics.[17] Increasingly, instead of the mentor controlling the process, learners are driving the mentoring engagement.

When managers are assigned as mentors, they tend to take their responsibilities more seriously when mentoring is one of the competencies for which they are evaluated on performance reviews. Training sessions for mentors and mentees to orient them to the process and to clarify ground rules can be conducted to support the process. Peer mentoring, the fastest-growing type of mentoring today, is offered when a coworker has experience or knowledge to share. Reverse mentoring, as when a Millennial coaches a boomer on social networking, has become more common, as well.

Some large companies maintain databases of managers who have volunteered to serve as mentors. Employees may review profiles of mentors on file and submit their choices in order of preference. To relieve the time demands imposed by having too many mentees, some companies facilitate small-group mentoring where four to eight mentees meet with one mentor. Often, such groups meet on a rotating basis with mentors who are expert in one area, such as e-commerce or cost accounting, and build their knowledge in a variety of areas.

Recognizing that many new leaders don't last two years in their new roles, many companies have also created "on-boarding" programs for newly hired executives to immerse them in the organization's culture.

> ## E-Mentoring at U.S. Bancorp
>
> To avoid losing the knowledge of boomers approaching retirement, U.S. Bancorp created Mentor Connect, which uses the Web to match mentors with those who want to be mentored. The program gathers demographic data and competency information from mentors and mentees, then suggests matches. Within the first week after the roll-out of the new Mentor Connect software, 152 relationships were established. Most mentoring takes place by phone between employees who are geographically separated.[18]

Engagement Practice #32:
Keep the career-development and
performance-appraisal processes separate.

Traditionally, performance-review forms have a section for summarizing appropriate career objectives for employees and for writing developmental objectives designed to close the gaps in current and required competencies. It makes sense to discuss career-advancement possibilities at performance-appraisal time, but such discussions are often counterproductive in the context of a discussion that has salary implications and may arouse defensiveness against perceived manager criticism.

In recognition of these potential limitations, many companies have directed managers to have discussions with employees about career opportunities at the six-month point between yearly performance reviews or at least once a year separate from the discussion of performance. Managers and employees typically report more positive outcomes when there is a dedicated focus on the employee's career development.

Engagement Practice #33:
Build an effective talent-review and
succession-management process.

The need for succession planning has gotten the attention of more companies in recent years as more older boomers have begun to retire. Only 34 percent of U.S. companies report that they are effective at identifying future leaders,[19] and four in ten senior leaders fail in their new jobs within their first eighteen months on the job.[20]

Many companies are using terms such as "talent-review process" or "acceleration pool development" to describe what was traditionally called succession planning. These newer terms reflect the increasing difficulty of preparing leaders and talented professionals for organizational opportunities that may not yet exist in a rapidly changing market environment. It is also widely acknowledged that many succession candidates are never promoted into the positions for which they were slotted.

Here are some succession-management strategies that are proving to be effective:

• Create alignment between projected company needs and individual aspirations and abilities by conducting in-depth assessments of targeted employees and comparing the results to the required competencies to assess promotability and developmental needs.

• Have the process codesigned by human resources and line management.

• Have higher levels of management review the assessments, eventually reaching a senior talent-review task force headed by the CEO. The most successful succession-management initiatives are usually driven not by the senior HR executive but by the CEO and are owned by a senior task force or committee that includes the top HR executive.

• Have managers of targeted employees inform succession candidates that they have been identified to participate in a high-potential acceleration pool, being careful to make sure they understand that no promotions are promised and that changes in organizational plans may result in their removal from the pool. One study revealed that, of the high-potential employees who were not formally told of their status, 22 percent were looking for another job. Of the high-potentials who were told, only 14 percent were looking.[21]

• Have managers work with high-potential succession candidates to follow through on customized developmental plans, often including training, internal mentoring, 360-degree feedback, external coaching, rotational assignments, and global and special-exposure opportunities.

• Delegate real responsibility. High-potentials thrive on challenging business assignments, so don't hesitate to "give them the keys to the car."

• Be careful not to overdo the requirement that high-potentials accept frequent overseas and travel-heavy assignments that severely limit the employee's time with family.

• Make sure that a review of developmental plans occurs yearly and that employees' potential is reevaluated with regard to various future roles and positions. It is important to give honest and constructive feedback to candidates who have been determined not to be candidates for higher advancement so that they may use it to make realistic alternative career plans.

• Assign groups of high-potentials to a "shadow board" where they will be presented with the very same issues the company's board is facing and asked to submit their ideas and recommendations for serious consideration by company leaders.

• To make sure high-potentials feel valued, spend lots of quality one-on-one time with them.

• When planning rotational assignments, consider bigger-scale responsibilities, bigger scope, line-to-staff and staff-to-line switches, start-ups, turnarounds, change management initiatives, and international assignments.

• Make sure they are well matched with effective and compatible mentors.

Do these practices pay off? According to Hewitt Associates, top-performing companies as measured by total shareholder return are more likely than are other companies to use a consistently formal approach to identifying, developing, and tracking the performance of potential leaders.[22] Yet, only 64 percent of companies, including only one-fifth of mid-size companies, have a management-succession committee or process.[23]

What About the B-Players?

In their effort to provide fast-track development to employees they see as A-players, companies often overlook the development of B-players—valued, stable contributors who make up the backbone of the organization but who often allow their own careers to take a backseat to the company's well-being.

One company that has made a concerted effort to develop its B-players is the luxury hotel chain Princely Hotels, which created a career-development committee to give opportunities to all managers, not just the stars. The committee has developed a career track that offers "lateral promotions" to managers among its sixty properties and makes sure they are getting the coaching they need.[24]

 Engagement Practice #34: Maintain a strong commitment to employee training and learning.

Many managers question the wisdom of spending money on training, especially during down business cycles. They worry that the money they spend on training will be wasted when the employees they train leave to go to work for other companies. Their worst fear is that they will become a training ground for their competitors.

Here are some findings that might help to assuage such fears:

• "Companies that spent $218 per employee in training and development had more than 16 percent annual voluntary turnover ... while companies that spend $273 per employee have less than 7 percent annual voluntary turnover."[25] Of employees who say their companies offer poor training, 41 percent planned to leave within a year, whereas only 12 percent of those with excellent training options had such plans.[26]

• Eight of ten employees in a Gallup survey cited the availability of employer-sponsored training as an important criterion in considering a new job opportunity.[27]

• Younger workers—Gen Xers and Millennials—have watched their parents lose their jobs after years of being loyal to their employers. So they no longer expect lifetime employment as their parents once did. Their more realistic expectation is lifetime employability, which means that training is of paramount importance to them. In their minds, learning new skills and acquiring new knowledge equate to increasing their value and sense of career security. It comes down to this seeming contradiction: You have to train your employees to the point where they know they are more marketable or else they'll leave. Put another way: What if you don't train them and they stay?

• Employers honored by their listing in *Fortune* magazine's annual "100

Best Places to Work" issue typically provide an average of forty hours of training per employee per year. As for the impact on the bottom line, companies in the top quarter of training expenditure per employee (an average of $1,595 per year) had profit margins 24 percent higher than those in the bottom quarter (an average of $128 per year).[28] More and more employers have concluded that training is an investment in employee productivity and retention, and they are making it available in a variety of ways.

One thing is clear: In order to reap the payoff, companies must design the training to support their business objectives. Two companies with very different business objectives—Kyphon and Jiffy Lube International—are good examples of this. Kyphon, which markets a device for correcting painful spinal conditions, depends heavily on its salespeople (called spine consultants), who teach surgeons about the product and how to use it in the operating room. Kyphon uses a combination of mentoring, classroom instruction, and fieldwork to train its consultants. After passing a test based on reading assignments, spine consultants receive two weeks of classroom training, then travel in the field with a supervisor for a few weeks before being assigned to their territories. Mentoring and classroom training continue at intervals. The company has even brought patients on site so that the administrative staff could see for themselves some of the dramatic results.[29]

While Kyphon's objective is to build long-term loyalty, Jiffy Lube's focus is on getting retail employees up to speed and preventing short-term turnover. Technicians have to be certified in safety and product knowledge within thirty days after hire. More than 95 percent of training is delivered online, with 150 hours available through the company's learning-management system, called Roadmap. Technicians can see their progress on a gas gauge. Since implementing its certification process, Jiffy Lube's turnover rate has dropped more than 50 percent in several locations.[30]

Cash Accounts for Employee Training

A great way to give employees more autonomy and choice in their own development is by providing individual learning accounts that provide employees with a set amount of training dollars they may spend per year on programs chosen from among a menu of company-sponsored training, including a course or two for pure self-enrichment.

The Horn Group, a public relations firm based in San Francisco, offers employees cash that they are free to spend on any type of training they feel would help them do their jobs better. Employees use the training dollars—called "a personal development fund"—to take courses in time management, writing, and many other subjects.[31]

Self-paced online training programs are now in wide use. Employees utilize a Web portal to access course information and content, as well as college courses offered online. Learning resources may be organized according to competencies needed by the employee. Media such as CD-ROMs, thumb drives, computer discs, videotapes, audiotapes, and textbooks have dramatically increased the variety of means available for delivering course content. Another effective practice is to create intranet-driven, knowledge-sharing networks where employees can ask and answer one another's questions via e-mail or bulletin boards or in real time.

Many companies offer "soft-skills" training—in communication, giving feedback, and negotiation—to technical staff. Such training is typically offered in classes where new skills can be tried out in face-to-face situations.

Most companies now reimburse tuition for college courses completed onsite or through e-learning. Reimbursement policies usually require that coursework relate in some way to an employee's current position or a foreseeable one. Larger organizations often have internal corporate academies or universities, such as the one at Seagate Technology, which, in addition to formal training sessions, offers site tours, job shadowing, and team-building sessions at several locations. Truman Medical Center in Kansas City features a cyber café that offers employees computer access and training. As an incentive, for every course an employee completes, Truman also gives "learning points" that can add up to paid time off. Smaller companies make the most of resources by having employees who attend industry conferences take detailed notes and make presentations to employees who could not attend. Others may start informal "brown-bag" lunch programs where employees brief one another on books they have read or share specialized knowledge on trends, products, processes, or clients.

Other trends in training include:

- Offering just-in-time training for new hires and for quick reassignment
- Conducting training-needs analysis to make sure training is tied to a real business need and can close a performance gap before offering the training

- Increasing outsourcing of training to outside vendors
- For global companies, making all training accessible worldwide twenty-four hours a day, seven days a week.

When It's OK to Train 'Em and Lose 'Em

UPS realizes that many of its young part-timers won't want to spend the rest of their lives loading and unloading packages. But that doesn't keep the company from helping them pay their college tuition and offering Saturday classes for computer-skills development and career-planning discussions. UPS recognizes that college students are loyal to their own skills development more than to their jobs or supervisors and that such perks will help ensure a continuing supply of applicants.

As for longer-term benefits to the company, Jennifer Shroeger, a UPS district manager, commented, "I'd like all those part-time workers to graduate from college and start their own businesses—and become UPS customers."[32]

What Employees Can Do to Create Their Own Growth and Advancement Opportunities

We have reviewed many areas where the organization can create career-growth opportunities for employees, but ultimately it is up to the employees to take charge of their careers. Managers can hold employees to their part of the bargain by challenging them to do the following:

- Master the job you have now, first and foremost. Remember that fortune favors those who do a brilliant job today.
- If you are in the wrong job, change to the right one. Love what you do, which means figuring out who you are in terms of talents, interests, values, and motivations.
- Know how the money flows through the organization, what factors cause profit and loss, and what part of that you can control.
- When no promotional options seem open, seek lateral or cross-functional assignments, or create a job that meets unmet company needs and makes use of your talents.
- Seek continual learning by formal and informal means.
- Familiarize yourself with career paths of those in positions to which

you aspire, gain their advice, get realistic previews of their jobs, and ask them to be a mentor to you.

- If a position you desire is not currently available, seek mini-assignments that will help prepare you and try out pieces of the desired job.

- Exhaust all options for enriching your current job by seeking new challenges and satisfying activities in your current job before pursuing applying for other jobs.

- Communicate your aspirations, talents, ideas, and plans to your manager so that he or she can provide appropriate feedback, coaching, or sponsorship.

- Re-energize your career by acting like an entrepreneur, starting a new service or line of business for the company.

- Before deciding to leave the company, communicate to your manager or to a trusted mentor the source of your career frustration, and ask for ideas and assistance.

Engagement Practices Checklist: Growth and Advancement Opportunities

Review the engagement practices presented in this chapter, and check the ones you believe your organization needs to implement or improve.

To provide career-advancement and growth opportunities:

Engagement Practice #23. __ Provide self-assessment tools and career self-management training for all employees.

Engagement Practice #24. __ Offer career-coaching tools and training for all managers.

Engagement Practice #25. __ Provide readily accessible information on career paths and competency requirements.

Engagement Practice #26. __ Create alternatives to traditional career ladders.

Engagement Practice #27. __ Keep employees informed about the company's strategy, direction, and talent-need forecasts.

Engagement Practice #28. __ Build and maintain a fair and efficient internal job-posting process.

Engagement Practice #29. __ Show a clear preference for hiring from within.

Engagement Practice #30. __ Create a strong mentoring culture.

Engagement Practice #31. ___ Eliminate HR policies and management
                                practices that block internal movement.

Engagement Practice #32. ___ Keep career-development and performance-
                                appraisal processes separate.

Engagement Practice #33. ___ Build an effective talent-review and succession-
                                management process.

Engagement Practice #34. ___ Maintain a strong commitment to employee
                                training.

Your next step: Resolve to take action on the ones you believe are most critical and appropriate for your situation and objectives.

Notes

1. Human Resources Department, "Talent Management Emerges as HR
   Department's New Leadership Challenge," *Management Report,*
   November 2002.
2. Robert N. Llewellyn, "The Power in Being a People Developer: Who Is
   the Best People Developer in Your Organization? Why Isn't It You?"
   quoting study by Lominger Limited, *HR,* July 2002.
3. Towers–Watson 2010 Global Workforce Survey—U.S.,
   http://towerswatson.com/global-workforce-study.
4. Adapted from David Noer, *Healing the Wounds: Overcoming the Trauma of
   Layoffs and Revitalizing Downsized Organizations* (San Francisco: Jossey-
   Bass, 1993).
5. Lindsey Gerdes, "The Best Places to Launch a Career," *Businessweek,*
   September 24, 2007.
6. Paula Santonocito, "Lands' End to Use PeopleComeFirst Solution for
   Learning Management," *HR Professional,* May 20, 2002.
7. Leslie Goff, "Dream It, and They'll Be It," in "The Top 10 Retention
   Tactics," *Computerworld,* November 22, 1999.
8. Robert N. Llewellyn, "The Four Career Concepts: Managers Can Learn
   How to Better Develop Their People by Learning How They're
   Motivated," *HR,* September 2002.
9. Stephenie Overman, "On the Right Track," *HR,* April, 2011.
10. Bruce Tulgan, *Winning the Talent Wars* (New York: W. W. Norton, 2001).
11. Right Management survey, December 2010 poll of more than 1,400
    workers in North America, http://www.right.com/news-and-
    events/press-releases/2010-press-releases/item20533.aspx.
12. Jena McGregor, "How to Make a Smart Lateral Move," *Fortune,*
    October 17, 2011.
13. Diane Stafford, "Best Leaders Retain Key Employees," *Kansas City Star,*
    August 10, 2000.

14. "Follow AT&T's Lead with This Tactic to Retain 'Plateaued' Employees," *Employee Recruitment and Retention,* Lawrence Ragan Communications, 2000.

15. Jodi Davis, "Leadership: The Role of Mentoring," presentation, Human Resource Management Association conference, Kansas City, Missouri, October 14, 1999.

16. Randy Emelo, "Creating a New Mindset: Guidelines for Mentoring in Today's Workplace," *Training + Development,* January 2011.

17. Randy Emelo, "Conversations with Mentoring Leaders," *Training + Development,* June 2011.

18. Bill Roberts, "Hard Facts About Soft-Skills E-Learning," *HR,* January 2008.

19. "Development Leaders for 2010," report, Conference Board, 2003.

20. Ibid.

21. Susan J. Wells, "Who's Next? Creating a Formal Program for Developing New Leaders Can Pay Huge Dividends, But Many Firms Aren't Reaping Those Rewards," *HR,* November 2003.

22. Ibid.

23. Ibid.

24. Thomas J. DeLong and Vineeta Vijayraghavan, "Let's Hear It for B Players," *Harvard Business Review* (June 2003).

25. Carroll Lachnit, "Training Proves Its Worth," *Training,* September 2001.

26. "The ASTD Trends Watch: The Forces That Shape Workforce Performance and Improvement," American Society for Training and Development, Alexandria, VA, 1999, http://www.worldcat.org/title/astd-trends-watch-the-forces-that-shape-workforce-performance-and-improvement/ oclc/55898392.

27. Ibid.

28. Susan J. Wells, "Stepping Carefully: Attention to Staffing Levels, Compensation, and Training Will Help Ride Out a Slowdown," *HR,* April 19, 2001.

29. Robert J. Grossman, "Developing Talent," *HR,* January 2006.

30. Jennifer J. Salopek, "Keeping Learning Well-Oiled," *Training + Development,* October 2011.

31. "Create a 'Personal Development Fund,'" *Employee Recruitment and Retention,* Lawrence Ragan Communications, 2000.

32. Keith H. Hammonds, "Handle with Care: How UPS Handles Packages Starts with How It Handles Its People," *Fast Company,* August 2002.

CHAPTER EIGHT

Reason #5: Feeling Devalued and Unrecognized

Make people who work for you feel important.
If you honor and serve them,
they'll honor and serve you.

—MARY KAY ASH

It's really quite simple: Everybody wants to feel important. So how do so many organizations manage to make so many people feel so unimportant? Selected comments from the thousands of exit surveys I read show that there are several ways that working people are made to feel unimportant. Here are some of those ways, in their own words:

Lack of Simple Appreciation

"They do not give to employees. On my first day of work I was not able to take a lunch. Also, I am not able to spend any money on my employees to show appreciation for a job well done."

"It's horrid to hear about an employee who had been with the company for 20+ years and did not even receive a card showing the company's appreciation."

"I believe ABC Company could do a better job of recognizing employees more. People tend to work better if there is an appreciation shown for what they are doing."

Belief That There Is Too Much Focus on the Numbers, Not Enough on People

"Everyone is treated as a number and not a person, you are a machine."

"Company leaders should recognize employees or understand that, despite all the focus on productivity, profits, and customers, they also should be flexible and appreciate the employees. It does not surprise me that there is a high turnover rate at XYZ Company."

Feeling That Some Employees Deserve Recognition and Don't Get It, While Others Do

"The evening shift should be paid more!"

"When you are in a remote office you are forgotten about."

"They do not show appreciation to the people who do the work, they give praise to the managers of the people that do the work. 'Thank you's are free."

"ABC Company hires new employees [who are] making more money than the people that have been here a long time. Then they want you to train the new employees that make more than you."

Feeling That No One Even Knows or Cares if Employees Exist

"This office never seems to receive any recognition in any kind of corporate newsletters or bulletins. Many of us feel isolated and ignored."

"When I came to ABC Company my manager never paid attention to the times I was available to work. Once a week, if not more, I would have to bring it to her attention the hours that I was available to work. Two months in a row she scheduled me wrong and made changes in the schedule without even asking me. I will never work at ABC again."

"Joining XYZ Company was the worst mistake I have ever made. When I was hired no one even knew I was starting."

Receiving Recognition That Is Too Late in Coming to Be Meaningful

"ABC Company rewards you for excellence, but when they do, it's months down the road before you hear anything."

Feeling That No One Is Listening to Employees

"We should be able to give input in regards to the new building. I believe that the employees know best how much meeting and storage space is needed."

"ABC Company takes a bulldozer approach to management. It is 'this is the direction we are going,' period, without asking for input from employees."

"XYZ Company initiates change without consulting the people who these changes will directly affect."

Feeling That Employees Are Worth Less Than Employees at Other Companies

"They don't stay competitive with other companies' pay scales. We have lost 75 percent of our employees to other employers that pay considerably more."

"The pay for our jobs is not enough to keep well-trained employees away from the competition. The small raises enable the competition to steal the employees away."

"Upper and middle management obviously don't have a clue what fair market value is for talented and experienced employees. After my two-year review I was so disappointed that I momentarily got nausea."

"Compensation is below market. A software developer with the same experience and skill in this city is paid $53,000. However, I am only being paid $32,000. I have received two offers that are paying close to average."

Believing That Employees Are Not Paid for Performance

"I have been given no incentives and no bonuses to show that I am appreciated."

"ABC Company needs a system to allow supervisors and managers to give raises based on merit or pay for performance. Their 'blanket' 2 percent and 3 percent raises are a joke and do nothing to encourage employees to strive for better performance."

"Bonuses are only given to whomever the manager likes."

Feeling That the Wrong Kinds of Rewards Are Being Given

"Bonuses should always be an option for rewarding employees instead of certificates or plaques."

"Forget all the cute gimmicks and 'jean day' and all the other childish improvements, and make the pay adequate enough to live off of—I have a mortgage to pay."

"They had a company picnic for the employees and instead of giving the employees the whole day off, we got to enjoy the horrible food for only a half an hour, and then go back to work."

Being Subject to Slow Pay and Changing Pay Plans

"There are too many changes in the compensation plans."

"My last payroll change took six weeks. 401K deposits were inconsistent."

"Reimbursement of tuition after four months is too long to have to wait!!"

"Highly dissatisfied with delay tactics of HR in resolving payroll/overtime issues. Instead of management resolving an issue, their words and attitude were 'if you don't like it—get a job elsewhere.'"

Feeling That Employees Are Treated Like Children Instead of Adults

"I did not appreciate having to keep tabs on every second of my time. I felt that as mature adults, we should be responsible for our time."

"At the call center they make a big deal about the employees dressing appropriately when customers don't even see them."

Feeling That The Company Doesn't Care about Employees' Physical Surroundings

"The noise level makes it very hard to do my job properly."

"A person cannot work in a 120-degree warehouse in the summer."

"The lack of workspace has become outrageous, to the point of employees having to sit on the floor to do necessary paperwork because lack of counter space. Yet requests for expansion [of existing services space] are continually denied. This has seriously impacted everyone and is the main cause of low morale."

"We have beautiful signs in the front of our banking office, but the insides of most of our buildings are dirty, outdated, and rundown."

Not Being Provided with the Right Tools

"Computers are horrible. They are always crashing."

"I think ABC Company's biggest problem is skimping on equipment and amenities for doing our work."

"It's like pulling teeth to get new equipment and supplies."

"XYZ Company does not supply the necessary equipment, i.e., computers, adequate work space, or file storage, or reference books needed daily to be efficient and quick in the performance of job duties. Give people the tools necessary to efficiently do their job! Days and weeks are wasted waiting for computer bugs to be repaired."

In all these ways, companies are not only missing opportunities to engage their workers, they are also giving them cause to become disengaged. Because these are the comments of employees who actually left their organizations, they serve as strong evidence that disengagement leads directly to costly turnovers.

William James once said that "the deepest craving in human nature is the craving to be appreciated." If that is so, why is there such reluctance on the part of managers to show appreciation?

Why Managers Are Reluctant to Recognize Employees' Efforts

Managers are reluctant to recognize the work of their subordinates because:

- The very qualities that result in people rising into management positions in most organizations often do not include empathy for others.

- They have worked for managers who taught them lessons such as "If you don't hear from me, that means you're doing a good job" and "Don't expect me to pat you on the back just for doing your job—I expect you to do your job."

- They are not paying enough attention to the performance of their employees to know when they have done something worth recognizing. (This raises a question: What *are* they paying attention to, if not the performance of their employees?)

- They don't know enough about an employee's job to know the difference between average and superior performance.

- They believe their people will think they are phony and insincere if they try to praise them.

- They are afraid they will recognize some employees and forget to recognize others.

- They believe that rewarding and recognizing employees are the responsibility of the human resources department.

It is rather discouraging to review these reasons. They are all too understandable. It makes one wonder how, with such obstacles, some companies are actually able to build cultures of recognition. The task of building such a culture is a formidable one, especially in organizations with a history of authoritarian leadership or in highly technical, scientific, or engineering organizations where thinking is more valued than feeling.

But thinkers have feelings, too, and if their employers do not make them *feel* valued, they will exercise their options to move on to employers that do. After all, the comments of lost employees reveal that, in all too many cases, disengagement really is about management's failure to consider the impact of its actions, or lack of action, regarding employees' emotions, especially when it results in an employee's feeling *worth less.* It should be said that many employees have overinflated views of their own worth. But I believe many more suffer from just the opposite affliction and need to be more frequently acknowledged as valued contributors.

Recognizing the Signs That Employees Feel Devalued and Unrecognized

There are many factors that may cause an employee to feel devalued or unrecognized, and there are just as many different indicators. Here are some suggestions of what to look for as precursors of potential disengagement:

- Valued contributor is overdue for a pay increase.
- Valued contributor is paid less than others in similar jobs in organization.
- Valued contributor is paid less than others in competing organizations.
- No bonus or incentive opportunity is available.
- Bonus or incentive offered is less than 10 percent of base pay.
- Nonperformers are receiving the same pay increases or bonuses as valued contributors.
- New recruits are making significantly more than more experienced, valued employees in similar positions.
- Valued contributor has not received informal recognition in the form of sincere expression of appreciation for contributions in the past ninety days.
- Employee is a B-player—a solid contributor who may feel overlooked or taken for granted.
- New hires seem to be ignored and disconnected.

- A valued employee has recently been passed over for promotion.
- A valued employee works for a manager who does not express appreciation or recognition.
- A valued employee works for an abusive manager.
- Valued employees do not have the right tools or resources to do the job right.
- Valued employees work in a cramped, noisy, messy, dirty, hot, cold, noxious, or unsafe physical environment.
- Employee surveys indicate that recognition and pay practices are top concerns.

Pay: The Most Emotional Issue of All

There is no more emotionally charged issue for employees than what they are paid for their contributions. What we make doesn't just pay the bills—it measures our worth in the most material way. We cannot help defining ourselves by the levels of our income, yet we go to great lengths to keep the information private.

In reviewing the comments of ex-employees about pay, we find that the root of their dissatisfaction runs deeper than the sums they were paid. They are bothered by inequity—knowing that they make less than others who are no more qualified, or even less qualified, than they are. They feel the injustice of getting the same pay raises as those who have contributed far less to the organization than they have. They interpret HR's unresponsiveness to requests for payroll changes as a sign that they are unimportant. They have no chance to receive a bonus, while others do. It all adds up to feeling "less than."

This is why pay and recognition are combined in this chapter—they are both tools for acknowledging the worth of those who work for us. We will look at best practices in both pay and recognition, as they must be considered "twins joined at the hip" for sending the right messages to employees about what we value. But it is helpful to remind ourselves of some key distinctions between the two:

- Recognition cannot replace pay; it can only add to it.
- Recognition is usually retroactive, acknowledging a contribution after the fact, while variable pay can be a powerful incentive for motivating future goal achievement.

- Recognition can happen at any time; it reinforces desired behaviors more effectively when it quickly follows an accomplishment by a team or an individual.

- Recognition can be customized or personalized to fit the person receiving it, making it more meaningful.

- Recognition in the form of material possessions carries the additional motivational power of reminding the individual of the company's appreciation.

- Any employee can recognize another employee, while only management can pay an employee.

- Recognition can take the form of a celebration, bringing some needed fun and excitement into the workplace.

- Innovative recognition practices may bring positive publicity to the company.

- Contests—a common recognition practice—can give every employee an equal chance for a payoff.

Both pay and recognition are powerful tools for reinforcing organizational values or changes in personal behavior and work culture. Together, they are more effective than either can be separately.

Pay Practices That Engage and Retain

Companies spend millions of dollars per year on compensation consultants to make sure that they are designing or redesigning their pay plans to fit their business cultures and objectives. So, it would be misleading to suggest that there are best practices that work equally well for organizations of all sizes and situations. However, there are definite trends in the way companies are choosing to pay their workers that appear to be more motivating and appropriate for the times and for newer generations of workers than the old system.

Companies have gradually replaced old pay practices with newer ones that meet new worker expectations. In the 1960s, 1970s, and even into the 1980s, most companies rewarded tenure over performance and created an entitlement mentality in much of the workforce. Workers "owned" their jobs, and most companies were stable and paternalistic. Companies absorbed pay and benefit costs regardless of their ability to pay.

With the late 1980s and 1990s came downsizings and the flattening of organizations and, with these, the loss of worker trust and loyalty. Workers were no longer "entitled" to their jobs and had to learn new skills to stay employable. People found more flexible ways of working—from home, part time, and in temporary positions. Pay and benefit costs were cut along with jobs. There was a severe loss of workforce commitment that has only grown worse since the economic meltdown of 2008.

Back when talent was scarce as job growth boomed in the late 1990s, companies actually started believing the words they had always mouthed— people really *are* a source of competitive advantage. Talented people had other options than working for companies that did not value them highly. Companies woke up to the fact that they needed to invest in their work- forces and form win-win partnerships. This meant more open communica- tion, more coaching, training, stock options, signing bonuses, creative perks, and generous benefits.

During the economic downturn of 2001 and again in 2008–2009, many employers began cutting back on perks, benefits, and signing bonuses. Employees started clinging to their jobs, in spite of the fact that they were asked to do more with less. At this writing, most experts believe the War for Talent will eventually return as the economy continues to grow while boomers retire in larger numbers. When this happens, employers will realize anew that people work for more than just pay and benefits—they work for what we now call "total rewards," the most meaningful of which are not related to pay.

Here, then, are some of the best pay practices that many preeminent employers have begun to embrace to better engage and retain their talent:

 Engagement Practice #35:
Offer competitive base pay linked to value creation.

The ongoing need to provide increased value to customers, combined with the need to control base-pay increases, have led many companies to link base pay more to value creation and less to rank or years of service. This new emphasis has resulted in some companies paying lower-ranked employees more than their managers because they judge that the employees' contribu- tions brought more to the bottom line. At The Container Store, for example, consistently ranked among *Fortune*'s "100 Best Places to Work in America," it is not unusual for a sales associate to make more than a store manager.

Another key is to communicate clearly to all employees how "value" is determined when making decisions regarding base pay. For example, in many companies, overall sustained value is based on three criteria:

1. Skills and competencies needed
2. Labor market supply and demand
3. Ongoing value to the organization[1]

Yet, employees in most companies could not explain, if asked, how value is determined because this has never been adequately explained to them. Besides communicating clearly how base-pay decisions are made, managers need to also be held accountable for making hard decisions about which employees are creating more value for the business and are keeping their skills aligned with company needs. There will always be a degree of subjectivity in such decisions, and many managers will try to please everyone by spreading pay increases evenly (like peanut butter) among all workers, often with disastrous results.

How salary decisions are made will depend on the goals of each organization. Some companies actually give base-pay increases for lateral moves within the organization, thus reinforcing the company's emphasis on employee development and preparation for future assignments.

Here are some other notable trends in base pay:

- *Payment for Skills and Competencies.* This has been a growing trend, resulting in more emphasis on paying the person, rather than the job. However, many companies have found that paying for results with lump sums and variable pay is the higher priority.

- *Less Emphasis on Internal Equity Based on Point Factors and Job Evaluations.* This trend is cyclical—the more competitive the labor market, the more companies de-emphasize internal pay equity in favor of staying competitive with other companies in the same industry. This can create problems of salary compression, as when new employees are recruited at starting salaries higher than those of experienced employees. Smart employers need to be disciplined enough not to get into bidding wars, remembering that pay is only one piece of the total rewards approach.

Some companies cannot afford to pay above-market base salaries but can still compete effectively for talent by giving employees more mentoring, no-cost recognition, additional vacation days, or whatever nonpay reward might be important to them. When employers reach the point where they feel they must pay a premium to capture new recruits, they will simply have to find creative ways to reward more experienced workers.

- *Less Reliance on Salary Benchmarking.* More workplaces are becoming less structured and more fluid in the way the work gets done. This means that some jobs are blended with other jobs, and some people are given broader roles, combining tasks that were formerly done by several other people. This means that when companies look to make market-based judgments about employees' value, they need to keep in mind that, when looking at salary surveys and benchmarking with other companies, they may not be "comparing apples to apples."

- *More Broad-Banding.* Many employers have drastically cut the number of salary grades and have created broad salary bands that reflect the fact that most organizations are flatter and less hierarchical than in years past. The growing popularity of broad-banding reflects the fact that it contributes to the attraction and retention of talent in several ways: It focuses employees on growing within a broad pay range, facilitates lateral career moves, emphasizes the person over the job, reinforces the use of dual career paths, and supports changes in work design.[2]

Increasingly, employers of choice understand that base pay, as a reward for individual ongoing value, is only one piece of a total-rewards approach. Employers of choice have gravitated toward the mix of variable pay to reward current value and nonpay rewards to complete the total rewards package.

 Engagement Practice #36:
Reward results with variable pay aligned with business goals.

Because of the increased focus on productivity during economic downturns, more companies are turning to new pay practices that require employees to put more of their pay at risk in exchange for greater rewards if they help the company meet its business objectives. While many employees will be uncomfortable with assuming the increased risk, many others, including top performers, will respond favorably to the opportunity for more "ownership" if it means being paid in proportion to their contributions. Data from one study showed that higher-performing organizations used more pay for performance vehicles than other organizations—among them spot bonuses, equity awards, other long-term incentives, and profit sharing, in addition to traditional vehicles such as base-pay increases and short-term incentives.[3]

Employee Ownership Reduces Employee Turnover

USA 800, Inc., a contact call center and fulfillment center with four hundred employees across the United States, had experienced turnover rates as high as 70 percent, resulting in the loss of significant training investment and in disruption of customer service. The owners decided to make the transition to 100 percent employee ownership. Within a year, the company's revenues increased by almost 30 percent and the employee turnover rate dropped to 23 percent. Company owners realized another positive by-product of giving employees a stake in the company: 80 percent of the company's managers have been promoted from within.[4]

Three Types of Variable Pay

There are three types of variable pay that many companies use in combination: short-term variable pay, long-term cash variable pay, and long-term equity variable pay.

Short-term variable pay, such as goal-sharing, win-sharing, gain-sharing, profit-sharing, team variable pay, individual variable pay, and combination plans, usually focuses on the achievement of business results within a one-year time frame. As a way of gaining more autonomy in directly rewarding employees for outstanding achievements, many managers now lobby for "spot award" money in their budgets.

Long-term cash variable pay is designed to reward business results over a sustained period of time, generally two or more years. Sustained performance requires a long-term focus, not just the short-term view adopted by so many companies in response to the expectations of the investment community. The longer-term perspective can also help keep key talent for longer periods.

Long-term equity variable pay means stock options. By making stock options available at all position levels in the organization, companies spread the feeling of shared ownership, reinforce teamwork, and promote longer-term retention.

The major attraction of variable pay is that it has the potential to fulfill employees' expectations of being paid for performance while allowing businesses to make additional payouts only if they achieve business goals.

Changing Workforce Expects More Customized Pay Options

With the impending retirement of Baby Boomers in ever-increasing numbers, employers will compete for Generations X and Y workers who will demand even more job freedom and flexibility. Gen Y (Millennial) workers will have shorter job tenures, request work-from-home arrangements, and seek quarterly bonuses, not yearly ones. To meet the changing expectations of younger workers, companies will increasingly customize rewards programs to the individual preferences of workers. Employers that provide customized rewards packages will have a decided edge in recruiting and retention over their competitors. Greenville Hospital System University Medical Center in Greenville, South Carolina, revamped its compensation structure to attract and retain nurses. In addition to merit increases, new nurses gain "experience increases" after their second year on the job. Nurses working 24/7 earn more than those working in clinics or outpatient centers. These changes, plus a boost in the pay levels for nurses overall, helped Greenville Hospital System cut its nurse turnover rate from 18 percent to 10 percent.[5]

For variable pay programs to work, they first depend on clear communication of the rationale, measures, and goals to be used both during and after the roll-out. This puts increased responsibility on senior leaders to openly discuss how bonuses will be figured and on managers to measure how well goals are being achieved. Second, the goals need to be realistic and achievable while still providing a reasonable stretch for the employee. Finally, the goals have to change as the business environment and priorities change.

 Engagement Practice #37:
Reward employees at a high enough level to
motivate higher performance.

Studies have repeatedly shown that there is a certain level at which employees become more willing to put forth the effort to achieve higher goals. Some experts argue that an award of 10 to 12 percent above base pay is required, which is significantly higher than the 7.5 percent that most companies pay.[6] Other experts report that variable pay in most companies averages about 10 percent of base pay for managers and sales professionals, 8 percent for exempt workers, and 5 percent for nonexempt workers.[7]

There are other factors to consider in determining the size of the variable pay opportunity. Generally, variable pay awards should be higher when:

- The bottom-line impact of the results is significant.
- The result is difficult to achieve.
- The result takes longer to achieve.
- Base pay is more at risk.

Engagement Practice #38:
Use cash payouts for on-the-spot recognition.

Many top employers reserve 1 to 2 percent of their base-pay budget for cash payouts or lump-sum payments to recognize top performers in the current time frame. One of the main reasons for the popularity of cash payouts is the increased motivation that comes when employees receive awards as quickly as possible after an achievement. Such awards also give organizations more flexibility in that they can be used to supplement team awards and recognize contributors whose value is acknowledged but who already have a high base pay or those who may be designated to receive minimal base-pay increases.

Engagement Practice #39:
Involve employees, and encourage two-way
communication when designing new pay systems.

Research consistently shows that employee satisfaction goes up when employees know how their pay is determined. One study found that 74 percent of employees who understood how their pay was determined reported being satisfied in their jobs. On the other hand, of those who did not understand how pay was determined, only 42 percent were satisfied. The same study found that only 28 percent of employees saw a link between their pay and their performance.[8]

For those in military service, pay is seldom an issue with anyone, since all know how pay is determined and what everyone else is making. Thus, it is not the distraction that it is in private corporations, where so much time and emotion are wasted speculating, gossiping, and being angry about pay.

The best time, but not the only time, to start the process of creating employee understanding is when designing a new pay system. Inviting the input of employees is the best way to create an understandable system that fits their needs and gets their buy-in. Forward-thinking companies begin the process by linking business objectives with the employee behavior they want the new pay system to reinforce. After developing a preliminary design, they may survey the workforce, conducting one-on-one interviews or focus groups to surface and clarify key issues and ideas. The initial roll-out meetings should allow plenty of time for two-way communication, with the most commonly asked questions solicited and answered.

Even if a pay system has been installed without going through this process, it is never too late to begin a campaign to communicate how pay is determined and to solicit employee feedback. One survey reported that half of employees felt that discussing pay was taboo in their organizations.[9] This is an obstacle to engaging and retaining talent that may be an uncomfortable one to tackle, but is worth making the extra effort to overcome the discomfort. We need to constantly keep in mind that, when it comes to pay, employees are just as interested in "how" as they are in "how much."

 Engagement Practice #40:
Monitor the pay system to ensure fairness,
efficiency, consistency, and accuracy.

As we have seen in the comments of employees, there are always questions about pay systems, and there always will be. Employees should be surveyed on a regular basis about the pay system, including the effectiveness of managers in coaching them through the performance measurement and management process discussed in Chapter 6. Continued monitoring will also be needed to ensure that pay practices stay aligned with business goals and that managers are making effective pay decisions.

The Total-Rewards Approach to Scarce Talent

When talent is scarce, many companies respond by increasing levels of base pay and short-term bonuses. This popular knee-jerk response often results in payment of generous sign-on bonuses and stay bonuses and in making counteroffers to people after they announce they are leaving. Treating talent as a commodity may serve to attract talent, but often cannot keep it in the absence of other "total-reward" attractions, such as a great boss, attractive work-life benefits, challenging work, and opportunities for career advancement. Another downside to this approach is that it serves only to drive up pay costs and to accelerate bidding wars with other companies.

Some companies put more of an emphasis on retaining scarce talent (as opposed to just buying it) by actually measuring their managers' success at keeping talent in the organization. "Percentage of employees retained" may be factored in when determining managers' pay. Other employers pay cash retention awards to key talent for each year they stay with the company. An employer may even pay stock options to employees who make referrals of candidates with scarce talents who are hired and stay for preset periods.

Employers that want to become true employers of choice typically pursue a more comprehensive strategy—they design a "total-rewards" approach that balances pay as a key attraction against a full range of non-pay factors. In other words, employers that pursue "total-rewards" strategies focus on delivering a compelling value proposition to prospective and current employees, one that is based on practices like those presented in all the chapters of this book.

More Words to the Wise About Pay

"Noncash rewards are the only real way to differentiate your employment offerings. Cash is a commodity, so it cannot differentiate one company's employment contract from another; it is the intangibles that distinguish. Besides, when it comes to money, someone will always pay more."

—TODD M. MANAS AND MICHAEL DENNIS GRAHAM[10]

The good news about showing people that we value them is that there are so many ways to do it that are absolutely free. At least they are free in the sense that you have to spend little or no money, but you do have to invest some time, energy, and imagination. So, the first key is to care enough to make those kinds of investments.

Next, it is important to understand what kind of recognition people want, that they don't all want the same kind of recognition, and that they don't all want the same kind of recognition that you do. Many studies on motivation and recognition have repeatedly found that managers thought employees valued good pay and job security, while employees themselves reported that they most valued intangibles such as managers who recognize their value, keep them informed, and are interested in their professional growth. When workers and supervisors were asked to rank a list of motivators in order of their importance to workers, workers rated "appreciation for a job well done" as their top motivator. Supervisors ranked it eighth. Employees ranked "feeling in on things" as number two in importance, while managers ranked it last.[11]

Of course, there are other noncash recognition methods in common use. One survey revealed the following breakdown:

Type of Award	Percentage of Companies Using
Gift cards or certificates	38%
Merchandise	19%
Dinners	19%
Special trips	19%
Trophies or plaques	18%
Top-performer listings	12%
Honorary sales clubs	7%
Special parking spots	2% [12]

Although 80 percent of organizations have a recognition program, less than a third of HR professionals (31 percent) believe that employees are satisfied with the level of recognition they receive for doing a good job.[13]

So, the question remains: Are any of these more effective than simply offering thanks for a job well done? Many workers would rather have more time off than additional pay or any of these noncash awards. Managers simply need to ask their people how they would like to be recognized, which seems so obvious that it's puzzling that more managers don't do it. Of course, there are some forms of recognition that all employees value, which brings us to our first recognition best practice.

 Engagement Practice #41:
Create a culture of informal recognition
founded on sincere appreciation.

Receiving simple and sincere thanks for their contributions is the primary form of recognition people want. In one recent study, 78 percent of employees said it was very important for them to be recognized by their manager when they do good work. Another 73 percent said they expected recognition to occur either "immediately" or "soon thereafter."[14] There are several ways of giving thanks; face-to-face conversation is the most preferred, but other possibilities are written, electronic, and public recognition. Many employees like written expressions of thanks, as they can be copied and kept. Not all employees like public recognition, however, so it is always best to ask employees whether they mind being singled out in front of others.

Many managers find it hard to give this simplest of recognition because they have developed the habit of taking the contributions of their employees for granted, perhaps because their own contributions have gone unappreciated. It is difficult to get managers to develop the new habit of giving thanks for good work. It is probably easier to change to a culture of recognition by hiring managers whom we know to be good at giving thanks to their employees than it is to train managers to build new habits. Still, managers can be taught the art of giving thanks, and many companies do include modules on how to recognize and show appreciation in their basic supervisory training. It takes practice to build new habits, so most effective training requires managers to actually try out new ways of expressing appreciation during training sessions.

There are different ways to say thanks, such as:

"I'm glad you're here."

"Thank you for being who you are . . . your role here is vital and much appreciated."

"You stayed late last night to finish that proposal, and I want you to know how much that meant to me and the whole team."

It also helps to have a list of different ways to express appreciation, like the following one:

- Send a gift certificate for dinner for two at a local restaurant with a note of thanks.
- Send out note cards with the words "You Done Good" or "Bravo" printed on them, along with your personal thanks.
- Give employees a way to recognize their peers, such as having them pass around an old trophy to coworkers for doing something they view as outstanding.
- Give employees an unexpected half day or day off.
- Take the employee to lunch.
- Give the employee a choice assignment.
- Pay for a massage or manicure.
- Send a gift basket to the home.
- At weekly leadership team meetings, have leaders come prepared to tell the story of an employee in their area who recently made a significant contribution or went above and beyond.

Whatever method you use, keep in mind that recognition works best when given in response to desired behaviors and performance. If you bring in donuts every Friday, it won't take long before employees see this as entitlement. People actually value recognition more when they have done something to earn it. For more ideas on how to recognize employees, read Bob Nelson's best-selling book, *1001 Ways to Reward Employees*, a great resource for managers who wish to start building new habits of appreciation.

There are more formal and elaborate ways of recognizing and saying thanks, which can require more sophisticated planning and financial investment. Yum Brands, the parent company of Pizza Hut, A&W Restaurants, KFC, Long John Silver's, and Taco Bell, has marching bands march right up to employees in recognition of their going the extra mile in the name of customer service. The recognition is just one part of the company's effort to "brand" itself as a great place to work, which also includes extensive training in how to resolve customer issues and listen better. After implementing the recognition and training programs, the turnover in Taco Bell restaurants went down from 200 percent to 98 percent.[15]

Nelson argues that many formal recognition programs have worn out their welcome because they look backward at what has been done instead of directing employees' attention forward to goals and the rewards that might motivate them to achieve those goals. In particular, he criticizes the incentive industry that continues to promote trinkets such as pen sets, coffee mugs, t-shirts, watches, clocks, paperweights, certificates of appreciation, and plaques, all of which today's employees value far less than being treated well on a daily basis.[16]

The bottom line is that informal no-cost recognition by an employee's direct manager, usually in the form of simple thanks in response to a job well done, does more to engage and sustain employee commitment than all other available options.

A New Habit in Action

"I try to remember that people—good, intelligent, capable people—may actually need day-to-day praise and thanks for the job they do. I try to remember to get up out of my chair, turn off my computer, go sit or stand next to them and see what they're doing, ask about the challenges, find out if they need additional help, offer that help if possible, and most of all, tell them in all honesty that what they are doing is important: to me, to the company, and to our customers."

—JOHN BALL, SERVICE TRAINING MANAGER,
AMERICAN HONDA MOTOR COMPANY[17]

Engagement Practice #42:
Make new hires feel welcome and important.

If we want employees to feel valued and important, the best time to start is during their first few days on the job. Increasingly, employers of choice are going to great lengths to welcome new hires in special ways:

- Sending gift baskets to their homes before they start
- Putting pastries or candy near their desks to encourage other employees to stop by, introduce themselves, and welcome them aboard
- Assigning "buddies," peer coaches, or mentors to coach new hires through the first few weeks on the job or to help them get settled into a new community
- Training managers to manage the new hire's first few days so that they know they are valued, that their contribution is vital to the company's success, and exactly what is expected of them
- Spreading out formal group orientation sessions so that they occur over a period of weeks instead of bombarding new hires with more information than they can take in during their first few days on the job

Many organizations make a special effort to make sure new hires more fully understand the significance of the work they do. John Sullivan describes the process of helping new employees appreciate the true value of their contributions as "walking them downstream."[18] There are several ways to do this:

Begin by first "walking them upstream" to see where the company's raw materials come from or how the customer makes first contact with the company. Then walk them downstream so that they can see how the product or service has an impact on the customer.

Let them talk directly with customers to find out how the product or service has an impact on them.

Let them sit in on a sales call with a satisfied customer.

Give the new hire testimonials and articles about the company and its products or services.

Orientation Program Slows New Hire Attrition

The Mid-America Program Service Center of the Social Security Administration in Kansas City, Missouri, had a new hire attrition rate of 9 percent and expectations of losing 1,400 employees to retirement. The center conducted a survey of new hires and learned that new hires felt disconnected and did not understand how they fit into the big picture. Within three months, a redesigned new hire orientation—NEON (New Hire Orientation and Networking)—was installed, focused on training managers how to interview and orient new hires. The program featured interactive group presentations and one-on-one sessions with managers designed to familiarize new hires with the SSA's mission, its history, and career development opportunities. Within eighteen months, new hire attrition had been reduced to 2.8 percent, and the center had saved more than $400,000 in turnover costs.[19]

Engagement Practice #43:
Ask for employee input, then listen and respond.

A sure way to instantly know whether we are being taken seriously is to observe how well others listen to us. We all have a basic need to know that others care what we think. When people ask our opinion, we feel respected. Yet, only 36 percent of workers say that their companies actively seek their opinions.[20]

One problem here is that many managers are not very good listeners and they know it. Many managers became managers because they see themselves as leaders who already know the best way to proceed, and they don't want to be slowed down by having to check in with their employees to get their input. "The workplace is not a democracy," I have heard them say, and they are right about that.

The U.S. Navy is not known as a democracy either, and yet one of the best examples of a leader listening and acting on the input of the average worker comes from the destroyer USS *Benfold*, as told in the pages of the *Harvard Business Review*. When Captain D. Michael Abrashoff took command of this ship in 1997, its 310 crew members were mostly demoralized, and the typical attrition rate in the Navy was 40 percent over the first four years. Captain Abrashoff set out to do something different to engage and retain his sailors.

What he did was to reject the Navy's traditional command-and-control approach to leadership. Captain Abrashoff had served under William J. Perry when he was secretary of defense and had been impressed with the way Perry listened intently to everyone he encountered. Abrashoff knew he wasn't a good listener, but he vowed that he would "treat every encounter with every person on the ship as the most important thing in my world at the moment."[21] It wasn't easy to begin with, but Abrashoff began asking crew members what they would like to change on the *Benfold*. The sailors responded with creative, cost-saving, workable ideas that Captain Abrashoff implemented almost immediately in many cases. He set up "get-to-know-you" sessions and met in his cabin with every sailor on the ship, asking a series of questions designed to get to know the crew personally and soliciting their ideas for improving things aboard the ship. He started placing more trust and responsibility in their hands, and they responded by doing their best so as not to let him down.

A result of Captain Abrashoff's steady efforts, the USS *Benfold* "set all-time records for performance and retention, and the waiting list of officers and enlisted personnel who want to transfer to the *Benfold* is pages long. It's a long wait because very few aboard the *Benfold* want to leave."[22]

Employees are hungry to be heard, and you can't afford not to seek, listen to, and implement their ideas. Here are several ways that organizations of all kinds are giving their workers more of a voice and showing them the respect of listening well:

- Hold 50/50 meetings with employees, where management speaks for 50 percent of the time about its goals, strategies, and ideas, then gives the floor to employees to respond for the rest of the meeting time. These kinds of meetings can be conducted over breakfast or lunch or during regular staff meetings.
- Conduct regular employee surveys, and be prepared to act on key issues surfaced. This boosts morale by letting employees know you take their ideas seriously and respect their input. Conversely, nothing

kills morale quicker than asking for input, then ignoring it. Surveys
don't all have to be expensive undertakings. Some companies build
morale by sending out e-mail surveys every month and acting
promptly to correct seemingly small but irritating problems.

- Conduct in-depth exit interviews that get to the root cause of
  why employees are disengaging and leaving; then take action to
  address the "push factors" that are driving good people out of the
  organization.

- Get out of the office and practice Tom Peters's MBWA principle—
  "Management by Walking Around." The key is that you have to be
  sincere and prepared to act on the suggestions you will get when you
  stop by and ask employees for their ideas on how to make things
  better.

- Let employees give anonymous written feedback to their managers
  on how they can improve their people management skills, not as part
  of a formal performance review but for developmental purposes.

- Publish the suggestions left in suggestion boxes, and act on the
  good ones.

Employees First, Customers Second Pays Off for HCL Technologies

HCLT, a $2.3 billion IT company with sixty thousand professionals in
twenty-six countries, encourages employees to ask questions, make suggestions, and offer solutions through a "value portal." The company has
implemented more than five hundred ideas, creating more than $25 mil-
lion in value. The company's revenues and operating profits more than
tripled over a five-year period after the company began putting employees first. What's more, the number of HCLT customers grew exponential-
ly—even during the recession. The CEO, Vineet Nayar, has written a
book, *Employees First, Customers Second*, which describes several steps he
took to give real power to all employees. The key to the "employees first"
model is to invert the traditional business pyramid and make management
and employees accountable to each other. As an example, any employee
with problems or complaints can "open a ticket," which is assigned to a
manager responsible for a solution. Only the employee can sign off on the
solution.[23]

Through Its Employees, Best Buy Listens to the Voice of the Customer

"My Customer" is the platform Best Buy created to unleash and amplify the powerful voice of its 100,000+ frontline employees to share what they have heard or learned from daily interactions with customers. Best Buy's employees engage in more than a billion customer interactions annually. The company reasoned that it should be possible to solve real problems that employees escalated to management on behalf of its customers in as close to real-time as possible. Employees are asked to be on the alert for ways to serve customers better, increase revenues, and cut costs and to submit their ideas expeditiously for senior leaders to consider. This invitation led to more than six thousand submissions of insights a week over the span of a year. Receiving such a volume of ideas and insights from customer-facing employees led Best Buy to make several key decisions and to put in place strategic shifts that helped retain customers it might have lost and increase customer traffic. Perhaps the biggest payoff was that employees became more engaged because the company made sure to let them know that something was being done with their insights.[24]

Engagement Practice #44: Keep employees in the loop.

Few things say "you're not important" more loudly than withholding information that employees want and need to know. Keeping employees out of the loop creates disconnection, alienation, and disengagement. On the other hand, companies that feed their employees a steady diet of vital information about the company build ownership and commitment.

Most employers are familiar with the story of Springfield Remanufacturing Company's success with "open-book management." After many frustrating years working at a company where information was hoarded at the top, Jack Stack started Springfield Remanufacturing Company and founded it on a key practice—opening up the company's operations data and financial information and teaching his workers to understand it, thereby empowering them to make decisions based on it. Stack also gave employees a financial stake in the game, which increased their sense of ownership in the business. The company's annual sales grew from $16 million to $83 million in just nine years, and Stack's book, *The Great Game of Business*, attracted such widespread interest that dozens of companies, such as Federal Express, Allstate Insurance, ExxonMobil, The Body Shop, and Hostess Frito-Lay, have adapted Stack's ideas to their own businesses.

One reason more companies have not adopted Stack's approach is their fear that giving information to employees would mean giving up their power. The thinking goes that "they wouldn't know what to do with it," or "they don't need to know," or "they will be overwhelmed with all this information," but, too often, underlying such statements is the assumption that employees are powerless children, too immature to be trusted with important information. The executive who hoards information may feel more privileged, important, and powerful, but the effect on the workplace is a negative one.

In the absence of information, employees fill the void with rumors born of anxiety. As rumors spread, productivity goes down and distrust goes up. Just the opposite occurs when the company decides to share information, often because the information it shares also happens to be important in achieving the company's goals. Cisco Systems openly reports all the bugs in its products on a public Web page as soon as any problem is reported. Rather than diminishing customer confidence in the company's products, this reporting builds trust and allows programmers to quickly correct the problem. Cisco's CEO, John Chambers, one of the most admired executives in American business, gives a Webcast management update every few weeks during which he responds directly to employee questions. Chambers wants his employees to learn about company news firsthand, not in the media.[25]

Here are some ways to keep employees in the loop:

- Openly discuss the company's strategic plan and what it means to each department and employee.
- Share articles that you read about the company, industry trends, and competitors.
- Give briefings about upcoming events that may impact employees' career options.
- Share information as soon as you possibly can to nip rumors in the bud.
- Share information face to face when possible.
- There will be times when information is confidential, proprietary, or otherwise sensitive, and you will not be able to share it. Those times will be the exception, however, not the rule.

- One final reminder: The more valuable and productive the employees, the more they want to be kept in the loop.

☑ **Engagement Practice #45:**
Give employees the right tools and resources.

Many employees are drawn to organizations by their anticipation of great relationships with their manager and colleagues. Yet, in one survey, 44 percent felt they were not given the tools and resources needed to succeed in their first days on the job.[26]

Whether it's something as simple as a hotel manager making sure the kitchen workers have better knives or a high-tech company having the latest hardware, it's obvious that people need the right tools to do the job. When they don't get those tools they need, it's not just that they become less productive; they also feel less important.

We may look to save money on hardware, software, furniture, and equipment, but if we are thinking of them as costs only, we are being shortsighted. Providing the right tools at the right time is an investment—not only in productivity but in sending a message to our employees that they are worth it.

The law firm Alston & Bird, selected as one of *Fortune's* "100 Best Places to Work in America," was also selected as the "most wired" law firm in America in a survey by *American Lawyer*. The firm makes sure that all associates have all the wireless devices they need for staying in touch while away from the office.[27] For Generations X and Y in particular, being able to perform their jobs while maintaining some semblance of lifestyle flexibility is a value of prime importance. Over and above the practical aspect, having the right connectivity devices also makes employees feel vital to the organization.

If you are not sure what tools and resources to provide employees, simply ask. Send out a monthly e-mail survey asking, "What do you need that would make you more effective in your job?" If you're not sure whether it's worth the expenditure, ask employees to present the business case for the purchase, showing how the new tool would pay off in the long run.

Many of the things employees need to be more effective are easy and inexpensive to supply, and when you respond quickly, it builds even more commitment.

Engagement Practice #46:
Keep the physical environment fit to work in.

This one is so basic that you wouldn't think it would need mentioning, but, time and again, departing employees complain of cramped, noisy, hot, cold, messy, dirty, noxious, or unsafe conditions. Ask yourself, "How would I like to work where my employees work?" Go to their workstations and spend some time talking with them about what in their physical surroundings could be improved. As with tools and resources, you may be surprised by how easy some solutions are—a fan, a heater, or an occasional cleaning may be all that's needed.

The environment you provide for your workers tells them how much you value them. When the Las Vegas casino mogul Steve Wynn designed a new hotel, he decided to spend the same amount of money per square foot to build the employee cafeteria as he spent on the hotel coffee shop. Wynn also decorated the back corridors that employees use in the same bright and cheery colors he used to decorate the guest corridors. Again, the message he sent was "You are important, you are worth it . . . because if you are happy, you will take care of the customer."

What Employees Can Do to Be More Valued and Better Recognized

There may be good reason why some employees don't feel valued or recognized—perhaps they have not made themselves as valuable to the business as they think they have. Research has consistently shown that the vast majority of employees feel underpaid and believe they are in the top 25 percent of all performers, which, of course, cannot be the case. This means that many employees have an inflated view of their value or feel unduly entitled to receive what they have not earned.

Here, then, are some guidelines for employees who want to get more recognition and pay:

- Ask your manager to define what results are required for excellence in your job.
- Ask yourself if you are willing to work hard and pay the price to achieve those results.
- Ask what criteria are used to determine bonuses and raises.

- Ask yourself if you are willing to put more of your pay at risk, to be paid bonuses based on achievement of targeted results rather than getting annual pay raises. If so, make them part of your performance plan, and commit to achieving them.

- Compete against yourself to achieve key results, not against your peers.

- Ask what new skills would make you more valuable to the organization.

- Tell your manager how you prefer to be recognized for your contributions.

- Ask to sit in on a sales call with a satisfied customer to better understand the value of your job.

- Present a cost-benefit analysis to your manager making the case for the purchase of tools and equipment you believe you need.

- If you feel you are being kept out of the loop, ask for more information.

- Don't wait for your manager to ask for your input—give him or her the benefit of your views and ideas.

Engagement Practices Checklist: Feeling Devalued and Unrecognized

Review the engagement practices presented in this chapter, and check the ones you believe your organization needs to implement or improve.

To make employees feel valued and recognized:

Engagement Practice #35. __ Offer competitive base pay linked to value creation.

Engagement Practice #36. __ Reward results with variable pay aligned with business goals.

Engagement Practice #37. __ Reward employees at a high enough level to motivate higher performance.

Engagement Practice #38. __ Use cash payouts for on-the-spot recognition.

Engagement Practice #39. __ Involve employees and encourage two-way communication when designing new pay systems.

Engagement Practice #40. __ Monitor the pay system to ensure fairness, efficiency, consistency, and accuracy.

Engagement Practice #41. __   Create a culture of informal recognition
founded on appreciation.

Engagement Practice #42. __   Make new hires feel welcome and important.

Engagement Practice #43. __   Ask for employee input, then listen and respond.

Engagement Practice #44. __   Keep employees in the loop.

Engagement Practice #45. __   Give them the right tools and resources.

Engagement Practice #46. __   Keep the physical environment fit to work in.

Your next step: *Resolve to take action on the practices you believe are most critical and appropriate for your situation and objectives.*

Notes

1. Patricia K. Zingheim and Jay R. Schuster, *Pay People Right! Breakthrough Reward Strategies to Create Great Companies* (San Francisco: Jossey-Bass, 2000).

2. Ibid.

3. "Real Pay for Performance Study," Sibson Consulting study of 140 for-profit (74%) and not-for-profit (26%) organizations, 2010, http://www.sibson.com/publications/perspectives/volume_18_issue_3 /Pay-for-Perf-Study.html.

4. Ruth Baum Bigus, "Ownership Option Helps Curb Employee Turnover," *Kansas City Star*, September 18, 2001.

5. Karen M. Kroll, "Let's Get Flexible," *HR*, April 2007.

6. Steven Kerr, "Risky Business: The New Pay Game," *Fortune*, July 22, 1996.

7. Zingheim and Schuster, *Pay People Right!*

8. Compensation study, Mercer Consulting, 2002.

9. Jeremy Handel, "Can Communication Boost Employees' Pay Satisfaction?" *HR Focus*, July 2002.

10. Todd M. Manas and Michael Dennis Graham, *Creating a Total Rewards Strategy: A Toolkit for Designing Business-Based Plans* (New York: AMACOM, 2002).

11. Bob Nelson, "The Top 10 Ironies of Employee Motivation Programs," *Employee Benefit News*, June 19, 2001.

12. Culpepper Pay Practices and Benefits Survey, 2008, http://www.culpepper. com/eBulletin/2008 /NovControlCompensationCosts.asp.

13. Rebecca R. Hastings, Society for Human Resource Management Online, June 29, 2011, citing *2011 SHRM/Globoforce Employee Recognition Survey* report, reflecting the input of 745 randomly selected HR professionals, http://www.shrm.org/Publications/HRNews/Pages/GloboforcePoll.aspx.

14. Bob Nelson, "Why Formal Recognition Programs Don't Work," *Update on Employee Recognition*, April 2004, http://nelson-motivation.stores. yahoo. net/ebooksarticles.html.

15. "Yum Stresses Trust, Recognition," Work and Family Newsbrief, December 2003.16. Nelson, "Why Formal Recognition Programs Don't Work."

17. Ibid.

18. John Sullivan, "Walk Them Downstream: Showing Your Employees They Make a Difference," Electronic Recruiting Exchange, April 1, 2002, http://www.ere.net/2002/04/page/2/.

19. Ruth Baum Bigus, "Orientation Program Stems New-Hire Attrition," *Kansas City Star*, July 22, 2003.

20. Catherine D. Fyock, "Retention Tactics That Work," citing Labor Day survey by Watson-Wyatt, White Paper, Society for Human Resource Management, March 1998, http://www.shrm.org/Research /SurveyFindings/Documents/2000%20Retention%20Survey.pdf.

21. D. Michael Abrashoff, "Retention Through Redemption," *Harvard Business Review* (February 2001).

22. Ibid.

23. Aliah D. Wright, Society for Human Resource Management Online, September 22, 2010, http://www.weknownext.com/workforce /recruiting-internationally-from-kansas-to-cameroon.

24. Steve Wallin, " Best Buy: Voice of the Customer Through the Employee," Management Innovation Exchange, September 1, 2011, http://www.managementexchange.com/story/my-customer-one-voice.

25. Frederick F. Reichheld, *Loyalty Rules: How Today's Leaders Build Lasting Relationships* (Boston: Harvard Business School Press, 2001).

26. Barbara Morris, "The Cost of a Bad Start," *Marketing*, October 27, 2003.

27. Lynne C. Lancaster and David Stillman, *When Generations Collide* (New York: HarperBusiness, 2002).

CHAPTER NINE

Reason #6: Stress from Overwork and Work-Life Imbalance

> What my business experience has taught me
> is that the key to competitiveness is innovation,
> and the key to innovation is people. Taking care of people,
> therefore, is an essential way of taking care of business.
>
> —RANDALL TOBIAS, CHAIRMAN OF ELI LILLY

> Employers that maintain a strong commitment to
> employee well-being even under difficult circumstances
> will have a distinct competitive advantage in
> their ability to attract and retain the very best staff.
>
> —DR. DAVID BALLARD, AMERICAN PSYCHOLOGICAL ASSOCIATION

The fact of stress in corporate America is no surprise, but it is sobering to consider all the things there are to be stressed about—overwork, personality conflicts, forced overtime, disorganized supervisors, gossip, harassment, prejudice, poor teamwork, manager abuse and insensitivity, other employees who don't pull their weight, inflexible work hours, illness in the family, child care, elder care, long commutes, the sacrifice of family dinners to stay late—the list goes on. The comments of Saratoga survey respondents are poignant reminders of the frustration and conflict that take their daily toll:

Doing More with Less

"ABC Company does not recognize the employees that work hard on a daily basis and take on extra responsibilities to compensate for the lack of manpower."

"XYZ Company does not employ enough staff. This results in high stress and high turnover of employees."

"They were not proactive in taking care of and keeping good employees. I have watched too many good employees leave ABC Company because they are not appreciated. The motto 'Do more with less' has been taken to the extreme."

"XYZ Company will go long periods of time without filling empty positions. This puts massive amounts of stress on the employees, and product development is stifled."

Abuse/Harassment/Insensitivity

"Does not deal well at all with sexual harassment and freaky, nasty remarks made by other employees."

"Management was the worst I have ever experienced in my fifteen-year nursing career. I had a death in my family, and the time was taken from my vacation time, that was incentive enough to start looking for another job."

"We're not getting paid enough for the type of abuse we take from the customers."

Sacrificing Family and Personal Life

"My number one complaint is that I do not get to spend enough time with my family. I have so much trouble being able to schedule time-off for certain events. All I would want is leave without pay. I will continue to give XYZ Company 110 percent, but I need more time."

"ABC Company does not acknowledge the fact that there is life outside of work."

"I feel that XYZ Company is a workplace for single people. It does not accommodate employees with families in regards to scheduling."

"I think they need to work on scheduling more weekends off."

Inflexibility of Work Hours

"Make working hours more flexible for those going to night school."

"Need to have flex-scheduling—something like any eight hours between 6 am and 10 pm you pick."

"There were not enough chairs for the RNs to sit and do their charts. Despite working on your feet for up to fourteen hours without sitting, we did not get breaks and were told that we didn't get paid for them. I was required to be in the building at lunch but without pay unless I took an urgent phone call. If I needed to leave at lunch, I needed to find a medical doctor willing to take calls and inform the receptionist. If you spoke what was on your mind you were considered a troublemaker."

"Family comes second to ABC Company—mandatory overtime on Saturdays!"

Impact on Customers

"XYZ Company expects employees to increase production while failing to realize that increased production may lead to unsatisfied customers."

"We are so short-staffed that we talk to one customer right after the other with no time in between. Customer service is decimated due to this fact."

"Our manager short-staffed us to the point that it jeopardized patients. She only cares about saving money in her budget."

No Fun

"We used to have Christmas parties and gifts. We never see anything like this anymore. Work should be a little fun, not so stressful."

Inadequate Benefits

"One personal day per year?! Other employers give as many as three."

"Employees should not have to wait five years to get more than two weeks vacation."

"I was very frustrated by ABC Company's health benefits. I was diagnosed with breast cancer—and I feel I have had to fight to get the bills paid."

"When people are sick they should not be penalized for it by receiving an occurrence. In fact, when there is a death in the family you should not be given an occurrence. We are given a certain amount of paid sick days and those should not be held against us in our raises. They are!!!!!!"

"Maternity leave is poor. An employee has to be with the company for a year before receiving any maternity leave."

How Big a Problem Is Stress?

These kinds of comments indicate that stress is indeed a problem in the workforce, but how big a problem is it really? Here are some findings from several surveys:

- Stress at work causes organizations to lose $300 billion a year though absenteeism, accidents, insurance costs, and medical claims.[1]

- 79 percent of respondents said their workload had increased as a result of the troubled economy.[2]

- More than a quarter of workers (27 percent) said their duties had doubled.[3]

- Among all those with extra work tasks, 51 percent said the extra work has had a negative effect on their well-being.[4]

- 77 percent of employees feel they are burned out.[5]

- 43 percent state that their job stress has increased recently.[6]

- 50 percent of adults feel stressed, fatigued, irritable, or angry or lie awake at night because of stress.[7]

- 30 percent of employees have fears of being laid off.[8]

- The 37 percent of workers that was found to be at risk for a sleep disorder experienced more negative work outcomes, and had higher absenteeism rates than the 63 percent that did not.[9]

- Less than 40 percent of employees feel their managers are genuinely interested in their well-being.[10]

- Only one out of ten employees feels that he or she is treated as vital corporate assets.[11]

Causes of Increased Stress

Judging by these survey results, it seems clear that one-quarter to one-half of all workers are feeling some level of dysfunction due to stress, which undoubtedly has a negative impact on their productivity and the probability that they will stay with their employers.

Several factors are contributing to current levels of employee stress: companies are squeezing as much productivity as they possibly can from all workers in a hypercompetitive global economy; companies are downsizing their workforces while not proportionately downsizing the work to be done; employees have continuing worries about job security as they read about downsizings, mergers, and acquisitions; there are heightened levels of free-floating anxiety that have persisted since the 9/11 terrorist attacks; and there is a continuing increase in two-career couples, working single parents, and workers with elder-care responsibilities.

Signs That Your Workers May Be Stressed Out or Overworked

There is a wide range of symptoms to watch for that suggest that employees are overstressed and overworked. Sooner or later, you may notice that workers:

- Consistently work late.
- Work through lunch.
- Work through sickness.
- Seem more fatigued than usual.
- Take work home.
- Rush to meet deadlines.
- Express frustration.
- Don't take vacations.
- Appear increasingly cynical, forgetful, or irritable.
- Try too hard to please a new boss.
- Have relocated from a distant location.
- Have recently experienced a disappointment or failure at work.
- Have experienced a significant family transition or trauma.

While most researchers agree that some workers are more easily stressed than others, most agree that negative working conditions spread the stress among all workers. Many of these conditions have been touched on in previous chapters—mismatch of the individual to the job, lack of worker participation in decisions, feelings of being left out of the loop, frustrations about the lack of career advancement, and unpleasant physical environments, to name a few. Other factors include infrequent rest breaks due to constant work demands, a constant hectic pace, stultifying routine, seemingly senseless tasks, and conflict and resentment among coworkers.

The ultimate question is whether the issue of worker stress is on the radar screens of managers and executives. Certainly it is from a personal perspective—most managers and professionals report feeling overworked, and work significantly longer hours than other employees. But do managers care enough to actually make plans to reduce worker stress as a means of increasing productivity, engagement, and retention? As we shall see, there are many managers who do, and their success stories inspire others to act in new ways.

Healthy versus Toxic Cultures

An organization's culture is a fact of life that must be faced, and many organizations need to face the fact that their cultures are toxic. Toxic cultures are simply unhealthy environments. They often are characterized by the following characteristics and practices:

- Force workers into choosing between having a life and having a career.
- See workers as costs, rather than as assets in which to invest.
- View workers merely as resources, not as people.
- Treat employees as if they are lucky just to have a job.
- Attempt to control employees rather than empower or form partnerships with them.
- Hoard information at top levels of management as means of maintaining power and control.
- Have leaders who are so self-involved or isolated that they are out of touch with employee attitudes and feelings.
- Tolerate infighting and conflict between departments.
- Behave in ways that are inconsistent with the company's professed values or rewarding and tolerating such behavior.
- Tolerate employees who blame others for their own mistakes or seek credit for others' accomplishments and ideas.
- Tolerate employees who lie, cover up the truth, or otherwise behave unethically.
- Constantly change direction, frequently driven by management fads but not committed to a consistent long-range strategy.
- Believe that employees cannot be trusted.

What's Your Organizational Civility Score?

Envisionworks, a Geneva, Illinois, management consulting firm, has created what it calls an Organizational Civility Index that surveys employees on how they treat one another. Questions on the index ask whether employees are reprimanded when they "are rude and disrespectful to other employees" and whether coworkers "shout at each other" or "block each other's success" or "compliment each other's work."

Founder and president Kevin Schmidt says that most of the companies that score poorly are headed by executives who put harsh demands on employees and belittle rather than praise staff. Schmidt says he has never met a monster boss but says he has told executives, "It must be awfully hard to be you because people hate you." When hit with this feedback, some managers break down.[12]

Any litany of toxic corporate behavior would be incomplete, as there are any numbers of ways a toxic organization might manifest a psychologically unhealthy culture. As we know, an organization might have a generally healthy culture but have managers who create toxic subcultures in their departments. Conversely, a manager might have built a healthy culture in a generally toxic organization, although this is less likely and more difficult to achieve.

The growing cost of health care is causing many companies to actually start assessing their "organizational health." A senior executive with Medstat Group, a health-care information management company based in Ann Arbor, Michigan, told the *Wall Street Journal* that corporations now realize their "psychological health" can be a major driver of costs. Their "health and productivity management study" of forty-three large corporations found that, during the height of the talent wars, "turnover-related costs rose to 37 percent of the health and productivity dollar."[13]

More Than Just the Right Thing to Do

Increasingly, companies are realizing that taking care of their employees as people is not just the right thing to do, it's also good for business. In the past decade, an overwhelming body of evidence has accumulated showing a strong connection between treating people right and achieving business profitability.

James Heskett, Earl Sasser, and Leonard Schlesinger, in their book, *The Service-Profit Chain*, persuasively diagrammed the links in the chain that lead from a starting point of internal quality of work life, to employee productivity, loyalty, and satisfaction, to quality customer service, to customer satisfaction, to customer loyalty, ultimately resulting in greater revenues and profits (see Figure 9.1).[14]

In his book, *Treat People Right! How Organizations and Individuals Can Propel Each Other into a Virtuous Spiral of Success*, Edward Lawler presents evi-

Figure 9.1.
Links in the service-profit chain.

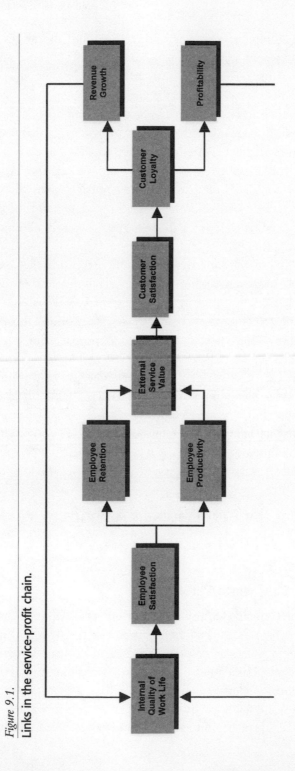

dence that strongly supports the logic of these links, but also makes an astute observation: "At the core of many people's concern about the wisdom of treating people right is the belief that there is an irreconcilable conflict between what is good for the business and what is good for employees."[15]

Some business leaders have been reluctant to embrace the idea that benevolent people-management practices can be a strategic driver of profits. They know that treating people well is a good thing but also believe that nice guys finish last, that the toughest and meanest survive, and that if employees don't like it, they can leave. I once worked at a company where the vice president of manufacturing, when asked if he was stressed, responded, "I don't *get* stress, I *give* stress." For such individuals, caring for people as a business strategy seems weak and softheaded.

There is a fast-growing information systems company that once made *Fortune*'s top-100-employers list but fell off it largely because of its demand that employees work sixty to eighty hours per week. There seems to be no shortage of young professionals who are attracted to working those hours in exchange for rapid advancement and good pay. A woman who worked there told me that, when she told this company she wanted to work part time, the employment representative responded, "A part-time job in this company is forty hours per week." In spite of this, young, talented professionals continue to be drawn to this company, attracted by the fast-track experience. They generally stay a few years and move on. The company has a good product and is profitable. But the question remains—is it building the kind of employment brand that will serve and sustain its business interests over the long term?

How Three of the Best Places in America to Work Do It

Here are profiles of a few companies that have taken a different path.

SAS Institute, Cary, North Carolina

Fortune magazine has named SAS the number one place to work two years in a row and placed it among the best for all thirteen of the years the Great Place to Work Institute has been giving the awards. The company provides high-quality child care at $410 a month, 90 percent coverage of its 5,500 employees' health insurance premiums, unlimited sick days, a medical center staffed by four physicians and ten nurse practitioners (at no cost to employees), a free sixty-six-thousand-square-foot fitness center and natatorium, a lending library, and a summer camp for children. CEO and cofounder Jim Goodnight has built a culture based on "trust between our employees and the company." All the perks have only strengthened SAS's business; the company is highly profitable and ranks as the world's largest privately owned software company. Turnover is the lowest in the industry at just 2 percent.[16]

Nustar Energy, Paulsboro, New Jersey

This company, which turns crude oil into asphalt, provides generous compensation and benefits and prides itself on a collegial environment that focuses on morale. When the house of an employee on medical leave burned down, NuStar immediately sent $3,000 to tide her over.

NuStar's 1,400 employees logged more than seventy-five thousand volunteer hours one year. Health and dental insurance are free. Everybody gets a bonus—or nobody does. There are merit pay and equity grants (of the $13.6 million awarded, $12 million went to employees below the executive level). Employees are intensely focused on efficiency, which helps to explain the fact that there's never been a layoff at NuStar. Executives visit field locations worldwide to strap on aprons and serve barbecue. The company's turnover rate is 2 percent. Chairman Bill Greehey says that he had seen employees treated shabbily early in his career, and he knew the kind of company he didn't want. He once fired a talented senior executive for berating his direct reports. CEO Curt Anastasio believes that the company's 65 percent total return for investors "is a direct result of our employee-focused culture."[17]

Zappos.com, Inc., Las Vegas, Nevada

This extremely successful and fast-growing online shoe retailer, now an Amazon.com subsidiary, has built a legendary culture in a short time. It is best known for offering $3,000 during on-boarding to any employee who may be doubting whether he or she will fit into the quirky, happy culture that is Zappos. Its 3,000 employees enjoy free lunches, free vending machines, and a life coach. After its acquisition by Amazon, CEO Tony Hseih and COO Alfred Lin told employees they would each receive a Kindle and a retention bonus equal to 40 percent of their annual salary. Job applicants at the 24/7 operation are interviewed in a room resembling a talk show set. As part of the company's Wishez Program, one worker's wish for a car was granted when an employee bought a new car and gave him his old vehicle. Zappos creates an annual Culture Book, which is free to anyone who asks for it, that contains the comments of employees who describe why they love working there.[18]

What These Employers Have in Common

What all these employers have in common is a philosophy of "give first, get second." In other words, these preeminent employers believe that if they take the first step in giving a desirable employment experience to its employees, those employees will respond by giving back. Thus begins a virtuous cycle of reciprocal commitment. Employers of choice understand that they are competing with other employers—both large and small—for talent and realize the importance of "branding" themselves as preferred places to work. It's no longer about passively recruiting by selling during job interviews—it's about proactively marketing one's organization as a great place to work.

Contrast this approach with that of employers who start employees on probation, wait to see if the employee is worthy of respect, judge new hires guilty until proven otherwise, and wait for employees to prove their commitment to the organization before demonstrating the organization's commitment to them. This is certainly the traditional approach, but, in a War-for-Talent economy, it can no longer keep your company competitive. The new employers of choice resolve to give before getting back and usually go to extra lengths to select the right people. This makes it so much easier to trust that the employees they hire will return their commitment in kind.

You're Not Competing Just with the "Big Boys"

When Tom Creal started his own company—First Biomedical—he had already given seventeen years of his life to a large company before he was let go in the fifth of five rounds of layoffs. The big-company environment had transmogrified into one where employees were no longer loyal to the company. It was a culture Creal didn't like. So he decided that someday he would operate his own company in a totally different way.

He didn't want to become a father figure, but Creal did want to develop company loyalty among his workers. He decided he would provide:

- Full medical, dental, life, and health insurance for the whole family
- Fifteen vacation and sick days, with carry-over of unused days
- IRAs with 3 percent matching and first-day vesting
- A seven-hour workday

- Free cell phones for employees on call
- Free snacks and Costco cards paid for by the company
- An onsite gym
- An incentive-driven wellness program
- Open sharing of the company's financial situation
- Two percent of employees' annual salaries paid as a bonus any month the company has a record gross-profit
- A year-end bonus of 4 to 5 percent of annual salary
- No job descriptions, with employees having the freedom to move on to different positions

Since opening its doors in 1998, First Biomedical has maintained very low turnover, which Creal believes has significantly increased productivity and revenues.[19]

Whether the company is benefits driven, culture driven, or great-manager driven, the best places to work choose the right employment branding strategy for their business objectives. The branding goal they choose is to be known for having cultures that are both high performance and high caring (see Figure 9.2). High-caring cultures never forget that employees are people, with basic human needs and widely varying family situations. They know that their employees want to have time to live rich lives beyond the bounds of work.

Figure 9.2.

Your culture equals your employment brand

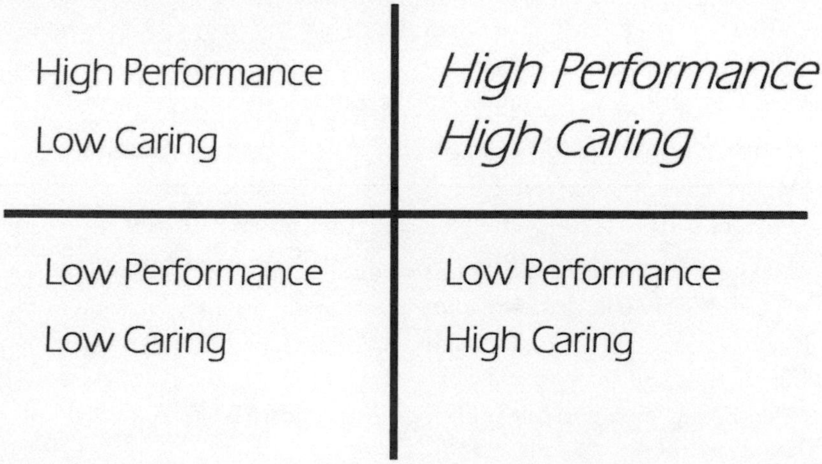

High Performance Low Caring	*High Performance* *High Caring*
Low Performance Low Caring	Low Performance High Caring

Employers of choice also seem to have the following engagement practices in common.

Engagement Practice #47:
Initiate a culture of "giving-before-getting."

Most companies initiate generous work-life and health benefits for their employees out of genuine, warm-hearted caring, but they also realize there will be a return on their investment—that doing so will help them attract, engage, and keep talent. My research and experience tell me that employers who genuinely care about the well-being of their employees generally arouse more commitment from them. That does not mean that taking a more cold and calculating approach based on anticipating the financial ROI of providing generous benefits cannot succeed; I believe it can, especially if the decision to provide those new benefits signals the beginning of a cultural transformation based on a more caring and respectful treatment of the workforce.

In researching the best practices of "destination employers" in the late 1990s for my first book, I was struck by how often the companies identified as employers of choice were led by CEOs with a sincere passion for taking care of their employees as people: Jim Goodnight at SAS Institute, Quint Studer at Baptist Hospital in Pensacola, Herb Kelleher at Southwest Airlines, Hal Rosenbluth at Rosenbluth Travel, and Wilton Connor at Wilton-Connor Packaging Company—to name a few out of a growing number.

What I noticed in all these leaders was their "if-we-build-it-they-will-come" faith in making the first move. What they all seemed to know intuitively was that if they demonstrated an initial willingness to trust their employees by giving valued services, then the vast majority of employees would willingly reciprocate. As astute business executives, they also certainly realized that well-treated employees take better care of customers, but that realization did not seem to be the prime driver of their generosity.

Owners Work Hard to Help Employees Battle Burnout

Working for a company like Spur Communications (formerly D-3, Inc.) a small, Kansas City–based marketing communications firm, sometimes requires long hours, including nights and weekends, to finish projects for big clients like Hallmark and Sprint. For owners David Svet and Mark Schraad, employee burnout was a very big concern. Both had previously worked for marketing firms where creative staffers would get burned out and leave. They were determined not to create the same kind of environment when they started their own firm.

"A steady diet of this schedule dulls your senses and the ability to think outside the box," said Svet. To prevent burnout, the owners established regular working hours of 8:30 A.M. to 5 P.M., and they try hard to enforce that schedule, clearing the office in the evenings if necessary. When client projects call for longer hours, employees are compensated with time off to refresh themselves. Spur employees also go on regular outings to parks and museums to stimulate their creativity and to break the workweek routine. The owners also pay for training conferences around the country and give spot bonuses and twice-yearly salary reviews.

Spur reports very low turnover and high morale. Employees appreciate having the extra hours for their lives away from work. The owners have actually turned away business because they knew it would impose an unhealthy workload on staff.[20]

The question most employers ask is this: What benefits and services can we afford to give that will allow us to attract and keep the talent we need while also reducing our employees' stress at work and allowing them to lead fuller and healthier lives outside of work? With the cost of benefits hovering at around 49 percent of total compensation, most companies look carefully at the cost-benefit equation and carefully consider the needs of their current and desired labor pool according to its demographic makeup.

In its 2011 Annual Benefits Report, the Society for Human Resource Management (SHRM) stated: "Today, organizations are managing ever-increasing costs amidst the uncertainty of the U.S. economy and the complex health care reform law. Given that the benefits allocation in HR budgets is typically fixed, or marginally flexible, it is not surprising that, according to this research, employers continue to remodel their benefits plans to give employees greater responsibility to manage their health care costs, retirement and financial security, and leave."[21]

Noteworthy findings included these:

- The percentage of respondents who reported that their benefits offerings had been negatively affected by the economy increased.
- Health savings accounts (HSA) are becoming more and more prevalent, while HMO plans continue to decline in popularity.

- A greater percentage of companies are offering health-care-premium discounts for employees who have an annual health risk assessment, participate in a weight loss program, participate in a wellness program, and/or do not use tobacco products.

- Employer-sponsored retirement plans continued to shift away from defined-benefit pension plans toward defined-contribution retirement savings plans and Roth 401(k) savings plans.

- Paid time off (PTO) plans continue to gain in popularity.

- Family-friendly benefits remained relatively stable.

- After gradually declining over the previous five years, flextime benefits experienced positive gains.

- There was a sharp dropoff in the number of companies that offered these employee services and benefits: executive club memberships, legal assistance and services, mentoring programs, organization-sponsored sports teams, professional development opportunities, and travel planning services.

- There was a significant decline over the previous five years in the number of companies that offered housing and relocation benefits, including assistance to employees in selling their homes in order to relocate, payments of cost-of-living differentials, down-payment assistance, location-visit assistance, mortgage assistance, rental assistance, spouse-relocation assistance, and temporary relocation benefits.

- Among the benefits and services that had increased significantly since 2007 were mental health coverage, rehabilitation assistance, and coverage for bariatric surgery for weight loss.[22]

To track changing trends in employer benefits and services, including comparison data based on company size, industry, and geographic areas, visit www.shrm.org.

Over the past several years, dozens of companies have conducted internal cost-benefit studies, which tend to link work-life programs to improved employee satisfaction, productivity, and attendance. Highmark, Inc., a twelve-thousand-employee health insurer based in Pittsburgh, conducted its own study of the return on investment (ROI) of its various wellness, preventive, and health-management programs for employees. Over the five-year period of the study, medical claims for the 1,900 employees who participated in Highmark's wellness programs were compared with the claims filed by employees with similar health risks who did not participate. The analysis revealed that the company had saved $1.3 million over the five-year period because annual health care expenses for participating employees were cut by $176 per employee.[23]

First Horizon National Corporation of Memphis, which has been honored for its pioneering work-life programs, found that, since it introduced flexible hours, it had reduced its response time to customer requests at its operations centers from ten days to four days. There were no significant cost savings, but customer satisfaction was increased, and employee retention rates were twice those achieved by offices where managers were less supportive of flextime. The biggest finding was that customer retention rates were 7 percent higher in the offices with flextime.[24] First Horizon has appeared on *Working Mother* magazine's list of the 100 Best Companies for sixteen consecutive years.

The New York–based financial services company Deloitte & Touche estimates that the flexible work arrangements it provides to its thirty thousand U.S. employees helped the company avoid $45 million in annual turnover-related costs.[25] Even during the long-term economic slump, most companies were unwilling to risk eliminating the very programs they have positioned as marquee items in their campaigns to brand themselves as good places to work. Many companies—such as Xerox, Charles Schwab, PriceWaterhouseCoopers, Lucent Technologies, and Sara Lee—kept their work-life programs intact during major layoffs.[26] Many other companies certainly have realized that maintaining benefits and services is even more important when they are asking their employees to work harder because of cutbacks.

Reducing stress and overwork is not all about providing formal benefits and services; it's also about creating an informal culture where executives and managers are thinking about what they can do for their employees at least as much as they are about what those employees can do for the company's customers.

Engagement Practice #48:
Tailor the "culture of giving" to the needs of key talent.

Selecting the kinds of benefits and work-life services to offer workers is not simply a matter of looking at benefit surveys and matching what other employers provide. The fact is that you may not be able to afford the kinds of benefits that other companies in your community provide, and yet you must still compete with them for the available talent. This means you must figure out a way to compete for talent that is more cost-effective; instead of offering onsite child care, for example, you might choose to focus on recruiting, selecting, and training managers so that they will manage people with respect and caring.

The other key to selecting the right benefits and services is matching them to the needs of your applicant pool and your current employees. Consider the case of Financial Associates, a thirty-one-year-old insurance brokerage firm that employs twenty-five people. The owner, Charles Stumpf, is a veteran in the insurance business and understands how competitive it can be. That is why he resolved to treat employees in such a way that they would not want to leave. "I made the conscious decision," he said, "to treat the people around me as family, not employees." So he put several practices into place that he thought would accomplish that end, including keeping records of employees' birthdays and hiring anniversaries and sending them cards on those special occasions, providing treats in the company kitchen, and putting signs on staff's office doors in recognition of their accomplishments.

Stumpf also thought about the fact that several of the women who work at Financial Associates have school-age children and some of them would prefer to work part time. So, he tailored a nontraditional work schedule to accommodate their needs. Working mothers are allowed to arrive a little later in the morning so that they can be home when their children leave for school. Others come in earlier in the morning so that they can get home and be with their children at the end of the school day. Stumpf also worked it out so that employees who wanted part-time work could share one job. He points out that one employee who works three days a week is one of his most productive workers.

When Stumpf made up his mind to move to a new location, he asked his employees what was most important to them in an office location. Their answer was "access to a major interstate highway" and "windows that open." He asked them what features they wanted in a break room and throughout the office, and he put them in place. The new office had a kitchen and access to a patio with a picnic table, a grill, and a telephone jack.

Stumpf also recalled that, early in his own career working for a trucking company, he always worried about whether he would have enough money to take along on a trip, so he gives employees a cash bonus before they go on vacations. He also gives them extra days off around the holidays.

As you might imagine, employee turnover is not an issue at Financial Associates. Stumpf knows he has saved time and money by maintaining a stable workforce. "When you have to hire, and retrain people, you know they won't know their jobs for a year, and that's time lost," he said. "By treating your people so they want to stay, you don't have to go through that cycle."[27]

Know Your Workforce!

The key is understanding the needs of the workforce. One of the best-known examples of this is SAS Institute, Inc. (briefly profiled earlier in this chapter), which CEO Jim Goodnight has built into one of the most successful software companies in the world by giving the right things to the right people. Goodnight knew that every other major software company gave stock options to its employees, yet he chose not to offer them. He knew that most other software companies offered extraordinary salaries, yet he decided to offer salaries that were merely competitive. Goodnight also knew that the work pace and style in most software companies was crazy and frenetic, so he deliberately set out to create a sane and relaxed campus environment.

What Goodnight understood was that there were hundreds of talented software professionals who were interested in a sane working environment and some semblance of balance between life and work. So that is what he created—a workplace with a generous variety of jaw-dropping attractions, not just because he wanted to be generous but as a strategic business decision. The company's environment is anything but lax—the work culture is built on accountability and results.

By its own calculations, SAS saves $67 million per year in avoided turnover costs because it maintains a 3 percent turnover rate in an industry that averages 20 percent turnover. This means the company can afford to keep adding new benefits, which it does on a regular basis. The strategy is working. SAS Institute has carved out a niche—a distinctive employment brand—by creating a work environment unlike any other in its industry. In so doing, the company has become a magnet for talent, especially Millennials and Gen Xers, who value a saner, more balanced life and tell stories of turning down higher salaries to come to work for SAS.[28]

Whether your company surveys the workforce yearly, as SAS does, or simply asks employees face to face, the key is to ask. Smart companies design their benefits, perks, employee services, rewards, cultures, and management practices to attract and keep the specific desires of the talent segments they need to meet their business objectives. In other words, they align their human capital strategies with their business strategies. In scanning *Fortune*'s profiles of the 100 Best Companies in America to work for, one is struck by the way so many top employers appear to have matched the right offerings to the right talent:

- Construction company *TD Industries* of Dallas offers upward mobility and respect to construction workers by calling them "partners" and offering 100 percent tuition reimbursement.

- *W. L. Gore*, inventor of Gore-Tex fabric and Elixir guitar strings, is a company built on innovation, so it offers the kind of work environment in which independent, creative people thrive. Workers get to choose their projects, and the process for selecting leaders is highly unstructured—most leaders are not appointed but rather emerge simply because other workers seem to follow their lead.

- *Starbucks* knows that many of the younger workers it needs to attract will work only part time but would not get health coverage for part-time jobs with other retailers. So, they offer health coverage to all workers who put in twenty hours a week and give stock options to those who stay for a year.

- *Boston Consulting Group* knows it needs to guard against consultants getting burned out. As a result, it instituted a practice whereby, when managers or colleagues notice someone working more than sixty hours a week and approaching burnout ("in the red zone," as they call it), a career mentor intervenes and typically encourages the individual to take some time off. They then do all they can to make sure their colleague's work gets done while the employee is away.

- Wireless tech supplier *Qualcomm* has employees in more than one hundred countries, so it offers a flexible holiday policy that allows their workers use ten company-approved days to suit their needs.

In all these examples, the common thread is the matching of what is given with what is valued and a faith that, if it is given, employees will give back.[29]

Engagement Practice #49:
Build a culture that values spontaneous acts of caring.

So far in this chapter, we have focused on benefits and aspects of culture that are within the power of business owners and chief executives to decide. But great employers are also characterized by managers who are empowered to act with spontaneous acts of generosity and caring. Here are some examples of how individual managers have helped relieve employee stress and have generated greater loyalty in return:

- Letting the team go out for a long lunch at the manager's expense on the condition that they not talk about work
- Sending cards, free movie tickets, or restaurant gift certificates to the homes of employees who have worked long hours to complete a project
- Bringing meals to the homes of workers who are grieving the death of a family member
- Providing a sympathetic ear when employees are going through divorces or child-custody problems
- Creating a Thursday ritual—free pizza in the office
- Giving an employee the rest of the day off after a particularly stressful morning
- Allowing employees to work from home when it isn't essential that they be at the workplace
- Pitching in to help with the workload on especially busy days
- Taking a break from communicating by e-mail, by having real face-to-face conversations with employees instead and concentrating on listening with genuine interest
- Offering a sincere apology for any past insensitive remarks or behavior

The point here is not to provide a prescriptive list of things to do but to describe the kinds of things managers do when they are being spontaneously sensitive to the needs of workers. Employees can tell when managers are going through the motions and when they are acting sincerely in the moment. As with so many other practices already covered in this book, the first requirement is to pay attention to the people you manage.

 Engagement Practice #50:
Build social connectedness among coworkers.

There is little doubt that a big part of the glue that binds people to workplaces comes from the relationships they form with other employees. I have heard employees say to coworkers, "You people are what's keeping me here," even as things are going from bad to worse in the other aspects of their work lives. Human beings have a basic need for belonging, as Abraham Maslow pointed out, and more employees look to the relationships they form at work as a source of the "family feeling" that might otherwise be missing.

We live in an increasingly transient society where workers stay in their jobs less than three years on average, and yet workers long for connection with coworkers. Most of us spend at least one-third of our workdays communicating by e-mail—time that in years past we spent in direct human contact. Many people now work from home or from remote locations and feel isolated from coworkers and alienated from their organizations. In toxic workplaces, employees often experience anxiety, distrust, unspoken conflict, petty jealousy, departmental infighting, incivility, and outright nastiness— conditions that make teamwork almost impossible.

What can a manager do about all this? Perhaps it is easier to start with what a manager cannot do—change the culture or suppress all conflict. Conflict, if openly and constructively expressed, can actually have positive consequences, leading to higher levels of trust and quicker, more open resolution of disagreements. Managers cannot expect employees to always get along, nor should they view themselves as referees in every personal dispute. Although manager interventions may sometimes be required, employees need to be able to resolve their own conflicts whenever possible.

Reducing Turnover Through Social Bonding

RiverPoint Group, a seventy-employee information technology group owned by Jon Schram and his wife, Jill Washington Schram, faced the challenge of a 60 percent turnover rate, made worse by the fact that most of its employees work offsite. The Schrams wanted to create a stronger common culture that would make employees feel more bonded to one another and to the organization. Among other initiatives, they created an associate management program, in which senior-level employees mentor their junior counterparts. Mentors and mentees talk several times a month by telephone and face to face at least monthly. Account managers are required to be on job sites once a week to ensure "face time" with associates. When employees start new projects, they are greeted with bagels from the owners and a cake on their birthdays. The owners also schedule quarterly staff meetings and social outings every three months so that employees can get better acquainted. Everyone stays connected through a corporate Web site.

Result: RiverPoint's turnover rate has fallen to 25 percent, well below the industry average. This has been critical to the retention of important clients.[30]

What managers can do is work to actively encourage harmony and social connectedness among workers. Here are some of the ways managers can help bind employees together in a positive way:

- Allow employees a reasonable amount of time to meet in the halls or at the water cooler to have personal conversations. Try not to always look at such gatherings as a drag on productivity but, rather, see them as time spent building connectedness among staff.

- Assign teams to work on projects together when possible, especially when there is an opportunity to bring together workers who have not worked together before.

- Create cross-functional teams, mixing staff from your department with employees from other areas or functions.

- Create a social networking site (like an internal facebook) that enables employees with similar interests to connect, chat, blog, and build relationships.

- Invite people from other departments to your staff meetings.

- Take the initiative to organize group outings such as picnics, softball games, offsite work sessions, group volunteer work, holiday parties, birthday parties, lunchtime card games, trips to sporting events, regular breakfasts or pot-luck lunches together, or informal meetings on Friday afternoons to review the week.

- Encourage several employees to join professional associations and attend meetings together.

- Ask employees to get up and go speak to one another more often or to take each other to lunch more frequently instead of depending on e-mails as their primary mode of communication.

- When an employee seems bogged down trying to solve a difficult problem, bring together several coworkers to brainstorm new ideas and possible solutions.

- Encourage the formation of employee interest groups, such as investment clubs, book clubs, informal parenting discussions, or travel discussions where employees can share photos from recent vacations.

- Get to know all your employees on a personal basis so that you will know enough to link those with common interests or to refer one employee to another who can help with a practical everyday issue, such as finding a good real estate agent.

- At staff meetings, ask members of the team to introduce themselves by mentioning one fact about themselves that most people would not know.

- As often as possible, bring onsite workers together with those who work from home or remote locations.

Research shows that employees who have good relationships with their coworkers are also more committed to the organization than workers whose relationships with coworkers are poor.[31] There may be times when those relationships are in need of repair, and you may require the services of a consultant who specializes in conflict resolution or team building. In the meantime, keep an eye out for creative ways to build the ties that bind among coworkers.

Engagement Practice # 51: Encourage fun in the workplace.

"Work should be more fun than fun," said the playwright Noel Coward, a statement that conjures images of the seven dwarfs marching off to the mines singing "hi-ho, hi-ho." Alas, for far too many employees today, the work itself is not fun, and the work environment is even less so.

Generation Xers noticed as children that many of their parents weren't having much fun working long hours and were neglecting their families in the process. Many of them made up their minds early on that, when they entered the world of work, they were going to make it more fun and less formal. In the late 1990s, when the War for Talent was most intense, Silicon Valley companies worked hard to create more fun for younger workers—putting in game rooms with foosball and pinball, throwing keg parties on Friday afternoons, creating quiet rooms with recliners for napping, and providing inflatable "stress-relief" punching dummies.

After the dot-com bust in 2000, many companies curtailed the "frivolity." Between 2001 and 2003, and again during recent years, the American workplace reached unprecedented levels of productivity, but at a price: People weren't having any fun. During these times, some companies felt that it was even more important to reinject some fun into the workplace to relieve the stress from overloaded work schedules.

Not everyone has the same ideas about what is fun, but most of us recognize that whether it is planned or spontaneous, fun activities and celebrations can be highly effective stress busters. In fact, the more stressful the workplace and the more employees are vulnerable to burnout, the more need there is for fun and celebration. Studies have actually shown that workplaces with higher "fun quotients" have lower health-care costs, higher productivity, and improved morale.

Here are some companies that have woven fun into their cultures:[32]

- At *ELetter*, a direct-mail company in San Jose, California, the CEO pledged that he would wear high heels to the office every day for a week if they met his ambitious sales goals. They did, and he did.

- To build teamwork and keep his executive team sharp, the CEO of *Demandline.com* of San Francisco told all five of them to meet at the airport with cold-weather gear for a five-day trip to an undisclosed location. They flew to Alaska, where they were met by two guides with ice axes and seventy-pound backpacks. They then proceeded to climb Matanuska Peak.

- During tax season at *Plante & Moran*, the accounting firm hands out "survival kits" with aspirin, stress balls, and candy, and each office throws an "end-of-tax season" bash.

- *Valassis,* of Livonia, Michigan, publisher of newspaper coupons and inserts, holds limerick contests and sponsors tail-gating parties at college football games.

- At *Simmons,* the Atlanta mattress manufacturer, employees break the stress by going on ropes-course training once a year. They even get to walk a high wire.

- *Republic Bancorp* of Owosso, Michigan, holds an annual Easter egg hunt.

- *Dreamworks Animation SKG* offers movie screenings, afternoon yoga, on-campus art classes, and monthly parties.

- *Third Federal Savings and Loan* of Cleveland threw a company-wide Mardi Gras party breakfast with Polish doughnuts, magicians, and caricaturists.

- Wireless pioneer *Qualcomm* sponsors staff baseball games, surfing lessons, kayaking tours, bonfires, and bowling.

- At *Network Appliance,* in Sunnyvale, California, a sign welcomes visitors to "Galactic Headquarters." At a company rally to kick off a new sales campaign, there were life-size cutouts of executives on the stage in Star Trek costumes.

- The auto lending company *AmeriCredit,* in Fort Worth, sent each of its branches a "fiesta in a box" with piñata and salsa music to celebrate reaching $15 million in loans.

- At *LensCrafters* in Cincinnati, managers and executives wore white gloves, bow ties, and top hats to welcome employees to the company party. They also opened their doors and parked their cars.

- At *Kimberly-Clark* in Dallas, one unit staged its own version of *Survivor.*

- At *Griffin Hospital,* in Derby, Connecticut, musicians and clowns entertain patients and staff, and, with each new birth, the Brahms *Lullaby* is played on the sound system.[33]

- *Capital One* provides each employee a quarterly "fun budget" to spend on such activities as white-water rafting.

- *CDW Computer Centers* gives employees free Krispy Kreme doughnuts once a month and free Dairy Queen every Wednesday in the summer. If the company meets sales goals, CDW offers an "old-timers" benefit to anyone with three years of service: a free trip for the employee and family anywhere in the continental United States (awarded every other year).

- *Southwest Airlines* organizes spirit parties, cake-decorating contests, barbecues, and chili cook-offs—all planned by local "culture committees."

- *Snapple* has "theme Fridays"—tie-dye day, silly-hat day. One year, it built a makeshift miniature golf course inside corporate headquarters.[34]

While most of these examples are planned, some of the best stress reducers are unplanned, such as sharing a cartoon with a coworker, deciding to rent a comedy video to watch over a lunch hour, having an impromptu contest to see who can cheer up the grumpiest person in the office, or buying a beverage on Friday evening for the person with the toughest experience with a customer.

It's worth remembering that not all stress can be relieved by a few moments of fun. More serious and concerted approaches are required to relieve the root source of stress—an individual struggling to perform a job for which she is not suited, a bullying manager taking out frustrations from a dysfunctional home life on his employees, or a management team that has simply pushed its workforce to the brink of burnout and exhaustion. All the fun committees in the world cannot remedy these kinds of problems.

Ultimately, it takes a balanced approach that combines both serious resolve and spontaneous fun that spells relief for the kinds of stress that are endemic in today's workplaces.

What the Employee Can Do to Relieve Stress and Overwork

Many employers have sponsored stress-management training for their employees in recent years, with most getting high marks from those who attend. But, because so much of a person's stress is self-imposed, employees must begin to take charge of managing their own stress levels.

Here are a few stress-busters that managers can encourage their employees to start doing or, to set the example, start doing themselves:

- Understand the basic truth that each of us has the freedom to choose how we respond to stressful events. Train yourself to become more conscious of and accountable for making those choices.

- Eat breakfast daily, drink less coffee and fewer caffeinated soft drinks, and start eating more healthy foods—if you're overweight, in smaller portions.

- Organize the work to be done the day before. Sort your in-basket according to priority, and work on high-priority items first.

- Establish set times in the day to review e-mail and voice mail.

- Let go of the need for perfection. Very few things really have to be done perfectly.

- Take all the vacation you have coming. Reserve those days on your calendar as far in advance as possible.

- Don't try to do two or three things at the same time. Chronic multitasking takes a toll.

- Don't bring work home with you every night. Instead, stay later or go in earlier occasionally.

- Let voice mail answer when you are extra busy and don't need the distraction. As someone said, "Just because someone throws you the ball doesn't mean you have to catch it."

- Block out your calendar ahead of time to make sure you will have the uninterrupted time you need to finish a large project or to complete several smaller tasks.

- If you are annoyed or angry, speak up in a diplomatic way. If you "gunnysack" your frustrations, they will fester and increase your stress levels until they come out in inappropriate ways.

- Don't hesitate to ask coworkers for help when you are trying to handle peak workloads.

- Take breaks to clear your mind and relax for a few minutes at a time. Go outside for fresh air if you can.

- Take lunch out of the office whenever you can, or just go for a lunchtime walk.

- Delegate more.

- Create a morning ritual—either quiet meditation or reading time—that can help set the tone for the entire day.

- Block out your calendar days before it starts to fill up to ensure that you will have the time you need between appointments or to work on important projects uninterrupted.

- Take a two-day getaway break to do what restores and energizes you—and not just on the weekends.

- Exercise every day, if possible.

- Don't be afraid to ask for flextime, part-time work, job sharing, or other family-friendly conditions if they can help to make your life less complicated and stressful.

- Seek sources of gratification other than your job—pursue a new hobby (or an old one), spend more time with friends and family, take more vacation days, travel more often, treat yourself to a massage, go for a drive to no place in particular—whatever works to give you more balance.

- If you are in the wrong job or are working for a manager who cranks up your stress levels, create a plan to change your situation, and start working on it today.

- Get enough sleep.

Engagement Practices Checklist: Overwork and Work-Life Imbalance

Review the engagement practices presented in this chapter, and check the ones you believe your organization needs to implement or improve.

To reduce stress from work-life imbalance and overwork:

Engagement Practice #47. __ Initiate a culture of "giving-before-getting."

Engagement Practice #48. __ Tailor the "culture of giving" to the needs of key talent.

Engagement Practice #49. __ Build a culture that values spontaneous acts of caring.

Engagement Practice #50. __ Build social connectedness and harmony among employees.

Engagement Practice #51. __ Encourage fun in the workplace.

Your next step: *Resolve to take action on the ones you believe are most critical and appropriate for your situation and objectives.*

Notes

1. Workplace Options survey of six hundred American workers, July 2011, http://www.workplaceoptions.com/news-top-stories.asp.
2. *Miami Sun-Sentinel,* September 11, 2011, citing Right Management survey, http://articles.sun-sentinel.com/2011-09-11/health /fl-job-stress-impact-20110911_1_workplace-stress-new-job-workers.
3. Workplace Options survey, op. cit.
4. Ibid.
5. CareerBuilder survey, December 17, 2009, http://www.careerbuilder.com /Article/CB-655-The-Workplace-5-Signs-of-Job-Burnout-and-What-to-Do-About-It/.
6. Ibid.
7. American Psychological Association, "2011 Stress in America" survey, released January 11, 2011, http://www.apa.org/news/press/releases/stress/index.aspx.
8. "In U.S., Worries About Job Cutbacks Return to Record High," *Gallup Management Journal,* August 31, 2011, www.gallup.com/poll/149261 /Worries-Job-Cutbacks-Return.
9. "Sleep, Performance and the Workplace," National Sleep Foundation "Sleep in America" poll, 2008, http://www.sleepfoundation.org/article /sleep-america-polls/2008-sleep-performance-and-the-workplace.
10. Tony Schwartz et al., *The Way We Work Isn't Working* (New York: Free Press, 2010).

11. Ibid.

12. Carol Hymowitz, "Bosses Need to Learn Whether They Inspire, or Just Drive, Staffers," *Wall Street Journal,* February 18, 1999.

13. Cited in "Business Briefs," *Wall Street Journal,* April 6, 2000.

14. James L. Heskett, W. Earl Sasser Jr., and Leonard A. Schlesinger, *The Service-Profit Chain: How Leading Companies Link Profit and Growth to Loyalty, Satisfaction, and Value* (New York: Free Press, 1997).

15. Edward E. Lawler III, *Treat People Right! How Organizations and Individuals Can Propel Each Other into a Virtuous Spiral of Success* (San Francisco: Jossey-Bass, 2003).

16. Milton Moskowitz, Robert Levering, and Christopher Tkaczyk, "100 Best Companies: The List," *Fortune,* January, 2011.

17. David A. Kaplan, "Undercover Employee: A Day on the Job at Three Best Companies," *Fortune,* February 7, 2011.

18. Kathy Gurchiek, "Delivering HR at Zappos," *HR,* June 2011.

19. Ruth Baum Bigus, "At This Company, It's All About Benefits," *Kansas City Star,* April 20, 2004.

20. "Marketing Firm Tackles Nagging Issue of Burnout," *Kansas City Star,* August 28, 2001.

21. Society for Human Resource Management Annual Benefits Report, June 25, 2011, http://www.shrm.org/Research/SurveyFindings/Articles/Pages/2011EmployeeBenefitsSurveyFindings.aspx.

22. Ibid.

23. Susan J. Wells, "Finding Wellness's Return on Investment," *HR,* June 2008.

24. Carol Kleiman, "Companies Assess Value of Work-Life Programs," *Omaha World-Herald,* June 24, 2001.

25. Henry G. Jackson, "Flexible Workplaces: The Next Imperative," *HR,* and Society for Human Resource Management Online, March 1, 2011, http://www.shrm.org/about/pressroom/PressReleases/Pages/GuidetoBoldNewIdeas.aspx.

26. Sue Shellenberger, "This Time, Firms See Work-Life Plans as Aid During the Downturn," *Wall Street Journal,* March 29, 2001.

27. Ruth Baum Bigus, "Firm's Policies Are Aimed at Retaining Workers," *Kansas City Star,* May 15, 2001.

28. Charles Fishman, "Sanity Inc.," *Fast Company*, January 1999.

29. "100 Best Companies in America to Work For," *Fortune,* January 23, 2006; January 22, 2007; February 8, 2010; February 7, 2011.

30. Ruth Baum Bigus, "Creating Bonds Between Far-Flung Workers," *Kansas City Star,* July 17, 2001.

31. Ibid.

32. Matthew Boyle, "Beware the Killjoy," *Fortune,* July 23, 2001.

33. Ibid.

34. Ibid.

CHAPTER TEN

Reason #7: Loss of Trust and Confidence in Senior Leaders

> Business begins with trust. . . . As companies abandon
> bureaucratic mechanisms, their leaders need to
> understand that trust is as important to management
> as it is to relationships with customers.
>
> —WARREN BENNIS

Having reviewed so many issues and practices that lie mostly within the sphere of managers to control or influence, we now consider the special challenge facing senior leaders—to create a culture of trust and integrity that strengthens the bonds of employee engagement. While this challenge is shared by all managers and every employee, it is incumbent on senior leaders to set the tone and the example.

The consulting firm Towers-Watson, which evaluates a company's employment brand by its share performance, reported that companies with high trust levels outperform companies with low trust levels by 186 percent.[1] Towers-Watson's *Global Workforce Study* of 4 million workers, released in 2010, asked respondents to name the five characteristics they desired in senior leaders. The most-desired trait by far was "trustworthiness" (followed by "cares about others' well-being," "encourages development of talent," "highly visible to employees," and "manages financial performance successfully"). However, when asked whether they agree that their companies' leaders are trustworthy, only 47 percent of American respondents agreed. Certainly the economy has played a role in dimming employees' view of senior leaders.[2]

If the bonds of trust between employees and senior leaders are weak, even the best efforts of gifted middle managers will not be enough to attract, engage, and keep the people needed for the business to achieve its goals. The direct managers themselves are less likely to be effective at engaging employees when they don't trust their leaders, as well.

Here are the comments from Saratoga's surveys that reveal the issues that workers find most troubling about senior leaders in their organizations:

Basic Lack of Trust and Integrity

"No follow-up from upper management: Do what you say you'll do and don't make promises you can't keep."

"The company asks lower-level employees to participate in community service while upper management never does it themselves."

"Trust is nonexistent within the company. You cannot believe anything that management says. They withhold information from employees."

"Weak, unapproachable HR department. Most of the staff thinks they are a joke. Nothing is ever kept in confidence. They have betrayed confidence before and the word has gotten out."

Isolated and Out of Touch with Day-to-Day Reality

"I don't think that upper management truly hears the voices and opinions of the staff. They are definitely not visible. Sometimes the human factor is forgotten, at least with the production staff."

"Take ideas from field teams who are a great deal closer to customers and know what's going on."

"I don't feel upper management really knows what is going on in the lower levels when things start getting bad."

"Upper management is ignorant of our day-to-day processes."

Greed and Self-Interest

"Top management is nothing but greed personified."

"High-powered managers were typically uninterested in anyone but themselves."

"Very poor support of employee morale. They are more worried about making money than anything."

"Post-merger management is too focused on protecting their own jobs that they have ceased being both advocates for the employees and the supervisors."

Lack of Concern and Appreciation for Workers

"Upper management tends not to take employees' needs into consideration when deciding changes. They also convey the attitude that if employees don't like what is going on, they can just look elsewhere for employment."

"Upper management doesn't even know that we are here."

"Upper management comes into our departments and doesn't even speak to us 'unknown' employees."

Lack of Trust and Respect for Workers

"Upper management has no respect for the people that do the work. They do not recognize their good employees. ABC Company management is all about the bottom line."

"XYZ Company has a vicious, cavalier attitude toward its employees that makes it hard for employees to feel important and valued. I felt constantly watched and threatened."

"Upper management are clearly the ones running the show. No one is allowed to make any decisions except for the upper management."

"They treat their employees like garbage. They use them up and then throw them out."

Isolated and Unapproachable

"Completely and utterly unknown, unseen, uncaring, unconcerned, and unapproachable upper management."

"Management needs more individual concern for each employee. They need to be able to talk with each employee and not judge through the eyes of another employee. Get to know the individual yourself!"

"Upper management never takes the time to communicate with the employees, to say 'hello.'"

Mismanagement of Change

"Provide consistent direction. In the past eight years, ABC Company has made too many management and corporate philosophy changes. Employees have whiplash!"

"XYZ Company doesn't initiate change well. They make drastic changes too quickly and do not properly prepare employees to adjust to the changes. But they never tell us why the change is happening."

"Stay with a plan long enough to see if it works before moving on to the next one."

Poor Communication

"ABC Company doesn't inform employees about decisions that would directly affect them. For the most part, most of the relocation decisions are not relayed to the departments that they affect. The company keeps too many secrets from employees."

"Upper management has a clear and direct set of objectives, but that message doesn't seem to filter down to the 'worker bees' that are the most important element of the upper management vision."

"XYZ Company doesn't communicate changes to the masses. Employees normally have to read about it in the newspaper."

A Crisis of Trust and Confidence

If these comments reflect the way departing employees feel about senior leaders, we can only wonder how the employees who stayed must feel. If we are to believe Gallup's surveys reporting that about 75 percent of the American workforce is disengaged, then we can only conclude that the lack of engaging leadership is a major root cause.

The corporate scandals that began and ended the first decade of this century only served to deepen the hole of distrust that had already been dug by the downsizings of the 1990s. Recent surveys of the American workforce provide ample evidence:

- Only 38 percent agreed that senior leaders have a sincere interest in employee satisfaction and well-being.[3]
- Only 12 percent said their leaders are extremely effective at meeting business goals.[4]
- Only 7 percent believe their leaders are extremely effective at retaining talent.[5]
- 82 percent believe executives help themselves at the expense of their companies.[6]
- Just 14 percent of respondents said they believe that their company's leaders are ethical and honest.[7]
- Only 12 percent believe their employer genuinely listens to and cares about its employees.[8]

- Just 10 percent of employees said they trust management to make the right decision in times of uncertainty.[9]

- Only 7 percent said that senior management's actions are consistent with their words.[10]

- Nearly three-quarters (72 percent) of workers say they trust their managers, whereas just about half (52 percent) express trust in their organization's top leaders.[11]

All these data point to not just a corrosion of trust but a crisis of confidence in the ability of senior leaders to lead their organizations to success—a basic requirement for engaging and retaining talented workers.

Reading the Signs of Distrust and Doubt

Watch for these signs in your company of growing distrust, cynicism, or loss of confidence in senior leaders:

- Lack of enthusiasm following announcement of new initiatives by senior leaders
- Increasing complaints and questions by employees about policies and practices controlled by senior leaders
- Questioning by middle managers of decisions and actions of senior leaders
- Increased grumblings among groups of employees
- Morale problems showing up in employee surveys
- Increased mention of senior leaders in exit interviews or surveys
- Active resistance to leader initiatives and change efforts

The Three Questions That Employees Need Answered

In reviewing survey comments, we find that workers have three fundamental questions on their minds when it comes to senior leaders:

1. *Will these leaders steer the ship to success?* Employees want to know whether their leaders have the right vision, the right strategy, the right people, and the personal character and competence to lead the organization where it

needs to go. For some companies, this can mean turning the company around to reverse its declining fortunes, while for others it means building on previous success to take the company to new heights. Regardless of the situation, talented employees want to know whether they have hitched their wagon to a star that is burning brighter or burning out.

2. *Can I trust them to do what they say?* No one wants to work for an organization where leaders are always saying one thing and doing another. This question gets right to the heart of organizational integrity and is directed as much toward direct supervisors as it is to senior leaders. Even if senior executives back up their words with action, if their actions don't reinforce the organization's professed values, trust is lost.

3. *Do they have trust and confidence in me?* Understandably, we all tend to trust and have confidence in those who have trust and confidence in us. The issue of who initiates the building of trust—employer or employee—can be debated, or you can say it doesn't matter. It seems clear, however, that senior leaders are in enough need of employee commitment that they should be willing, even eager, to initiate the reciprocal commitment process.

Criteria for Evaluating Whether to Trust and Have Confidence

As I conduct post-exit interviews, former employees increasingly mention disappointment with senior leaders among their primary reasons for leaving. As consumers of a future work experience with a potential employer, job seekers seem particularly interested in checking out the reputation of senior leaders before accepting an offer. Because they have been sensitized by the spectacle of corporate CEOs betraying the trust of their constituents on a large scale, employees now view their leaders through different lenses. Here are three criteria by which employees now judge senior leaders:

1. *Servant mentality versus selfish greed.* As we have seen in the survey comments, employees suspect that leaders have mainly their own interests in mind as they go about their daily business. Many workers see business leaders as interested mainly in maximizing their stock options and building their personal wealth, not in pursuing what's best for the long-term interests of shareholders, customers, and employees. As evidence supporting this belief, they cite

the disproportionate rise in executive compensation. Between 1983 and 2001, the ratio of average CEO pay to average worker pay rose from 42 to 1 to 342 to 1.[12]

Yet, there are also plenty of leaders who see their calling to leadership as one in which they will serve those they are called to lead. They do all they can to serve the needs of employees so that the employees, in turn, will better serve the customer. Such leaders are interested in building an organization that serves the business community, makes lives better, and makes a profit, not in exploiting others for personal gain. These "servant leaders" (see Robert Greenleaf's classic book, *Servant Leadership*) are striking a chord that resonates among today's workers.

2.   *Shareholder value versus employee value.* Employees have heard the mantra about maximizing shareholder value for so long and seen so many corporate mission statements that speak almost exclusively about it their eyes have glazed over. When employees hear and read this, they get the message that the CEO's only real responsibility is to serve the interests of the shareholders. Who are these shareholders? They are mostly anonymous mutual fund managers and day traders who never get to know the company or its products or services, employees, or customers. Shareholders' interests are important, certainly, but employees know when they are being given short shrift.

Contrast this obsession with shareholders with the attitude of CEOs like Jim Sinegal, the master merchandiser and retailing hall-of-famer who retired in early 2012 after spending twenty-eight years building Costco into the largest U.S. retailer of its type. In an interview with the *Wall Street Journal*, he was asked about Wall Street's perception that Costco puts a higher priority on meeting the expectations of employees and customers than on meeting those of shareholders. Sinegal's response: "That's not the case. We want to obey the law, take care of our customers, take care of our people, and respect our suppliers. And we think, if we do those four things pretty much in that order, that we're going to reward shareholders." Sinegal's philosophy of giving customers a break on prices was also questioned. He was asked whether it was worth it to take a hit on profits. His reply: "There are all sorts of opportunities where you can try to sneak in a little more margin here and a little more profitability there, but that's not what we're about. When you start suggesting that it's not important to save the customer money on this because they'll never know the difference, you start to fool yourself. The customer trusts us. You don't want to give up on that type of reputation."[13] Once, when speaking to Wall Street analysts about the way he ran Costco, he said: "Wall Street is in the business of making money between now and next Tuesday. We're in the business of building an organization, an institution, that we hope will be here fifty years from now." [14]

In the business press, we read more and more reports about CEOs with similar employee-first attitudes and approaches. Interestingly, most of their companies seem to be building strong reputations for excellent customer service provided by committed front-line employees.

3. *Lean and mean versus nice workers giving great service.* With the great recession of 2008–2009, "lean and mean" came back in style as businesses looked for new ways to cut costs. Companies cut to the bone, laying off thousands of workers. Many of these downsizing companies gave little thought to how they might redeploy or retrain these workers before cutting them loose. Remaining workers felt lucky to still have their jobs but quickly realized they were doing the jobs of two or three people. Before long, employees (and managers) were starting to feel abused and burned out—not exactly the best formula for putting them in the mood to provide world-class customer service.

As Sam Walton, the founder of Wal-Mart, said years ago, "It takes a week to two weeks for employees to start treating customers the same way the employer is treating the employee."

Smart CEOs intuitively know what Sam Walton knew. One of those CEOs is David Neeleman, CEO of the Brazilian airline Azul. Neeleman, a serial entrepreneur, launched Azul in 2008 after leaving Jet Blue Airways, which he had founded in 1999 and led to twelve consecutive quarters of profitability and the highest percentage of seats filled of any other airline.

The story of how Neeleman achieved such dramatic growth at Jet Blue is worth recalling here. From the start, Neeleman was committed to running lean but not mean. To reduce costs, Jet Blue's reservations agents worked from home instead of working from an expensive call center. Yet, Neeleman knew many of his six thousand employees by name, asked about their personal lives, pitched in to pass out snacks when he flew, and stayed behind to help clean the plane. Neeleman was obsessed with reliability and customer service but said the real secret weapon was the crew. Whenever Neeleman and his senior executives considered making a major change, they would first ask, "How will this affect crew members' morale?" If they concluded it would hurt morale, they would elect not to make the change because it would not be worth it—"employees treat customers the way they are treated themselves," he said.

When a company survey revealed that one-third of the crew members were unhappy with the abrasiveness and favoritism of their supervisors, Neeleman and his COO realized that they were promoting people without teaching them how to manage. That's when Neeleman decided to create a five-day training program called "Principles of Leadership," taught by senior executives. One of the five key principles of the program: "Treat your people right."

Neeleman's decision to make an upfront commitment to his employees was returned in kind. Said one of his pilots, "I would walk through a burning building for him."[15]

How many "lean and mean" companies have created this kind of loyalty? Mean leaders make for mean employees who are often mean to customers. It is a formula that is destined to fail in the long term.

> "Companies which, perversely, don't put shareholders first, do better for their shareholders than organizations that only put shareholders first."
>
> —ROBERT WATERMAN, *THE FRONTIERS OF EXCELLENCE*

Engagement Practice #52:
Inspire confidence in a clear vision, a workable plan, and the competence to achieve it.

One of the first requirements of trust is competence. We will follow only those leaders we judge to be capable. Traditionally, leaders were selected from among the most skilled functional specialists, but that is certainly not the case today. Leaders have to be more like orchestra conductors, blending the efforts of the most skilled performers.

So what kind of competence do employees expect from leaders today? At the most basic level, they simply want to know that the organization will be successful, ensuring that they will have a job and a future. Because so many businesses fail, this is unfortunately a promise that many employers cannot deliver. So, as a prerequisite for becoming a first-class employer, the leader must inspire the confidence of workers that the company will be successful going forward.

It is natural that we look to the leaders for this assurance. We want our leaders to have a clear and achievable vision, confidence in their capacity to achieve the vision, the ability to inspire and mobilize followers to achieve the vision, the ability to transform the vision into a workable strategy and plan, the right team of people in place to carry it out, and the ability to follow through with persistence to achieve the plan. And, while they are at it, we require complete honesty and integrity, and, yes, please show us you care about us as individuals. This is a tall order, but we demand nothing less.

We may want servant leaders, but we do not want "soft" leaders. In his best-seller, *Good to Great: Why Some Companies Make the Leap and Others Don't,* Jim Collins studied the leaders of companies that achieved and sustained exceptional financial performance over a fifteen-year period. He describes them as "Level 5" leaders—executives who "build enduring greatness through a paradoxical blend of personal humility and professional will."[16]

As an example, Collins profiles Cork Walgreen, CEO of Walgreen Drugs, a man of fierce resolve who saw that the company's future lay in convenient drugstores, not in the food-service business it had built. He challenged his executive team to get the company out of the restaurant business within five years. At the time, Walgreens had five hundred restaurants, but the CEO was firm and fanatical in his vision, which turned out to be correct.

Walgreen and all the other CEOs of the good-to-great companies did not fit the mold of the attention-seeking, heroic CEOs who were glorified in the press during the 1980s and 1990s. In fact, all these executives were described by their associates as rather quiet, self-effacing, and humble. "It's not that Level 5 leaders have no ego or self-interest," writes Collins. "Indeed, they are incredibly ambitious—but their ambition is first and foremost for the institution, not themselves."[17]

Humble, yet passionately determined, Neeleman, Walgreen, and the other chief executives briefly profiled here, including Vineet Nayar of HCLT, discussed in Chapter 8, are the kinds of leaders that today's workforce seems to find most engaging. Bottom line: It's not about ego, quick results, and personal ambition—it's about patiently, quietly, but tenaciously executing a shared compelling vision with a valued and dedicated team.

> "Followers are more interested in our integrity than in our speeches about integrity, and their antennae are sensitive and efficient to any possible incongruities."
> —LANCE SECRETAN

Engagement Practice #53:
Back up words with actions.

One of the greatest sources of employee cynicism and disengagement is the failure of leaders to do as they say. We have grown tired of CEOs who say "people are our most important asset" but cut back training budgets without blinking, who survey employees as if they intend to follow through with corrective action but never do, who say quality is number one but push employees to do the work in a third of the time it takes to do it right, or who say that treating people right is a priority for all managers but fail to hold managers accountable for abusing employees. It's all just more fodder for Dilbert cartoons. Leaders who can't or won't back up their good intentions with actions might as well be deliberately driving people out of their organizations.

Words and Deeds out of Synch

A major international corporation that claimed to be committed to work/life values drew up an excellent plan to help managers incorporate work/life balance into the business. The company gathered its top eighty officers to review the plan—but scheduled the meeting on a weekend.[18]

Someone once compared trust to money in a bank account. If people meet our expectations over time, we put coins in the bank, and, after a while, the bank has earned our trust. If it doesn't meet our expectations, we take coins out. When it comes to our employers, the more coins we take out, the closer we come to closing our accounts and walking out the door for good.

Some leaders are so externally focused that they make feel-good statements in speeches and annual reports with no apparent awareness that what they are saying may be inconsistent with internal realities. One company displayed its code of conduct in its lobby, proclaiming that "trust" was a driving principle, yet it searched employees' belongings each time they entered and exited the building.

Everyone has a story to tell about the mixed signals companies send. What can employers do about it? Probably the best insurance is to have a CEO who places a high value on integrity and insists on carefully selecting executives and candidates for all positions on the basis of character first and capabilities second.

Some companies conduct surveys in which employees are asked to rank a variety of cultural factors according to how strongly they desire them and how much they believe them to exist in the organization. The larger the "gap" scores, the greater the discrepancy between the actual and the desired culture on those factors. Follow-up employee focus groups conducted by outside consultants can help bring to the surface specific issues that senior leaders need to face and reconcile. While this process may be facilitated by HR staff, it needs to be owned by senior line managers.

Often, the mixed signals may be created by executives who espouse one thing and middle managers who do another. Some managers believe that, because of their privileged status, they are exempt from the rules that govern everyday life in the organization, such as having to be at work on time or taking reasonable "lunch hours."

It's Not Just What We Do . . . It's What We *Won't* Do

Companies earn trust points not just for the consistency of their internal behavior but also for the things they will and won't do in their interactions with the outside world. Employees at CenterBeam, Inc., in Santa Clara, California, are proud to tell their stories.

The company was trying to recruit enough talented people to support its rapid start-up and had made an offer to a qualified candidate when the résumé of a superstar candidate came across the desk of the hiring manager. Managers asked the CEO, Sheldon Laube, if the offer could be rescinded so that the company could hire the superstar. Laube's response: "No way. We made a promise to the first candidate. If we're going to be the kind of company that people trust, we've got to keep our promises."

Shortly after that, the company ordered $500,000 worth of tape drives from a distributor. Before they could be unpacked, the company found out that a rival distributor was offering comparable machines at a price that could save the company almost $100,000 per year. A few engineers wanted to refuse delivery of the more expensive tape drives, but CenterBeam executives treated the shipment as binding.

CEO Laube has seen these decisions pay off by deepening the commitment of CenterBeam employees: "It's amazing how many employees have come up to me and said, 'It's great to work at a company that has integrity. Many employees tell me that at their old companies, 'people promised things that they just didn't deliver.'"[19]

In one company, senior leaders solicited employee feedback and invited "different ideas and perspectives" about how projects should be completed, but some project managers summarily shot down many of the new ideas employees suggested. In these situations, multirater feedback from managers, exit surveying, and regular employee surveys can help uncover these demoralizing situations so that they can be corrected.

 Engagement Practice #54:
Place your trust and confidence in your workforce.

To demonstrate trust in people before they have even earned it is a risky proposition. We may find out later that our trust was misplaced or even betrayed. We may risk giving away our own power as leaders. We may trust employees too much to make important decisions before they are ready, thus jeopardizing a customer relationship. And yet, employers of choice routinely take these risks and make a habit of trusting employees before they have earned it.

Nordstrom department stores is famous for trusting its salespeople with the power to make on-the-spot decisions that build customer loyalty, even if it means spending the company's money to do it. When Bill Gore left DuPont to start W. L. Gore and Associates in the basement of his house, he recognized the importance of trusting employees with the independence to make decisions that serve the interests of the organization.

To formalize this philosophy, Gore sent out a company memo outlining the concept of "the waterline," likening employees to the crew of a ship. Understandably, no employees would be allowed to drill holes below the waterline, as that would endanger every crew member. They would be allowed to drill holes above the waterline but not below. In other words, with every decision they faced, employees would ask themselves, "Is this decision above or below the waterline?" If they concluded that the decision might significantly impact other crew members, they would be obligated to consult further with more senior colleagues. If, however, they concluded that the impact on other crew members would be negligible, they were free to make their own judgments without consulting more senior crew members.[20]

In his book *Making the Grass Greener on Your Side: A CEO's Journey to Leading by Serving*, Ken Melrose tells the story of taking over as CEO at Toro Company when the emphasis was on getting bottom-line results at all costs. The company had been pushing so hard to get bigger that, somewhere along the way, its reputation for quality among its distributors and customers had eroded so badly that it was on the brink of bankruptcy.

Melrose and his executive team decided to put the emphasis on quality and product excellence and aggressively reduced high field inventories. Customer satisfaction became the new byword. At the same time, Melrose became a convert to a servant-leadership philosophy and began "driving power down to the people who do the actual work and make things happen."

He established what he called "four leadership imperatives—building trust through openness; fostering risk-taking, innovation, and creativity; practicing a coaching and serving role; and creating win-win situations." He also installed an Employee Stock Ownership Plan so that the title of "owner" became more than symbolic.

Melrose credits the servant-leader approach for the company's revival, pointing out that it runs against the grain of traditional corporate leadership, which concentrates power and control at the top. "Ego addiction is the main cause of management failure because it causes people in management positions to suppose they know all, to hoard power, and to destroy trust."[21]

Sometimes managers learn by trial and error. When Gerald Chamales founded Rhinotek Computer Products, in Carson, California, he admits he was "completely green" as a manager and found himself behaving in a dictatorial way with his employees. He screamed at employees who didn't follow orders precisely and threw temper tantrums when employees failed to measure up to his standards. As a result, he alienated his workforce. When he began to notice the company's high turnover, he asked himself whether it might be connected to his own management style.

Chamales decided to change his approach; he learned to control his temper and started walking around his office and plant floor soliciting feedback from his two hundred employees. Turnover declined dramatically thereafter. "I've done everything in this company from sweeping floors to typing invoices, yet it is important to have humility and realize that the people doing the jobs have the solutions."[22]

Ultimately, it boils down to simple human respect. In her book with a one-word title—*Respect*—Sara Lawrence-Lightfoot describes her father's secret: "He gained respect by giving it. He talked to the fourth-grade kid in Spring Valley who shined shoes the same way he talked and listened to a bishop or a college president. He was seriously interested in who you were and what you had to say."[23]

When senior leaders invest so much energy in their own self-importance that they cannot adopt this humbler attitude, they lose the opportunity to engage and inspire. Many will never change their authoritarian, micro-managing styles because they are not comfortable with the idea of giving away power. The irony is that, when leaders give power away, they increase the collective power of the organization to innovate and meet new challenges, thus enhancing their own power in the long run.

What the Employee Can Do to Build Reciprocal Trust and Confidence

What could a "lowly employee" possibly do that would cause a senior leader to inspire more trust and confidence? At first, we might respond "not much." But, while many employees may not have much control, all employees have some degree of influence. Here are some actions you can take to exercise the influence you do have:

- Respond honestly on employee surveys. Point out how the actions of senior leaders do not match their words and professed values. Describe specific instances of management behavior that have created distrust or caused you and other employees to lose confidence.
- Speak up in meetings and express your convictions firmly.
- If you are asked to take part in something unethical or dishonest, refuse to go along, report it to a superior, or be prepared to resign.
- Be willing to take the risk of counseling your managers against taking an action that is unethical and will damage the company's reputation.
- When a leader or manager puts trust and confidence in you by giving you the freedom to do the job without constant oversight, be prepared to take the initiative.
- Show that you are interested in having an "ownership mentality." Learn how the business makes money and what you can do to make it more profitable and perhaps share more in that profitability.
- Earn your manager's trust by constantly looking for ways to take the initiative to meet customers' needs or by improving your own skills so that managers will trust you to handle new challenges.
- Give new leaders the benefit of the doubt. Give them time to

communicate and begin to execute their new vision before judging them to be unworthy of following.

- If you feel called to become a leader yourself, resolve to do everything in your power to gain and keep the trust and confidence of your employees.

Engagement Practices Checklist: Building Trust and Confidence

Do senior leaders in your organization do what it takes to build trust and confidence among employees? Review the engagement practices presented in this chapter, and check the ones you believe your organization needs to implement or improve.

To inspire trust and confidence, senior leaders should:

Engagement Practice #52. __ Inspire confidence in a clear vision, a workable plan, and the competence to achieve it.

Engagement Practice #53. __ Back up words with actions.

Engagement Practice #54. __ Demonstrate trust and confidence in the workforce.

Your next step: *Resolve to take action on the ones you believe are most critical and appropriate for your situation and objectives.*

Notes

1. Research study cited in Rachel King, "Great Things Are Starting at Yum," *Workforce Management,* November 2003.
2. Kathy Gurchiek, "Recession Alters Relationship Between Employers," *HR,* March 17, 2010.
3. Ibid.
4. "Aon Hewitt Survey Shows Gap in Leadership Effectiveness," *Talent Management,* Talent Survey of 1,328 U.S. employees, May 4, 2011, http://talentmgt.com/articles/view/aon-hewitt-survey-shows-gap-in-leadership-effectiveness/2.
5. Ibid.
6. The Gallup Organization, 2002.
7. Maritz Research, 2011 Employee Engagement Poll of 1,857 American workers, July 11, 2011, http://www.maritz.com/Press-Releases/2011/Americans-Still-Lack-Trust-In-Company-Management-Post-Recession.aspx?intPage=0&Pagesize=10.

8. Ibid.

9. Ibid.

10. Ibid.

11. Blessing & White, Employee Engagement Report, March 2011.

12. Len Boselovic, "CEO pay up 23% to $11.4M," *McClatchy-Tribune Business News*, April 20, 2011.

13. Kris Hudson, "Boss Talk: Turning Shopping Trips into Treasure Hunts; Surprises, Bargains Keep Sinegal's Costco Humming, But Should He Boost Prices?," *Wall Street Journal*, August 27, 2007.

14. Roseanne Harper, *Supermarket News*, July 18, 2011.

15. Chuck Salter, "And Now the Hard Part," *Fast Company*, May 2004.

16. Jim Collins, *Good to Great: Why Some Companies Make the Leap and Others Don't* (New York: HarperBusiness, 2001).

17. Ibid.

18. Pamela Babcock, "Is Your Company Two-Faced," *HR*, January 2004.

19. George Anders, "Honesty Is the Best Policy—Trust Us," *Fast Company*, August 2000.

20. Lance H. Secretan, *Reclaiming Higher Ground: Building Organizations That Inspire Excellence* (New York: McGraw-Hill, 1997).

21. Chuck Hutchcraft, "Toro Chairman Sows Seeds of Restructuring," *Chicago Tribune*, November 21, 1995.

22. Carol Hymowitz, "Bosses Need to Learn Whether They Inspire, or Just Drive, Staffers," *Wall Street Journal*, February 18, 1999.

23. Sara Lawrence-Lightfoot, *Respect: An Explanation* (New York: Perseus Books, 1999).

CHAPTER ELEVEN

Planning to Become an Employer of Choice

The great French Marshall Lyautey once asked
his gardener to plant a tree. The gardener objected that
the tree was slow-growing and would not reach maturity
for one hundred years. The Marshall replied, 'In that case,
there is no time to lose; plant it this afternoon.'

—John F. Kennedy

CEOs polled by PriceWaterhouseCoopers in its fourteenth annual global survey in May 2011 reported that their top priority was managing talent, overtaking the previous year's top concern—risk management. PWC said that 55 percent of U.S. CEOs planned to increase their headcount over the next twelve months but were concerned that they might not have access to people with the right skills even after several years of slow labor-market activity. According to PWC, 75 percent of U.S. CEOs planned "some change" or "major change" to their company's talent management strategy over the next twelve months.[1]

When the competition for talent gets heated, many companies begin to scramble and cast about for ideas on how to plug the talent gaps or stop the bleeding. Some just put more time and money into their recruiting efforts, which is like speeding up the pace of the blood transfusion while the patient is bleeding to death.

Many companies know they need to stop the bleeding first, but, in their search for answers, it seems not to occur to them to look for the root causes. Instead, in many cases, the CEO asks the HR department to do something about the worker shortage or turnover problem, and the search begins for "what other companies are doing." The only problem with that approach is that the practices that fit the business strategies of other companies may not fit your company.

For example, it may not be appropriate to implement engagement practice #2—increase hiring of temps, adjunct staff, and part-time workers—if there are already too many of these workers in the company. In such a situation, customer service may begin to suffer because there are too many temps and part-timers and not enough full-time employees with solid customer service experience. Increasing hiring from within (engagement practice #6) may not be advisable for companies that are pursuing a business strategy focused on innovation and product development and already know they don't have enough innovators and product developers currently on board.

Yet the instinct to find out what other companies are doing and to copy-cat their practices is irresistible to many otherwise conscientious professionals. I can even recall seeing several articles during intense periods of competition for talent that listed the "top 20 effective retention strategies" in broad terms, like this:

1. Training
2. Flexible Work Arrangements
3. Tuition Reimbursement
4. Sabbaticals
5. Extended Parent Leave

and so on through all twenty items on the list.

First of all, these are not strategies. Second, they may not be the right practices for your company. Third, these lists are usually dominated by pay-and-benefit practices and typically feature very few intangibles, such as cultural or management practices, which, as we know, may have a much bigger impact.

Part of the problem is that it is tempting to select short-term, tangible practices over long-term, intangible ones (see Figure 11.1). Being only human, we prefer short-term solutions to long-term ones. Besides, we are impatient to get results and believe we need to score a quick success. Likewise, the intangible stuff seems just too soft, too squishy, too hard to implement, and too difficult to change in a reasonable time frame. Or so the thinking goes.

Actually, there is plenty of evidence now to support the conclusion that the greatest drivers of employee engagement and retention *are* intangible—mostly related to the way managers treat employees. In fact, in reviewing the

Figure 11.1.

Four necessary employer-of-choice elements.

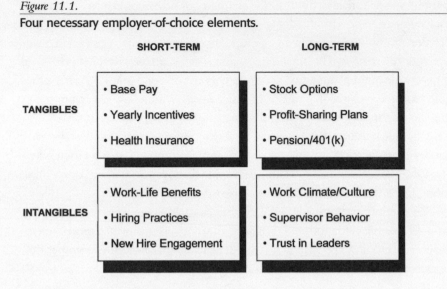

list of fifty-four engagement practices in Appendix A, you will see that most of them are intangible and within the power of the manager to implement. In the end, it doesn't matter whether they are short term or long term, tangible or intangible. What matters is whether they are the right practices for your current situation.

So, as you consider the fifty-four engagement practices in this book, think of them as items in a cafeteria. Some you have already tried and found satisfactory. The ones you have not tried and now choose to put on your tray may be few, but they will be the right ones.

Talent Engagement Strategies in Action

The strategies companies use to engage their workers depend not only on their business strategies but also on the size and complexity of the organization and its workforce. Here are several examples of companies big and small that have implemented talent selection and engagement strategies differently, but successfully.

United Parcel Service (UPS)

The Challenge: Engaging and retaining the young, mostly part-time workers who load, unload, and sort packages in the company's 270,000-square-foot

Buffalo, New York distribution center. The turnover rate was 50 percent, creating customer service disruptions and proving to be costly in several ways.

Strategic Actions: The new district manager, Jennifer Shroeger, created a five-part strategic plan, as follows:

1. *Meet the expectations of applicants.* Instead of hiring anybody that walked in the door, which it had been doing, UPS started asking applicants if they were hoping for full-time jobs. If the answer was "yes," then they were probably going to be disappointed at some point because full-time jobs rarely open up. It usually takes six years to work up to a full-time driver's job. "I can't hire workers who want full-time work if there aren't any full-time jobs," Shroeger said. Instead, the company sold part-time work for what it was—short, flexible shifts that could fit the schedules of students from the many colleges in the area.

2. *Communicate differently to different groups of workers.* To better understand the needs of her entire workforce, Shroeger analyzed information that broke down the worker population into five distinctive groups, closely paralleling their age and the stage of their careers. She realized that those older than thirty-five valued different motivators than their younger co-workers. Understanding these differences, the company tailored its recruiting and re-recruiting messages accordingly.

3. *Take better care of the new hires.* To make the warehouse environment less intimidating to new hires, UPS improved the lighting, upgraded the break rooms, and installed more personal computers on the floor, which provided access to training materials and human resources information on the company's intranet. The best part-time supervisors became trainers, spending a week shadowing new workers. Shroeger initiated an employee-retention committee, composed of both managers and hourly workers, to track new hires through their first few weeks on the job and to fix small problems before they become bigger ones. The committee also plans fun social activities, such as after-hours baseball games and floor-wide "super-loader" contests.

4. *Give supervisors the freedom and training to manage people their own way.* The company let managers figure out their own best way of motivating different workers. Supervisors completed training in how to handle difficult situations and respond to different career questions. They also learned how to

have more flexibility with students and moms, who have frequent changes in their schedules, and were challenged to find out and remember something about the personal lives of workers.

5.   *Let them move on with new skills and good will*. Shroeger realized that young, part-time workers are going to move on with their lives. But, having given them the opportunity to build their skills via tuition-reimbursement, Saturday computer classes, and career planning discussions, she expected they would leave with good feelings about UPS and perhaps become customers someday, as many have.

The Results: Within four years of implementing these practices, part-time turnover dropped from 50 to 6 percent, meaning that about six hundred workers who would otherwise have left remained on the job. Annual savings due to lowered hiring costs totaled $1 million. Lost work-days due to work-related injuries dropped by 20 percent, and the percentage of packages delivered on the wrong day or at the wrong time dropped from 4 percent to 1 percent.[2]

Mike's Car Wash, Inc.

The Challenge: This Indianapolis-based company has 650 employees (450 work part time) in thirty-seven locations throughout central Indiana and in Dayton and Cincinnati, Ohio. The average turnover rate in the car wash industry is 75 to 80 percent.

Strategic Actions: CEO Mike Rice had his HR department spend six months analyzing three years' worth of employee records, comparing the applications of employees who had quit with those who stayed. The department also reviewed assessment scores from hiring managers and notes from exit interviewers. This analysis uncovered what Rice called "twelve red flags," such as applicants who had left more than two jobs in the previous twelve months without a reasonable explanation for leaving, such as a layoff.

"We got much better at hiring the right person from the start," says Rice, explaining that, now, only 1 percent of applicants are hired. "If we hire the right person, we know we'll get much longer tenure out of them and better performance."

Because the car-washing business is customer-service intensive, another red flag among applicants was a lack of prior experience in jobs that required customer service interactions, such as stocking shelves. So Rice asked his HR staff to develop a program called Hire the Best. All hiring managers were retrained and given an interview script to help them identify red flags or other past behavior that might help predict applicants' future job performance.

So that applicants have a realistic preview of the job, they watch an eight-minute video (viewable on the company's website) "showing everything that would steer you away from the job," said Rice. "Most of it talks about the work environment, being on your feet all day and working in the heat and cold. About the last third says, 'If you can live with this, here's what's in it for you.'"

Because the company hires mostly Millennials (those born between 1982 and 1995) who like structure, lots of feedback, and clear expectations, Mike's provides two performance appraisals per year and frequent employee focus groups where policies and other concerns are addressed.

Result: Mike's turnover hovers around 55 percent—about one-third less than the industry average. The average length of stay for a Mike's employee has been two years, with nearly half of the turnover planned, such as high schoolers who graduate and go off to college.[3]

Motek Software

The Challenge: This southern California company, now a part of AFS Technologies, customizes industrial computers for use on warehouse forklifts and dominates its market niche. From the beginning, the goal of Motek's founder and CEO, Ann Price, was to attract the very best IT workers and make them want to remain in a work environment that allowed them to have a life outside work.

Strategic Actions: Price expects her twenty employees to keep 9 AM to 5 PM hours. She also buys lunches for them at the best restaurants, brings in a hairdresser for employees once a week, and gives new employees one month vacation per year. When employees postpone taking their vacation, Price has been known to book it herself and go along with them to make sure they take it. "We're robbing ourselves of the best years of our lives," she says. "I'm living proof that you can achieve the same goals and not give that all up."

The Results: A turnover rate of less than 1 percent and a highly stable workforce, which helps to avoid disruption of service to the company's clients.[4]

IHS Help Desk

The Challenge: Even though this IT consulting and training company was growing and succeeding, owner Eric Rabinowitz realized that a 113 percent turnover rate was threatening the future of the business. On further inspection of company data, he found that 20 percent of turnovers were happening in new hires' first month on the job.

Strategic Actions: Rabinowitz began asking employees what he might do differently, and he got an earful. He had expected that offering full-time work and good benefits would be enough, but his employees saw themselves as temp workers with no career path and were always looking for their next job. Because most of them worked off-site, they felt as if they were working for the client. They also mentioned that they wanted more training and a clearly defined career path.

Rabinowitz realized that most employees would not stay with the company more than two years, but he resolved to give them whatever training would motivate them to stay at least that long. He surveyed employees to find out what kind of training they wanted, then set up Web-based training programs that met their needs. He also started a communication program to make workers feel less isolated at remote locations; he created a newsletter and hired an employee advocate to visit work sites once a week and create a stronger bond between the company and its employees. The company also improved its benefits plan to include dental and life insurance and started incentive and employee recognition plans.

The Results: Within a year, the company had lowered its turnover rate to 19 percent.[5]

American Home Shield

The Challenge: American Home Shield, the major appliance warranty arm of Service Master, with 1,500 employees based in Memphis, Tennessee, was experiencing 89 percent turnover in a critical department. The cost: $250,000 annually, plus erosion of employee morale and customer loyalty.

Strategic Actions: The company recognized that it first needed to understand why some employees leave and others stay. To capture this information, an employee turnover project team surveyed a sample of employees who had already left the organization. AHS also surveyed those who left the organization after the initial survey and surveyed remaining employees on a quarterly basis to discover which factors had caused them to stay or to consider leaving.

The team found that the key factors were having supervisors available to employees, job training, and clear communication of job requirements, but these were also the most dissatisfying aspects of working at American Home Shield. The team recommended and led the implementation of these steps:

- Reorganized the training schedule to match the typical learning curve of the specific job.

- Increased the autonomy of front-line employees, freeing up supervisors to handle higher-level issues.

- Streamlined the procedure for communicating job-requirement changes by (1) giving only department managers the authority to make job-requirement changes and (2) assigning department employees e-mail accounts through which all job-requirement changes would be communicated.

The company also improved the hiring process by having a trained interview team ask prescreened behavioral questions.

Results: American Home Shield was able to reduce turnover from nearly 90 percent to about 35 percent in one year. The company's retention-management plan allowed management to control employee turnover on an ongoing basis.[6]

Steak and Shake

The Challenge: When Peter Dunn took over as CEO of this fast-casual restaurant chain, earnings had slipped, and crew turnover stood at 200 percent—markedly higher than the 129 percent average reported by other restaurants in its category. At 50 percent, management turnover was also excessive.

If Dunn was going to achieve his goals to turn around the company and fuel an expansion, he knew he was going to have to reduce the high turnover among store employees because it was negatively impacting guest satisfaction scores. The company told investors that it could save $2 million to $4 million per year by increasing the retention of front-line workers. He also estimated that bringing manager turnover under control could save another $1 million to $2 million per year.

Strategic Actions: Dunn planned to build customer retention by increasing employee retention, an idea known as building a "virtuous cycle," similar to "the service-profit chain" described in the book by that title. One of the ways the company planned to do this was by giving store managers more freedom to make decisions about how to increase revenues and efficiency. For the first time ever, Stake and Shake provided managers with statistics on each store's operations, including turnover rates, customer satisfaction data, drive-through efficiency, and most profitable items. Managers were challenged to create their own business plans for their stores and to share them with employees.

The company also decided to increase benefits to front-line workers, starting with a 50 percent reduction in their vision and dental expenses, in addition to the health-care insurance and a full range of other benefits it already offered. One of these benefits was life insurance, which the company believes produced the greatest reduction in turnover for the money spent. Stake and Shake also increased new-hire orientation time, relying on industry data showing that restaurants that give four or more hours of orientation enjoy turnover rates 34 percent lower than those that provide only an hour or two.

The Results: In less than a year, manager turnover had dropped to 30 percent, and turnover among front-line workers was down twenty-four points. Guest satisfaction had improved from 81 percent to 86 percent, and same-store sales had increased by 12 percent.[7]

FleetBoston Financial (now Bank of America)

The Challenge: To reduce annual turnover in the bank's retail operations, which had reached 25 percent overall, with rates as high as 40 percent among tellers and customer service representatives. Such high turnover rates had put the bank's customer-focused strategy at risk. An analysis of the bank's employee survey and exit interview data suggested that employees were leaving because of low pay and heavy workloads. Despite raising pay rates and installing more flexible pay arrangements, the bank found that turnover rates continued to rise.

Strategic Actions: The bank suspected that the reasons employees were giving for leaving during their exit interviews were safe and superficial responses and that they were reluctant to discuss the real reasons. Fleet retained a consulting firm to conduct a comprehensive analysis of workforce characteristics and management practices that most directly influenced employees' decisions to stay or leave.

One of the first discoveries was that the bank's active history of mergers, acquisitions, and consolidations had resulted in the closing of some branches, which had raised employees' worries about job insecurity. To counter these concerns, the bank decided to focus on broadening career opportunities within the organization. The idea was that if employees could improve their mobility, they would see that as also enhancing their marketability, making them less concerned about possible future layoffs.

By examining the career paths of employees, the bank learned that those who progressed most rapidly through different jobs were most likely to stay. This finding was surprising to some managers who believed that employees who broaden their experience in the company and become more marketable are most likely to pursue outside opportunities.

Managers began paying more attention to career development needs and encouraged employees to consider a broad range of possible movements within the bank, operating on the hope that they would receive their share of mobile new employees to replace those who moved on. The bank also learned that there were two categories of employees at greatest risk of leaving: high-performers who had been in the same position for two or more years and employees who had just completed undergraduate or graduate degrees. Managers were encouraged to initiate discussions with these employees in particular to address the sources of their concerns.

Another interesting and valuable finding was that nonexempt employees who had progressed into exempt positions tended to stay longer and earned more frequent promotions than those who entered as exempt employees. As a result, Fleet clarified and publicized its policies outlining how nonexempts can become exempt employees and began providing career coaching to nonexempt employees to encourage them to pursue new growth opportunities.

Further analysis of employee data revealed that employees whose managers left the bank were themselves more likely to leave. To address this, the bank decided to raise the amount of variable pay that managers can earn in the form of higher performance-based cash bonuses. Fleet also replaced departed supervisors with internal candidates who were already known and trusted by current employees.

In exploring the reasons for high first-year turnover, the bank realized it needed to enhance its new-hire orientation process and began giving more frequent feedback and more training during the first year of employment. Recognizing that it might also have been giving new hires more work than they could manage, the bank also reduced workloads.

Finally, the bank examined hiring-source patterns and discovered that employees who had been referred by other employees were more likely to stay than employees recruited through agencies or want ads. Fleet decided to lower its investment in recruiters and to increase the bonuses it paid employees for referring new hires who stayed at least six months.

The Results: Within eight months of implementing the new retention initiatives, FleetBoston found that its turnover rate had decreased by 40 percent among salaried employees and 25 percent among hourly employees. The turnover rate among first-line supervisors declined to 6 percent, and first-year turnover dropped by 10 percent. These combined improvements are estimated to have saved the company $50 million.[8]

My Maid Service

The Challenge: When Derek Christian acquired this Lebanon, Ohio–based home cleaning company several years ago, he was faced with the challenge of how to keep hourly, unskilled, low-wage employees engaged in an industry with a 300 percent turnover rate. Many of the jobs are monotonous, physically demanding, and dirty. Employees often unexpectedly quit in search of higher pay or better opportunities, leaving employers scrambling for replacements.

Strategic Actions: "I'm not naive enough to think that everyone is going to want to clean houses for the rest of their lives," Christian told HR Online, adding that he addresses employees' short-term and long-term goals during monthly performance reviews. "As long as they spend two good years with me and do a good job, I've got no problem helping them find [other] jobs." To get those two good years, Christian decided to help many of his forty-five employees build computer skills to help prepare them for their ideal job— an office job. He sends them to training classes at the local community college or helps them find online programs and even helps them apply for jobs when the time comes. Christian taught one employee who wants to launch a pet-sitting business how to create a business plan and operate a small business.

He offers flexible hours to all workers, which is appreciated by the employees who also attend college. He also made the strategic decision to pay his maids $12 an hour, well over the average $9 hourly rate. Most employees, who are either high school graduates or dropouts, are "very loyal," Christian said. "But when they leave, they refer their friends, so there are usually three people to replace them."

The Result: The company experienced zero turnover in 2009, and only one employee left in 2010. "It wouldn't be that hard for big companies to adopt a similar program," says Christian. "I get really good people, people who can potentially do better things because they know I'm going to help them get somewhere else."[9]

What Do We Learn from These Success Stories?

There are common threads that run through all these stories and are worth pointing out. Though there were significant differences in company size, industry, circumstances, and range of solutions, all shared a common approach:

- Resolving to take action without delay as soon as they recognized there could be a serious threat to the fortunes of the business
- Recognizing key employees on whom the business depended and attempting to understand how to better meet their needs
- Implementing targeted initiatives to meet the needs of those key employees
- Tracking improvements to demonstrate progress and measure success

In some cases, the approach was straightforward and based on common sense. Other companies pursued a more sophisticated approach, relying on complex analytical tools that produced some unexpected findings and led to a wide range of solutions. In every instance, the commitment of the CEO was the driving force for the new initiatives.

Linking Talent and Business Objectives

These stories remind us of the business imperative for achieving "preferred employer" status. In order to reach our business objectives, we must consistently compete for talent and win, not just in terms of attracting talent but also in terms of engaging and retaining it, as well, knowing that current employees, especially the best, will always have the option of moving elsewhere.

Yet, while most corporate executives say they see the importance of linking business and talent strategies, a recent survey found that only two in ten companies have systematic talent-management practices in place to try to collect such metrics. The same study found "sizable gaps between what companies said they should measure to determine the effectiveness of their talent-management practices, and the metrics they actually collected." For example:

- 59 percent said they should measure ROI per employee, but only 11 percent actually did.
- 77 percent said they should measure the separation rates of high-performing employees, but only 24 percent actually did.
- 75 percent said they should measure quality of hire, but only 16 percent actually did.
- 64 percent said they should measure time to full productivity, but 16 percent actually did.
- 64 percent said they should measure promotion rate, but only 21 percent actually did."[10]

Part of the problem lies in the fact that, in many organizations, senior leaders look to the HR department to focus on increasing efficiencies and reducing costs when it should instead be focused on creating value for the business by linking talent strategies with business objectives. A prime example of a focus on efficiency at the expense of value is a company that measures cost per hire but makes no attempt to measure quality of hire.

Linking the Right Measures to Business Results

Instead of simply benchmarking the efficiency of human resources and cost measures against those of other companies, many businesses are taking a broader perspective. They are focusing internally, but in a more strategic way, and are measuring the company against itself, not against other companies that may have very different strategies.

The first requirement is for the business to actually have a clear and detailed business strategy. Next, the organization must target the job roles that are most critical to achieving the plan. As we know, as few as 20 percent of the workforce can contribute 80 percent of the value. In the case of a national restaurant chain with a business strategy that depends on improvements in customer service, the front-line workers have to be considered pivotal to the success of that strategy.

There are many questions to ask: Are there enough of these people on board? Do they have the right competencies and, if not, how will they be developed? How will we attract people with the right talents for these critical roles? Do we have the right human resources systems and practices in place to engage and retain these people? Are they receiving the right rewards? And what about the noncritical employees and B-players we depend on—are we focused on keeping, re-engaging, and rewarding them, as well?

Another important lens to look through is the growth phase of the business. For example, a start-up retail venture will concentrate on selecting and rewarding its top executives but focus more on middle managers as it begins to expand nationally and open up new stores. Similarly, employers of choice stay attuned to the career phases of their employees. The recruiting pitches, rewards, benefits, and management practices they use to attract, engage, and retain new hires are different from those used with more experienced workers, with women, and with other demographically diverse populations of workers.

One definite trend indicating a more proactive approach to talent management is that more companies seem to be conducting comprehensive "talent review" processes, often beginning with in-depth assessments of high-potential employees. Senior officers and department heads then review the capabilities of specific individuals deep inside the organization, not only to discuss their readiness for promotion but also to assess their strengths against strategic talent needs. Following these sessions, managers are expected to create action plans for employees and talent strategies for their units.

Ultimately, managers and human resources leaders need to be focused on linking talent-related outcomes to customer measures. For example, tracking employee retention as a leading indicator of customer retention and revenues has proved to be particularly compelling.

The good news is that, armed with more sophisticated and robust IT capabilities, more companies have increased their investments in tracking the impact that metrics such as turnover rates, productivity, and employee morale have on the bottom line. The evidence justifies the new focus; for example, more than half (52 percent) of higher-performing companies have reported that they focus on measuring employee engagement, whereas only about one-third (32 percent) of the lower-performing organizations do so.[11]

Creating an Employer-of-Choice Scorecard

Rather than try to benchmark themselves against other employers, some companies are creating ways of measuring their own progress toward becoming employers of choice. In other words, they are starting to track year-over-year improvements by creating their own dashboards of talent-management indicators. One way of doing this is to track measures of the four things every organization must do with talent: attract, select, engage, and sustain engagement (see Figure 11.2).

Figure 11.2.

Four key things we MUST do with talent.

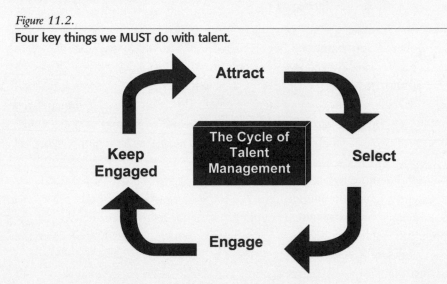

Measures of *attraction* could include the following:

- Ratio of Employment Applicants to Open Positions
- Percentage of Applicants Considered "A" Candidates
- Average Days to Fill Vacancies
- Ratio of Acceptances to Offers
- Applicant Dropout Rate
- Number of Recruiting Sources Used
- Percentile Rank of Total Compensation When Measured against Competitors for Talent
- Percentage of New Hire Referrals Who Stay at Least Six Months
- Average Monthly Percentage of Open Positions

Employers of choice, for example, typically have ratios of employment applicants to open positions of at least 20 to 1, some as high as 100 to 1. New-hire referral rates of 30 percent are considered healthy, usually indicating that current employees speak well of the company to their friends and feel comfortable recommending the organization as a good place to work.

Measures of *selection* might include:

- First-Year Voluntary Turnover Rate
- First-Year Involuntary Turnover Rate
- First-Year Performance Results
- First-Year Performance Evaluation by Managers
- First-Year Absenteeism Rate
- First-Year Employee Engagement Survey Scores
- Percentage of Candidates Hired after Behavioral Interviewing
- Percentage of Selection Decisions Based on Competency Analysis

Engagement surveys have become an important tool for many companies, which are using them as a primary indicator of how well talent is being managed. Most see engagement as a much more meaningful measure than employee satisfaction because it encompasses satisfaction and dimensions of performance, along with commitment or intent to stay with the organization. As you would expect, engagement survey scores are a key measure in the next two categories.

Measures of *new-hire engagement* might include:

- Percentage Completing Comprehensive Orientation Process
- Percentage Completing "Entrance Interview"
- Percentage Coached by Buddy or Mentor
- First-Year Employee Engagement Scores
- Percentage of New Hires Considered "Outstanding" Performers
- First-Year Voluntary Turnover Rates
- Results of Surveys of First-Year Employees
- Percentage Whose Supervisors Leave or Are Reassigned in First Year

Some companies that are especially concerned about quick turnover among new hires might want to track some of these measures during the first 30, 90, or 180 days.

Measures of *sustained employee engagement* could include:

- Voluntary Turnover Rate
- Top-Performer Voluntary Turnover Rate
- Performance and Quality Results
- Absenteeism Rates

- Employee Engagement Scores
- Training Hours per Employee
- Ratio of Internal to External Hires
- Percentage of Employees Who Complete Individual Development Plans
- Percentage of Rehires among All Hires

There are dozens of similar measures that a company might begin to track and report. As shown in Figure 11.3, the scorecard becomes more meaningful in the second and subsequent years as improvements and dropoffs become apparent at a glance. The next logical step would be to begin showing the relationship between some or all of these measures and business results, such as revenue per employee (including outsourced operations) or customer retention rates.

Figure 11.3.

Sample employer-of-choice scorecard.

EOC Indicators	2012	2011
Voluntary Turnover Rate	11.9%	13.2%
Employee Referral Rate	21.2%	17.4%
Ratio of Jobs Filled Internally	39.8%	33.5%
New Hire Retention Rate	76.3%	71.8%
Quit Rate	13.5%	14.4%
Ratio of Acceptances to Offers	64.7%	59.7%
Percentage of Engaged Employees	36.6%	27.9%
Absenteeism Rate	4.0%	5.1%

The Plan Works . . . If You Work the Plan

You may have seen the Dilbert cartoon where Catbert asks Dilbert's boss if he has a plan for retaining employees, and the boss responds, "I whittle at their confidence until they believe no one else would ever hire them." The bad news is that there really are such bosses. The good news is that you are now armed with fifty-four engagement practices from which you can choose to create a better plan for your employees. And the really good news, as we have seen in the success stories presented earlier in this chapter, is that if you work the plan, the plan will work.

When I ask audiences what they hope to get from my presentations, often someone says, "I was hoping for a magic bullet." The urge to slay the two-headed monster of employee disengagement and turnover is primal and hard to resist, but we must. There is only one "magic bullet," and that is the steady commitment to a plan that is made up of several well-targeted practices.

As Jim Collins points out in *Good to Great,* good companies become great not through quick changes but through patient and determined application: "Sustainable transformations follow a predictable pattern of buildup and breakthrough. Like pushing on a giant, heavy flywheel, it takes a lot of effort to get the thing moving at all, but with persistent pushing in a consistent direction over a long period of time, the flywheel builds momentum, eventually hitting a point of breakthrough."[12]

Using Talent Analytics to Outperform the Competition

The era of human-capital metrics has arrived. Leading-edge companies are increasingly adopting advanced methods to analyze workforce data and leverage it to boost employee engagement, retention, and business per-formance. Google, Sysco, JetBlue, Dow Chemical, Harrah's Entertainment, Starbucks, and many others are leading the way in mining company data to find trends, patterns, and new insights that pay off.

A few examples:

- Google even has a talent analytics function with its own director and thirty analysts. One of this team's investigations studied annual employee surveys, performance-management scores, and other data to isolate the attributes of the company's most and least successful managers. They identified eight behavioral characteristics of good managers and five behavioral characteristics of bad managers that can be used for hiring, management training, and succession management decisions.

- Sysco, the Fortune 100 global food-service company, measures employee satisfaction, productivity, retention, customer loyalty, supervisor effectiveness, diversity, and quality of life for each operating unit. Units that score higher on employee satisfaction also have higher revenues, lower costs, and superior customer loyalty. Analyzing the data helped Sysco identify management actions that increase employee satisfaction and engagement. In six years, the company improved the retention rate of delivery associates from 65 percent to 85 percent and saved nearly $50 million in hiring and training costs.[13]

- JetBlue asks its crew members one crucial question—"How likely are you to recommend JetBlue as a good place to work?"—then tracks the response percentage into "Promoters," "Passives/Neutral," and "Detractors." By subtracting the percentage of Promoters from Detractors, JetBlue uses the resulting "Net Promoter" score to monitor employee engagement and predict financial performance. The company has shown that higher employee Net Promoter scores on flights and locations drive customer Net Promoter scores, which drive loyalty, which drives revenues. JetBlue topped J. D. Power's annual customer service survey six years in a row.[14]

One study revealed that Starbucks, Best Buy, and Limited Brands agree that they can precisely identify the value of a 0.1 percent increase in employee engagement at a particular store. Best Buy estimated that value at more than $100,000 in the store's operating profit.[15]

Partners in Working the Plan

Becoming a destination employer is an achievable dream for every company, no matter how big or how small it may be. But, if it were easy, every company would be one. It takes a team effort, with everyone pushing on the flywheel—senior leaders, human resources leaders, managers, and employees.

Senior leaders make the commitment, enlist the support of the board; build a culture of trust, competence, and caring; approve sufficient budgets; and hold all managers accountable for engaging and retaining talent.

Human resources leaders link talent strategies to business objectives, balance value-creating activities with those that cut costs, create the right support systems for managing talent, partner with marketing to build an "employment brand," help the organization understand the true reasons people stay and leave, recommend the right best practices, support line managers in the implementation of those practices, and track the right measures.

Managers bear great responsibility, for they directly control or influence many of the reasons most employees decide to stay or to go. The great managers are the ones that can make their departments employers of choice long before the organization as a whole gains that status. And, yet, great managers of people have not been honored as the heroes they are.

Companies need to select more of the right people to become managers in the first place, be more rigorous in the selection process, and take greater care not to promote good technical performers above their level of competence. Managers must be challenged to be great managers, given the tools and training they need to become great, and rewarded in meaningful ways for engaging and retaining valued workers. And managers must be relieved of some of the loads they are bearing—doing the work of two or three people in addition to managing their direct reports. Too many managers are simply too busy managing budgets and "getting things done" to spend quality time with their employees.

Finally, many managers have to start taking more responsibility for their role in engaging or disengaging employees. They need to understand that pay is not the reason most employees leave and accept that their way of managing *may be* the number one reason. For many, that means that they must stop blaming senior leaders for not paying more (when low pay is not the culprit) and stop depending on human resources to do all the recruiting and recognizing. In short, managers need to own all four phases of the talent management cycle: attract, select, engage, and sustain engagement.

As for *employees,* they may need to be reminded that no manager has as much power to engage them as they do to engage themselves. Even so, senior leaders in many companies now survey employees to track the percentages that are engaged and not engaged, then challenge department managers to do whatever it takes to better engage their people and improve their scores in the next survey. While this does engender accountability for managing people with skill and emotional intelligence, there is a potential downside.

It is simply this: The responsibility for being engaged does not fall just on the shoulders of the manager—it is the employee's responsibility, as well. One manager once asked me, "What about the employees? They shouldn't just be waiting around for the manager to engage them. Why don't we just score employees on how well they are keeping themselves engaged?!"

By overemphasizing the manager's role in engaging employees, organizations risk creating an environment where employees may become passive, expecting all motivation and incentive to come from external sources. It is easy enough for many employees to fall into a victim mentality and assume an attitude of entitlement, especially when organizations habitually fail to seek active employee input and put off confronting poor performers.

Maintaining the fine balance between engagement and entitlement is a shared partnership between company leaders and employees. The need for both parties to meet halfway in the process makes it all the more important for organizations to spell out exactly how they expect employees to keep themselves engaged, as well as how managers should work to engage their employees.

Notes

1. PriceWaterhouseCoopers Fourteenth Annual Global CEO Survey, May 2011.
2. Keith Hammonds, "Handle with Care," *Fast Company*, August 2002.
3. Carol Patton, "Tackling Turnover: Creative Benefits and Screening Techniques Can Keep Hourly Workers on the Job," *HR Exec OnLine*, December 1, 2010, http://www.hreonline.com/HRE/story.jsp?storyId= 533326583.
4. Bob Calandra, "Finders Keepers," *Human Resource Executive*, June 2, 2000.
5. Ibid.
6. David G. Allen, "Retaining Talent: A Guide to Analyzing and Managing Employee Turnover," SHRM Foundation, 2008.
7. Rachael King, "Turnover Is the New Enemy at One of America's Oldest Restaurant Chains," *Workforce Management*, April 2004.
8. Haig R. Nalbantian and Anne Szostak, "How Fleet Bank Fought Employee Flight," *Harvard Business Review*, April 2004.
9. Patton, "Tackling Turnover."
10. "Talent Management Metrics Get an F," based on a survey of 426 HR professionals, released by the Institute for Corporate Productivity, Seattle, May 2010.
11. Ibid.
12. Jim Collins, *Good to Great: Why Some Companies Make the Leap and Others Don't* (New York: HarperBusiness, 2001).
13. Thomas H. Davenport, Jeanne Harris, and Jeremy Shapiro, "Competing on Talent Analytics," *Harvard Business Review*, October 2010.
14. Human Capital Management Institute Report, "Workforce Metrics and the Employee Engagement Linkage to Revenue," virtual workshop, March 29, 2011.
15. Davenport et al., "Competing on Talent Analytics."

Summary Checklist of Employer-of-Choice Engagement Practices

The following checklist is provided for readers interested in reviewing all fifty-four engagement practices presented in Chapters 4–10. Because it is difficult to focus on implementing several practices all at once, you may wish to use the checklist to put items in order of importance or urgency as you begin to plan your employer-of-choice strategy.

To Match Candidates' Expectations with Work Realities

1. Conduct realistic job previews with every job candidate.
2. Hire from the pool of temp, adjunct staff, interns, and part-time workers.
3. Hire candidates referred by current employees.
4. Create a realistic job description with a short list of the most critical competencies.
5. Allow team members to interview candidates.
6. Hire from the pool of current employees.
7. Create a way for candidates to "sample" the work experience.
8. Survey or interview new hires to find out how to minimize new-hire surprises in the future.

To Match the Person to the Job

9. Make a strong commitment to the continuous upgrading of talent.
10. See that all hiring managers perform talent forecasting and success-factor analysis.
11. Cast a wide recruiting net to expand the universe of best-fit candidates.
12. Follow a purposeful and rigorous interview process.
13. Track measures of hiring success.

To Match the Task to the Person

14. Conduct "entrance interviews" with all new hires.
15. Work to enrich the jobs of all employees.
16. Delegate tasks to challenge employees and enrich jobs.

To Provide Coaching and Feedback

17. Provide intensive feedback and coaching to new hires.
18. Create a culture of continuous feedback and coaching.
19. Train managers in performance coaching.
20. Make the performance-management process less controlling and more of a partnership.
21. Terminate nonperformers when best efforts to coach or reassign don't pay off.
22. Hold managers accountable for coaching and giving feedback.

To Provide Career Advancement and Growth Opportunities

23. Provide self-assessment tools and career self-management training for all employees.
24. Offer career-coaching tools and training for all managers.
25. Provide readily accessible information on career paths and competency requirements.
26. Create alternatives to traditional career ladders.
27. Keep employees informed about the company's strategy, direction, and talent-need forecasts.
28. Build and maintain a fair and efficient internal job-posting process.

29. Show a clear preference for hiring from within.

30. Eliminate HR policies and management practices that block internal movement.

31. Create a strong mentoring culture.

32. Keep the career-development and performance-appraisal processes separate.

33. Build an effective talent-review and succession-management process.

34. Maintain a strong commitment to employee training.

To Make Employees Feel Valued and Recognized

35. Offer a competitive base pay linked to value creation.

36. Reward results with variable pay aligned with business goals.

37. Reward employees at a high enough level to motivate higher performance.

38. Use cash payouts for on-the-spot recognition.

39. Involve employees and encourage two-way communication when designing new pay systems.

40. Monitor the pay system to ensure fairness, efficiency, consistency, and accuracy.

41. Create a culture of informal recognition founded on sincere appreciation.

42. Make new hires feel welcome and important.

43. Ask for employee input, then listen and respond.

44. Keep employees in the loop.

45. Provide the right tools and resources.

46. Keep the physical environment fit to work in.

To Reduce Stress from Work-Life Imbalance and Overwork

47. Initiate a culture of "giving-before-getting."

48. Tailor the "culture of giving" to the needs of key talent.

49. Build a culture that values spontaneous acts of caring.

50. Build social connectedness and cohesion among employees.

51. Encourage fun in the workplace.

To Inspire Trust and Confidence in Senior Leaders

52. Inspire confidence in a clear vision and a workable plan and the competence to achieve it.

53. Back up words with actions.

54. Place your trust and confidence in your workforce.

Guidelines and Considerations for Exit Interviewing/Surveying and Turnover Analysis

Exit survey and interview data should be seen as a valuable source for the analysis of turnover root causes, but too often they are regarded as superficial and relatively meaningless because of the way they are gathered and who does the gathering. When viewed as a strategically important retention practice, conducted skillfully, and incorporated with other relevant organizational data, exit survey and interview data can help organizations develop effective, on-target solutions to the "push factors" that too often, even unintentionally, drive good people out of the organization.

The Traditional Exit Interview

As traditionally practiced in many organizations, the exit interview is a perfunctory, multipurpose exercise, conducted on the employee's last day by an HR staffer. The agenda usually includes collecting the employee's keys, badges, or other equipment, completing forms, discussing separation benefits, and interviewing the employee about his or her feelings about working at the company and reasons for leaving. The employee may also be asked to fill out an exit survey form. A few companies use third-party online post-exit surveys.

As discussed in Chapter 1, the employee is often reluctant to reveal the true reasons for leaving to a company representative; in addition, the interviewer may have never been trained in the art of exit interviewing, and the collected data may never be (1) analyzed, (2) made available to management, and (3) used to adapt strategy. These are serious limitations that undermine the legitimate purposes of exit interviewing and surveying.

The Best Reasons to Conduct Exit Interviews and Surveys

Many organizations have decided not to conduct the exit interview at the same time as employee's keys are collected and benefits are discussed because these agenda items may set the wrong tone and conditions for an open discussion of the real reasons for leaving. They also muddy and detract from the true and varied purposes of an exit interview, which include:

- Bringing any "push-factor" root-cause reasons for leaving to the surface
- Alerting the organization to specific issues to be addressed
- Giving the employee a chance to vent and gain a sense of closure
- Giving the employee the opportunity to provide information that may help colleagues left behind
- Providing information about competitors and their practices
- Comparing information given with the results of past surveys and employment data
- Detecting patterns and changes by year or by quarter
- Obtaining information to help improve recruiting
- Possibly heading off a lawsuit
- Planting the seed of possible rehiring
- In some situations, offering a final opportunity to eliminate the "push factor" reason for leaving and convince the employee to stay

Most Favorable Conditions for Conducting Exit Interviews and Surveys

Whether interviews or surveys (paper, online, phone-voice-activated) are used, there are certain optimum conditions that tend to increase the chances of achieving the greatest benefits for the individual and the organization:

1. *Trained, Independent Interviewers.* The critical skills needed for successful exit interviewers—putting the employee at ease, creating rapport, and asking probing, follow-up questions, instead of accepting the individual's initial

surface response—do not come naturally for many. Interviewers must also understand the distinction between asking employees why they are leaving and asking why they didn't stay. No matter how well company representatives may have been trained or how trusted they may be, there will always be those departing employees who do not feel comfortable opening up with any representative of the organization.

This is why more companies have elected to use independent third-party consultants to conduct the interviews by phone, in person, or through secure Web sites. The downside is that employees become more difficult to reach once they have left the company. Another alternative is to have all employees complete a written survey on their last day, then notify them that they will be receiving a phone call from the third party to obtain clarification on some of their responses.

2.   *Offered on a Post-Exit Basis.* Because departing individuals may still have unresolved emotions and be preoccupied with other personal, coworker, family, or financial concerns on the day of their departure, many employers have a third party contact the employee during the evening or on weekends at home a few days or sometimes weeks after the employee's last day. This allows the employee time to gain perspective and to speak with the benefit of time for reflection. There is a countervailing case to be made that it is better to contact departed employees soon after their leaving, when they are feeling the emotions that caused them to leave most intensely.

It is more expensive to have third-party consultants conduct phone interviews than to have departed employees complete a post-exit Web survey. This is why many companies have third parties conduct actual interviews only with those highest-performing employees the company most regretted losing and invite all others to complete a confidential, password-protected Web survey.

3.   *Guaranteed Confidentiality and Anonymity.* Departing employees need to be assured that they can provide frank and candid feedback without fear of retribution by their former manager or a coworker. Many employees are more likely to accept such assurances when they come from a third-party interviewer or surveyor than from a company representative.

This is a more difficult issue for smaller organizations that conduct interviews with fewer employees and can therefore more easily identify departed employees by their comments and demographic information. CEOs at these smaller companies therefore cannot confront managers with specific information that is critical of them without revealing the identity of the departed employee. Smaller companies typically resolve this problem by not acting on the specific information about the manager until five or more exited employees have also responded to surveys, a number considered sufficient to protect the anonymity of all departing employees.

Some companies provide departed employees the option of remaining anonymous or being identified by name. They know that many employees don't mind being identified and are perfectly happy for the former manager to read what they have to say, with emotion. The problem with giving employees this option is that the more people who choose to be identified, the smaller the pool of those choosing anonymity, making it easier for them to be identified. If the employer is large enough that many dozens of employees are leaving in a given year or quarter, then this issue is of less concern. In a smaller organization, it is a tougher decision. Many managers are not as open to feedback from departed employees who choose to remain anonymous, rationalizing that many of them may be poor performers or the chronically disgruntled.

4. *Conducted with All Employees Who Leave.* To have the broadest possible understanding of all reasons for employee turnover among all categories of employees, it is important to survey all departing employees in one form or another. All employees may not complete and return surveys after their departure or be reachable by telephone, but they should at least have the opportunity to participate.

It is also a good idea to interview or survey employees who leave the company involuntarily because they may have valuable insights to share. However, they may also be more emotional on the day of their separation, so a post-exit survey will usually be more effective. Special approaches may need to be developed for those who are laid off or terminated for cause. Another category of employee not to be overlooked is that of workers who are transferring from one location to another within the company. Having them complete exit surveys is another way to capture potentially valuable information about their work experiences and feelings even though they are staying with the organization.

5. *Consistent Survey Questions.* Once the survey has been designed, it is important not to keep changing the questions, at least not the core questions.

This will help ensure that the data received are reliable. Many organizations also intentionally adapt many of the same questions from their employee engagement surveys for use in their exit surveys, thus allowing comparisons to be made and patterns to be detected.

6. *Sufficiently Probing to Discover Potential Legal Exposures.* Interviewers should do enough probing to find out if there may be potential legal issues that may put the company at risk if the employee makes a charge of harassment or discrimination. Third-party interviewers are obligated to let interviewees know upfront that, if they bring up a potentially illegal issue, the interviewer will be obligated to report it to the company. If the company encounters a situation where the employee files a charge later and exit interview records show that the employee made no mention of the problem in the exit interview when given the opportunity, the courts will allow that fact to be made part of the company's defense.

7. *Findings Reported to Management.* Because "push-factor" reasons for leaving are within the control of managers and senior leaders, these employees should have the opportunity to see the findings in both summary form and in more detailed reports so that they may take corrective action. Senior leaders will certainly need to see these data in order to hold their direct reports accountable for making appropriate corrective changes to prevent the regrettable departures in the future of valued employees. Larger companies that do regular exit surveying typically provide managers and senior leaders quarterly and annual reports of findings. Assuming that enough exit surveys have been done to warrant a report, providing quarterly (instead of annual) updates sends the message that the information is not just "nice to have" but critical. Alas, most companies do exit interviewing or surveying (mostly by internal staff), but far fewer even bother to share the information with leaders. I believe this happens mainly because most managers are skeptical that the departing employees have given the real reason for leaving. This problem is greatly lessened when there is a third-party survey provider or interviewer.

8. *Exit Findings Combined with Other Organizational Data.* Exit survey data by themselves can be quite revealing, but to ensure a more rounded view of organizational issues and trends, they are best reviewed in combination with data from surveys of current employees and other organizational trend data. Such data may include the average tenure of employees in various positions,

performance data, hiring source, the number of years with the company at which various employees are most at risk of leaving, quit rate, average vacancy rate, and other data of this kind. This type of comprehensive analysis can help identify predictors of turnover among various groups of employees so that actions can be taken to keep it from occurring.

9. *Leaders and Managers Taking Action Based on Findings.* As mentioned in Chapter 1, 95 percent of companies conduct exit interviews or surveys, but only 30 percent report that they ever take corrective action based on what they learn. There we have one more reason why most companies are not employers of choice. Employers of choice view every avoidable turnover of a valued employee as a failure to be analyzed and understood in terms of its true causes in order to prevent such future turnovers.

This means that every piece of data at the disposal of company leaders must be taken seriously. However, if senior leaders and managers do not believe that the information gathered is based on the skilled questioning of candid departing employees, they certainly cannot be expected to trust the findings or take action based on it.

One Last Chance to Reclaim a Valued Employee

There are times during an exit interview when it may become obvious that an employee who has decided to leave is really heartbroken at the prospect of leaving but feels there is no alternative. For example, an employee may love the job, the work environment, and the colleagues but have nonetheless decided to leave because the boss would not grant flexible hours. In these situations, an alert and proactive exit interviewer may be able to intervene to help change the boss's mind or report the situation to higher-ups who may be able to assign the individual to a different manager, give her a new assignment, or take whatever action may be appropriate to re-engage her. Some companies even conduct exit interviews as soon as possible after the employee gives notice because they believe there may still be a chance the employee can be saved if the reasons for leaving can be addressed.

In her book, *HR from the Heart,* Libby Sartain, senior vice president of human resources at Yahoo! Inc., recommends always asking departing employees, "Is there anything we could have done to keep you here?"[1] You may discover that there may still be a sliver of a chance to keep valued talent and to save the company money in avoided turnover costs.

Sartain also recommends trying to connect with departing employees on a deeper, more human level by asking such questions as:

- If you had the past three months to live over again, what do you think you would do differently?
- What have you learned that you can take with you to your next job?
- What are you proud of from your time here?
- What goals did you meet?
- What accomplishments will you be able to take with you?[2]

Just One More Question

One question that should be on every company's survey is "Would you consider returning to the company and, if so, under what conditions?" Of course, asking this question requires that the company, as a general policy, be willing to rehire former employees. As amazing as it may seem, there are still companies that will not rehire. Employers of choice, however, realize that former employees are to be viewed as alumni—to be kept in touch with and considered for rehire if and when the time is right.

Departing employees who answer this question affirmatively should be listed in a special recruiting database and contacted periodically by e-mail. There are few things more gratifying than welcoming back to the company a former employee who thought the grass might be greener, found out it wasn't, and has come back to tell and retell that story to their colleagues.

Note to Readers

To view our own post-exit survey, visit www.keepingthepeople.com and click on "surveys," then on "decision to leave." Visitors to the website are encouraged to complete this survey as part of our ongoing research into the root causes of avoidable employee turnover.

Notes

1. Libby Sartain, with Martha I. Finney, *HR from the Heart: Inspiring Stories and Strategies for Building the People Side of Great Business* (New York: AMA-COM, 2003).
2. Ibid.